Chris Leadbetter and Stewart Wainwright

Cambridge IGCSE

ICT

Coursebook

Completely Cambridge – Cambridge resources for Cambridge qualifications

Cambridge University Press works closely with University of Cambridge International Examinations (CIE) as parts of the University of Cambridge. We enable thousands of students to pass their CIE exams by providing comprehensive, high-quality, endorsed resources.

To find out more about University of Cambridge International Examinations visit www.cie.org.uk

To find out more about Cambridge University Press visit www.cambridge.org/cie

CAMBRIDGE UNIVERSITY PRESS
Cambridge, New York, Melbourne, Madrid, Cape Town,
Singapore, São Paulo, Delhi, Mexico City

Cambridge University Press
The Edinburgh Building, Cambridge CB2 8RU, UK

www.cambridge.org
Information on this title: www.cambridge.org/9780521179119

First published 2010
6th printing 2013

Printed in the United Kingdom by Latimer Trend

A catalogue record for this publication is available from the British Library

ISBN 978-0-521-17911-9 Paperback with CD-ROM for Windows® and Mac®

Cover image: Computer key. Return or enter key on a computer keyboard.
Adam Gault / Science Photo Library

IGCSE® is the registered trademark of University of Cambridge International Examinations

Contents

Introduction

Welcome to the new, full-colour *Cambridge IGCSE ICT* (Information and Communication Technology) *Coursebook*. This new text has been extensively overhauled and revised from the previous edition, for two main reasons:

- to focus clearly on the University of Cambridge International Examinations (CIE) IGCSE examination in ICT (syllabus 0417);
- to update the content with recent developments in ICT and its effects on our lives.

In making these changes, we have:

- created a brand-new accompanying CD-ROM loaded with materials to improve student success in the examination;
- ensured that all explanations are accessible to students;
- included practical examples of the devices, processes and methods being explained;
- included brand new short, self-assessment questions throughout the text;
- revised and updated the exercises for homework and class discussion;
- refreshed the design, making full use of colour and photographs where possible.

The coursebook is designed to help students studying for the CIE IGCSE examination in ICT sections 1–8, which is the examined section. On the CD-ROM, we have supplied practical coursework projects with exemplar answers and ***our*** examiner's comments to provide practical help on how to tackle the remaining two parts of syllabus, the practically assessed exercises. Other material on the CD-ROM provides revision of the coursebook material.

The text follows the syllabus contents as closely as possible, varying only where needed to assist with the narrative flow and reduce duplication between sections. Each Module begins with a list of learning objectives (headed 'When you have finished this module, you will be able to:') and ends with a summary of the specific points that have been covered. The learning outcomes are intended to provide a skeleton upon which to hang the detail which is covered in the text. The summary, by contrast, is intended to assist students when they revise, by providing a short overview of the contents to let students be confident in their grasp of the material.

Throughout each Module, specific syllabus codes are shown alongside subheadings to show which parts of the syllabus are being addressed in each case, as follows.

The text aims to encourage an active learning style and includes many self-assessment questions as well as varied longer-answer questions and tasks, while maintaining a structured approach to the learning process.

Self-assessment questions require short answers only, and are intended to allow students to check their understanding of the material as they move through the coursebook. Answers to these questions are provided at the end of the coursebook. The self-assessment questions are indicated in the text with an icon like this.

Longer-answer questions are of two types. These questions are contained within a box labelled 'Questions', as follows.

Questions

Some questions are related directly to the requirements that students will find when they sit their examination.

These questions are intended to stretch the students more than the SAQs do, and let them demonstrate their understanding of the concepts being taught. These questions are related to the text and are intended to form a starting point for activity in class or for individual work. They are indicated in the text with an icon like this.

Other questions are more broadly based and are intended to encourage students to find out about a small area of the course, and are often suitable for classroom discussion as well as independent thinking. We find this type of work to be especially effective because it allows students to formulate their own answers – there is often no single right answer to the question. These questions are indicated with an icon like this.

Finally, there are Extension questions and tasks. These include concepts, examples or thinking that fall beyond the strict boundaries of the syllabus. However, addressing these questions will deepen students' understanding of and appreciation for the concepts being presented. Each of these pieces of work is meant as a starting point which may interest students, particularly the more able, and encourage them to carry out some independent enquiry into a topic. **It must be stressed that this work is not an integral part of the syllabus requirements and can be omitted without prejudicing attainment in the examination**. These Extension materials are contained within clearly marked boxes, headed like this.

Extension

The CD-ROM contains several categories of material.
- Real CIE past exam papers (Papers 1, 2 and 3).
- Our exemplar answers for the CIE past papers, including our mark scheme for Paper 2 (Practical test A). We have also provided comments, indicating common pitfalls or giving some explanation of why certain answers are correct or how the marks are awarded.
- Revision questions (without answers).
- Revision notes and tests to ensure that students' revision goes smoothly.
- A Learning and Revision Guide with useful tips on study skills and exam technique.
- A Glossary of Key Terms and their definition.

We hope that this resource is both useful and interesting to the reader, and helps students achieve a good grade in the CIE IGCSE in ICT.

Chris Leadbetter and Stewart Wainwright.

Acknowledgements

I would like to thank the staff at Cambridge University Press for their patience and advice; My son James for some of the illustrative documents that can be found in the text, particularly those relating to commercial documentation between companies; and my wife for her forbearance and the copious cups of coffee which simply appeared on my desk as if by magic.

Chris Leadbetter

I would like to thank Cambridge University Press for their constructive help and advice during the editing process. I also wish to thank my wife and daughter for their patience whilst I have been busy co-authoring this book and CD.

Stewart Wainwright

The authors and publishers acknowledge the following sources of copyright materials and are grateful for the permissions granted. While every effort has been made, it has not always been possible to identify the sources of all the materials used, or to trace all copyright holders. If any omissions are brought to our notice, we will be happy to include the appropriate acknowledgments on reprinting.

p. 1 Andy Lauwers/Rex Features; p. 2tl © D. Hurst / Alamy; p. 3 © Chris Cooper-Smith / Alamy; p. 4 iStock/300dpi; p. 5 © MCNG Photography / Alamy; p. 8cl Colin Cuthbert / Science Photo Library; p. 8tr © Chas Spradbery / Alamy; p. 8cr Ton Kinsbergen / Science Photo Library; p. 8br Geoff Moore/Rex Features; p. 9t Shutterstock/Elner; p. 9b Shutterstock/Zsolt Nyulaszi; p. 12tl Shutterstock/gabor2100; p12cl Shutterstock/Ximagination; p. 12bl and 12tr Shutterstock/carroteater; p. 14tl Shutterstock/Bojan Pavlukovic; p. 14br © Mark Sykes / Alamy; p. 15tr © RTimages / Alamy; p. 15br © Eyebyte / Alamy; p. 16 Mike Devlin / Science Photo Library; p. 17tl © bluudaisy / Alamy; p. 17br © Anthony Hatley / Alamy; p. 18l © Art Directors & TRIP / Alamy; p. 18r © Maximilian Weinzierl / Alamy; p. 20l iStock/© FineCollection; p. 20r iStock/© Suprijono Suharjoto; p. 21l © BrazilPhotos.com / Alamy; p. 21r © ICP / Alamy; p. 22 iStock/© Chris Beddoe; p. 24bl © Glowimages RM / Alamy; p. 25tl © Corbis Premium RF / Alamy; p. 25cr Shutterstock/Dr_Flash; p. 26 iStock/© Midhat Becar; p. 27tl Shutterstock/36clicks; p. 28tl © Maximilian Stock LTD / PHOTOTAKE / Alamy; p. 28cr iStock/© Falk Kienas; p. 28br © Aleksandr Ugorenkov / Alamy; p. 29 © cambpix / Alamy; p. 30t iStock/© Klaas Jan Schraa; p. 30c iStock/© Greg Nicholas; p. 30b © Ted Foxx / Alamy; p. 32tl iStock/© Bruce Riccitelli; p. 32br Ton/Kinsbergen/Science Photo Library; p. 33 © CreativeAct - Technology series / Alamy; p. 38tr Shutterstock/Joachim Wendler; p. 38cr Shutterstock; p. 39cr Shutterstock/Chudo-Yudo; p. 41 © Justin Kase z08z / Alamy; p. 54tl © Art Directors & TRIP / Alamy; p. 54bl © Hugh Threlfall / Alamy; p. 54cr Shutterstock/Sergei Devyatkin; p. 54br iStock/© Andres Balcazarp; 55 iStock/© Krzysztof Kwiatkowski; p. 57 iStock/© Rich Legg; p. 59 BBC Bitesize;

p. 60 Reproduced with the permission of Portland Secondary School, Australia; p. 62 iStock/Thumb; p. 71 iStock/© Stefan Matei Lungu; p. 73 iStock/© Stefan Matei Lungu; p. 75 iStock/dwphotos; p. 77 iStock/© Timur Arbaev; p. 78tl iStock/© Karen Harrison; p. 78bl iStock/© Ugur Bariskan; p. 78br iStock/© Andres Balcazar; p. 81tl © Streetfly Stock / Alamy; p. 81tr © Eric Carr / Alamy; p. 85 iStock/© Pali Rao; p. 87tl iStock/© Alan Crawford; p. 87tr © Rob Walls / Alamy; p. 87cr © Alan Oliver / Alamy; p. 92b Shutterstock/Viktor Gmyria; p. 93 Shutterstock/Pixachi; p. 94 Screenshot of CALMA software by Julia Bowder, Michael Clarke and James Saunders. Department of Music, University of Huddersfield (www.hud.ac.uk/mh/music/calma.int/html); p. 95 Steinbergnorthamerica.com; p. 97 Facebook is a trademark of Facebook Inc. (screenshot of Facebook Principles page); p. 102 School report from 2005 reproduced by permission of Xaverian College, Manchester; p. 104 iStock/Parema; p. 106tl iStock/© Xavier MARCHANT; p. 106bl © Tony French / Alamy; p. 106tr © Royal Geographical Society / Alamy; p. 107l iStock/MistikaS; p. 107r © PCN Photography / Alamy; p. 109 © Transport Picture Library/Paul Ridsdale / Alamy; p. 110 © imac / Alamy; p. 113 iStock/© Nick M. Do; p. 115 © Duane Branch / Alamy; p. 118 Cordelia Molloy / Science Photo Library; p. 119tl iStock/© Sascha Burkard; p. 119cr iStock/© Pierre-Emmanuel; p. 119br © Nigel Cattlin / Alamy; p. 120 iStock/© Steve Snowden; p. 122t © Crown copyright 2010, the Met Office; p. 122b © imagebroker / Alamy; p. 124 iStock/© Zoran Milic; p. 130 iStock/© Willie B. Thomas; p. 131 Shutterstock/Rezachka; p. 132l iStock/© Ricardo Azoury; p. 132r © Network Photographer / Alamy; p. 137 Shutterstock/Stephen Coburn; p. 139l iStock/© Andrew Howe; p. 139r iStock/Neustockimages; p. 140 iStock/© Els van der Gun; p. 142 © Fancy / Alamy; p145 Shutterstock/Sudheer Sakthan; p. 146 Adams Picture Library/John Powell; p. 150 Shutterstock/Konstantin Chagin; p. 154 Alamy/Ali Arman; p. 156 iStock/© Andrey Prokhorov; p. 158 iStock/© Chris Schmidt; p. 160 Shutterstock/Monkey Business Images; p. 164 © Gary Doak / Alamy.

l = left, r = right, c = centre, t = top, b = bottom

1

Types and components of computer systems

When you have finished this module, you will be able to:

- define and give examples of hardware and software, and describe the difference between them
- identify the main hardware components of a computer system
- identify the need for an operating system, and describe various user interfaces associated with operating systems
- identify different types of computer ranging from mainframes to PDAs.

Overview

As you look around the world today, you will see information and communication technology (ICT) being used almost everywhere. This module will help you to learn and understand more about different ICT systems, what these systems can do and how they affect society.

One of the first electronic computers was invented in the 1940s by a team of code breakers working at Bletchley Park in the UK. They were trying to decode messages sent by German forces during World War II. The machine was called Colossus (Figure 1.1).

In the years since then, many different types of computers have been developed – mainframes, personal computers and laptops. More recently smartphones, mobile phones that are also computers, have become prevalent (Figure 1.2).

Not so obvious are the computers embedded in equipment such as automatic washing machines or the control systems for greenhouses or factories. You will learn about all these applications of ICT in this course.

This first module focuses on basic computer systems and their components. First you will learn about hardware and software, and the difference between them. You will look at the main hardware components of a computer system, then at some of the different operating systems (software) that computers need in order to work.

Figure 1.1 The Colossus machine at Bletchley Park, UK, was one of the first electronic computers. It was invented in the 1940s. Because valves (large electronic components) were used, Colossus was huge, filling the room.

Figure 1.2 A smartphone – a mobile phone that is also a handheld computer. Since the 1940s, computers have become smaller and more powerful because of developments in electronics.

Finally, you will look in more detail at different types of computer and how computers have developed over time.

1a,b,c ## Hardware and software

The physical parts of a computer system – the parts of the system that you can feel or touch – make up the computer's **hardware**.

Sometimes this is obvious: a monitor screen is obviously hardware because you can touch it. A printer, a mouse and a pen drive are all examples of hardware because you can see and touch them. The computer case itself is hardware, as is a handheld device or palmtop computer.

Less obvious is the computer inside a mobile phone; that too is hardware. You might think that it is not hardware because you cannot touch it. However, if you took off the case it could be touched just like any other sort of computer, so it is still hardware.

The set of instructions that make the computer system do something is called the **software**. However advanced or expensive the hardware of a computer system, it is useless unless it has instructions it can follow that make it do something.

microprocessor

Figure 1.3 Examples of hardware.

There are two main types of software:

- Some software will rarely make itself known to users, but will still be essential to keep the computer usable – this is the computer's **operating system** or **system software**.
- Other software will allow users to use the computer to play a game, for example, or to write a letter. These are called **applications**; sometimes we refer to them as **programs**.

Here are a few examples of general-purpose applications and what they can be used to do:

- Word-processing applications are used to produce letters, reports and memos.
- Database programs are used to store and retrieve information.
- Spreadsheet applications are used for tasks that involve calculations or graphs and charts.
- Presentation applications are used to create slide shows and presentations.
- Desktop-publishing (DTP) packages are used to produce posters, newsletters and magazines.
- Graphics programs are used for artwork.
- Computer-aided design packages are used to produce detailed designs and plans.
- Communications software such as web browsers and email programs are used to access the Internet and send and receive email.

Figure 1.4 Sometimes, general-purpose programs are combined into a single integrated **package**. Word-processing, spreadsheet and presentation programs are often bundled in this way.

- Web page editors are used to create web pages.
- Audio production and editing programs are a common way of producing high-quality music at low cost.

In contrast to general-purpose applications, specialist, custom-made software can only be used in one particular situation. Examples include applications for payroll, accounts, stock control, route planning or weather forecasting.

A key point is to remember the main difference between hardware and software:

- You can touch hardware – it is made of physical objects.
- Software relates to ideas and instructions for using the solid objects.

This covers most cases, but you will return to this idea in Module 3.

? SAQs

1 Sort the following into hardware and software:

   monitor, mouse, web browser, spreadsheet program, joystick, flight simulator game

2 You have taken some digital photos and you want to edit them on your computer. What free photo editing program could you use? Besides editing photos what else can you use it for? So is it a package?

1d Main components of a general-purpose computer

So far we have looked briefly at different types of computer, and at hardware and software. But what exactly is a computer?

A **computer** is a device, or a group of devices, designed to do something, such as process information or control a system.

The hardware of most computers can be divided into several types of device:

- An **input device** is used to put data into the computer.
- A **processor** does something with the data given by the input device.
- An **output device** is used to tell someone or something the results that the processor came up with.
- A **storage device** keeps all this data and the software that is used. If the computer did not have somewhere to store things it would forget everything when it was turned off.

Figure 1.5 shows how these devices are normally thought of.

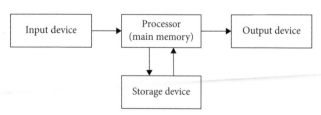

Figure 1.5 The main components of a computer. The arrows show the flow of data around the system.

Input and output devices

Input and output devices are looked at in more detail in Module 2. To help you start thinking about them, try the following question.

Question

1 Look at Figure 1.6. List all the input and output devices that you can see. Try to divide them into different types.

Can you think of other input or output devices not shown in Figure 1.6? Add those to your lists.

Figure 1.6 A typical multimedia PC (personal computer). There will often be a printer as well, or a combined printer and scanner.

Processor

People often use the word 'processor' to refer to the **central processor** or the **central processing unit (CPU)** of a computer.

The CPU contains a number of parts, most of which are beyond the scope of this course.

Extension

A **microprocessor** is a single integrated circuit (chip) that performs the functions of a CPU. Microprocessors are used to control devices such as washing machines, video players and burglar alarms.

Investigate the use of microprocessors in household devices. What are the advantages? What are the disadvantages?

What is a graphics processing unit (GPU)? What does it do?

Main or internal memory

One important part of the CPU is the **main memory**. This is used to store all the data and instructions which the computer is going to use or the answers that it has produced.

The main memory is sometimes called other names, but they mean the same thing. Some of these names are: **internal memory** or **primary memory** or **immediate access store (IAS)**.

The main memory is electrical. This means that when the computer is switched off, it will forget everything. So when you next switched the computer on it would just sit there, a useless lump of metal and plastic, because it had forgotten all its instructions! This is why you have to reload all the programs when you switch the computer back on and also reload the work which you were doing.

However, in order to reload the programs and data, the computer must be 'working' – in other words it must be ready to do things. This means that when you switch it on the computer must already have some software in it so that it can understand what you want to do. This software is stored on a special type of main memory called **ROM (read only memory)**. ROM cannot be changed, even by switching off the power.

ROM would be useless for doing work or running programs, though, because we normally want to change things. We might use a word processor to type up a piece of coursework for school and then we want to check our emails or play a game. This means we want to change what the instructions are for the computer. We could not do that if there was only ROM, because we could not change its contents. So another sort of memory is needed.

This other form of memory is called **RAM (random access memory)**. RAM stores anything that needs to be changed. All the programs and all the data being used are stored here.

Normally a computer's RAM is much bigger than its ROM because it needs to hold far more. However, the ROM is bigger in some computer systems; these include everyday microprocessor-controlled devices such as washing machines.

Two words of warning:
- Do not confuse main memory ROM with a CD-ROM or DVD-ROM; they are different (Module 3).

- Do not confuse memory with backing storage. One name for memory is 'internal memory' because it is inside the computer, closely connected to the CPU. Backing storage is outside the processor.

Module 3 will look further at the differences between memory and storage devices.

Module 3 will look further at the differences between memory and storage devices.

Question

2 ROM and RAM are two different types of memory found in computers.
  a What does ROM stand for?
  b What does RAM stand for?
  c What is the main difference between ROM and RAM?

Measuring the size of memory

Computers store and process data using binary numbers. For example, a computer might store the letter B as 10000011.

Data is stored in a computer as a series of 0s and 1s. The computer does not understand things like 'a' or 'hello' or '23'. It can only understand electrical signals being turned on or off. These signals can stand for 0 (no signal being sent) or 1 (an electrical signal). Everything else has to be made up of combinations of these electrical signals or no electrical signals. We can't keep talking about electrical signals or no signals so we need a name for a single unit (a 0 or a 1). It is called a **bit**, which stands for **b**inary dig**it**. By putting a number of these bits together the computer can represent many different types of data. For example 10000010 might stand for 'A' and 10000011 might stand for 'B'. We shall be studying this in some depth later in this book.

Notice that the examples of A and B that were given both contain 8 bits. This is not an accident. Quite often 8 bits are grouped together like this. A group of bits like this is called a **byte**.

Computer memory is measured in **bytes**. One byte is commonly made up of eight bits.

A computer's memory will contain a large number of these bytes otherwise it could not store very much data. Generally, the more bytes that can be stored, the more useful the memory will be.

The size of a computer's memory (and backing storage – see Module 3) is normally measured in **kilobytes (kB)**, **megabytes (MB)** or **gigabytes (GB)**. Table 1.1 shows how these relate to each other.

Table 1.1 Common units for measuring the size of memory.

Unit	Abbreviation	Size
kilobyte	kB	1 kB = 1024 bytes
megabyte	MB	1 MB = 1024 kB
gigabyte	GB	1 GB = 1024 MB
terabyte	TB	1 TB = 1024 GB

 SAQs

3 Complete the following sentences by using the correct words from this list: memory, megabytes, eight, gigabytes.
  a A school computer has 512 .... of memory.
  b A byte is a unit of computer .... and it consists of .... bits.
4 Put the following in order of size, smallest first:
     1 terabyte, 2048 kB, 1.2 GB, 16 bits, 1.5 MB.

Backing storage

A **storage device** is used to store programs and data when the processor is turned off. The programs and data must be put back into the processor's memory when needed for use. This is why there are two arrows on Figure 1.5, to show programs and data going into and out of the storage device.

Figure 1.7 Inside a PC.

Storage devices are sometimes called **backing store**, **secondary storage** or **external storage**; these all mean the same thing.

You will learn more about storage devices in Module 3.

Question

3 A question in a maths book tells you to add together the two numbers 5 and 3. You write the question in your notebook and start to work it out. You are called away to have your meal with the family. After eating, you go back to your homework and write out a full solution to be handed to your teacher the next morning.

Think of everything mentioned so far in this module and imagine that you are a computer. Try to identify which components of a computer match the different steps in solving the maths problem.

Extension

In ICT, there is a distinction between the meanings of the words 'data' and 'information'.

- 'Data' is used to describe numbers, words and anything else that has not yet been processed.
- 'Information' describes the outcomes from a process. In the sum $2 + 3 = 5$, 2 and 3 are the data, and 5 is the information. But what are the $+$ and $=$ signs?

Try to define the data and information for some processes you use in real life, such as setting a central heating system, or washing clothes in a washing machine.

Operating systems

In the last section we focused particularly on the hardware components that make up a computer.

We now turn to an important set of software programs that 'bring the computer to life'. They make the computer able to do useful things. This software is called the **operating system (OS)**. It can also be called **system software** or **operating system software**.

There are many different types of operating system. Each one makes a computer act in a slightly different way. To start to understand this, imagine a high-powered sports car. If you were to drive it around a racing track then it would be very different from your aunt driving it down into town in order to do her shopping. It is the same car but the person driving it and the reason why it is being driven are different, and so the outcome is different.

The same is true for computers. Two computers can look identical but depending on how they are controlled they will be good at different things. The operating system is what controls them.

User interfaces

The operating system is the set of programs that do all the things needed to make a computer work. One of these programs controls what users see on the screen. This is called the **interface** or (in full) the **human–computer interface (HCI)**.

There are many different types of interfaces. Which one is chosen depends on:

- the jobs that the computer has to do;
- the type of user and their abilities.

A **graphical user interface (GUI)** is one which uses graphics to stand for more complicated actions that the user wants the computer to carry out (Figure 1.8).

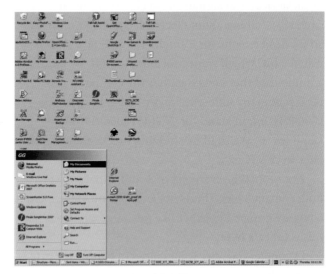

Figure 1.8 A graphical user interface.

GUIs are typified by the use of little pictures (called **icons**) to stand for things that can be done. These icons can be **pointed** at by an arrow (or cursor) on the screen, controlled by a **mouse**. The screen can be divided into different areas which can have different things in them; these areas are called **windows**. Put the four elements (windows, icons, mouse, pointer) together and you get **WIMP**. Graphical user interfaces are sometimes called WIMPs.

Pointing using a mouse and clicking on pictures is simple to do and requires little IT knowledge, so a GUI is an interface that can be used by a young child or by someone who knows nothing of computers.

A **command-line interface (CLI)** is also an interface for communicating with a computer (Figure 1.9). However, this time you have to type in specific commands to tell the computer what to do. This is far more difficult to use for two main reasons:

- the user must know all the commands;
- the user must be careful not to make any typing errors – otherwise the computer will not be able to understand the commands and carry them out.

Figure 1.9 A command-line interface.

Command-line interfaces are used by people like technicians looking after computer systems. The technicians know the commands and are able in this way to access the whole of the system. However, someone using a GUI can only get to places on the system that they have been given icons for.

? SAQ

5 a What is an operating system (OS)?
  b Describe the features of
    i a graphical user interface
    ii a command-line interface.

Questions

4 Many other types of interface can be used on computer systems.
  a Find out about menu-based interfaces and form-based interfaces. For a menu-based interface, find an information system at a local train station or bank. For a form-based interface, look at a typical website for booking a hotel room: http://www.ichotelsgroup.com/ is a good example.
  b For each one try to find some uses and explain why they are used.

5 Find out what experience members of the class have of different interfaces.

  What types of user interfaces are used by different people in school? Why do they each need the type of interface which they use?

Extension

- Try to find out about some more types of interface. What, for example, is a 'natural language' interface?
- Are the type of user and the job that is to be done the only factors dictating what a computer interface will look like?
- A washing machine uses a computer processor to control the wash cycle. What does the user interface look like? Why is it not a GUI?

(1f,g) Types of computer and their development over time

People have been building calculating devices for centuries. In the 20th century, electronic computers became possible. As you saw at the start of this module, one of the first, Colossus, was invented in the early 1940s by a team of code breakers working at Bletchley Park in the UK. They were trying to decode messages sent by German forces during World War II.

Although Colossus worked far faster than any people could do, compared with computers today it was very slow. It was massive, filling a room (Figure 1.1), and very unreliable because it used valves rather than solid-state technology.

The development of computers was very slow to start with because nobody could think of a use for them. In the late 1940s the President of IBM stated that there would never be a need for more than five computers in the whole world. He was talking about different computers from those we have now, but he still got it wrong.

In the late 1950s and 1960s, companies and universities began to invest in large computers (they were big but still very slow) called **mainframes** (Figure 1.10). People had to bring their work to the computer, which was in a different room or even a different building, and then the work was done when the computer could find the time to do it!

Figure 1.10 A mainframe computer.

In the 1970s, companies started to fit terminals to mainframes. A **terminal** is usually a keyboard and a monitor screen which lets a person have their own connection to the computer. The users of these terminals could then all share the power of this single mainframe. Many mainframe computers are still being used today.

Most people nowadays want to have their own machine. This first became possible in the late 1970s and the 1980s. These computers were called **personal**

computers (PCs) because they belonged to and were controlled by a person rather than a large company (Figure 1.11).

Figure 1.11 Personal computers: **a** from the 1980s, **b** from the 1990s, **c** from 2009.

In the 1990s, portable computers became popular. They became known as **laptops** (and later as **notebooks**) (Figure 1.12). Laptops have their own power supply (e.g. a battery) and screen. They are also completely portable while still having the same hardware as a PC.

Figure 1.12 An example of a netbook computer.

Recently, **netbook** computers have become popular. These are small, usually cheap, less powerful laptops used mainly to browse the Internet.

When batteries were developed that combined a smaller size with a longer life, smaller and smaller laptops became possible. Eventually some laptops were small enough to fit in the hand and became known as **palmtops**.

One kind of palmtop uses a stylus to operate symbols, including a keyboard, on a screen. Sometimes the stylus is used for handwriting which will be understood by the machine; more often it is used like a mouse. Basic software is built in so that standard computer applications can be used. These devices are commonly referred to as **personal digital assistants (PDAs)** (Figure 1.13).

If a mobile phone is included, which in turn allows connection to the Internet and to other networks, the device is often called a **smartphone**.

Figure 1.13 A PDA. The stylus is used as a pointing device or to enter text.

Questions

6 Name four different types of computer. For each one, explain the context where it would be used and who would use it.

7 In the 1940s, if I wanted to take some notes on what I was doing when I was visiting a site as part of my job, I would take out a notebook and write some notes that I could use later. Nowadays, in the same situation, I take out a PDA and, using the stylus, I write some notes that I can use later.

Has anything really changed? Does this represent a great improvement?

8 Over the 60-odd years since Colossus was built, computers have become smaller and gained more processing power. What will happen over the next ten years?

Extension

Try to find out about some of the machines that appeared between 1960 and 2000. To get started, go to http://oldcomputers.net/zx80.html. This is an example of a machine from right in the middle of the timeframe. Other useful sites are http://www.computinghistory.org.uk or http://www.computerhistory.org/timeline/ You might find other, equally useful sites.

What were the sizes and processing speeds of these machines?

Summary

- The physical parts of a computer system make up its hardware.
- The instructions given to a computer system are its software.
- Software enables computer hardware to do something useful.
- A computer consists, generally, of devices for input, processing, output and storage.
- The main processor (CPU) contains two types of memory: RAM and ROM. RAM stores data and software while processing is occurring; ROM stores essential software needed when the computer is first switched on.
- Backing storage is different from memory.
- Storage devices store software and data when the computer is switched off.
- Different computers have different operating systems that control them.
- One part of an operating system is the user interface.
- Mainframes, PCs, laptops, palmtops, PDAs and smartphones are all types of computers.

2 Input and output devices

When you have finished this module, you will be able to:

- identify a number of input devices, such as keyboards, pointing devices and sensors
- identify a number of output devices, such as monitors, printers and control devices
- explain where each device is used.

Overview

In Module 1, you saw how the hardware of most computers can be divided into several types of device:

- **Input devices** are used to put data into the computer.
- A **processor** does something with the data given by the input device.
- **Output devices** are used to tell someone or something the results that the processor came up with.
- **Backing storage** keeps all the data and the software that is used.

You learnt about processors in Module 1. In Module 3 you will focus on backing storage.

In this module you will look first at input devices, then at output devices. You will also see how input and output devices can be integrated in a system, for example to control an automatic washing machine.

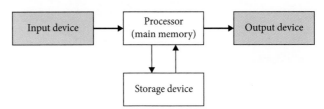

Figure 2.1 The main components of a computer. This module focuses on input and output devices.

Input methods and devices

You will look at many different kinds of input device in this module (Table 2.1).

Some devices are used by people to enter data themselves. Keyboards, pointing devices, cameras, scanners and microphones are examples. These are sometimes called **manual input devices**.

Some devices, such as optical mark readers, enable data to be entered directly, without human intervention.

Table 2.1 Different types of input device.

Manual input devices	Direct input systems	Sensors
Keyboards	Systems using:	Temperature sensors
Pointing devices, e.g. mouse, touchpad	• magnetic ink character recognition (MICR);	Pressure sensors
Scanners	• optical mark recognition (OMR);	Light sensors
Cameras, including webcam, video camera	• optical character recognition (OCR)	
Microphones	Magnetic stripe readers	
Musical keyboards	Chip readers, used in chip-and-PIN systems	
Remote controls	Bar code readers	

These **direct input** or **direct data entry** methods are used when large amounts of similar data need to be entered, often in commercial or business applications.

Sensors make up the third type of input device. These collect data automatically.

2a,b Keyboards and keypads

Keyboards are input devices used to enter fixed values, often characters, into the computer system. There are many different types of keyboard. This section looks at qwerty keyboards, concept keyboards and numeric keypads.

Figure 2.2   Qwerty keyboards.

Most people think of keyboards being used to type letters, numbers and punctuation into a computer. Typically this means the use of a **qwerty keyboard** (Figure 2.2).

This type of keyboard gets its name from the arrangement of letters on the top line of keys. This is the most common of all keyboards because it was the way that the keys were arranged on old-fashioned typewriters (Figure 2.3). Most keyboard operators had been trained to use typewriters before computers became popular so the keyboard had to stay looking the same or all their skills would have been lost.

Figure 2.3   An old mechanical typewriter. Many people believe that the qwerty arrangement of keys was devised to make the input of data as simple as possible. In fact the keys were deliberately arranged to try to slow the operator down so that the typewriter did not jam.

On a qwerty keyboard each key always means the same thing. When you press a letter Q it is always a letter Q.

Keyboards are typically used with monitors to show an immediate output of what has been typed in. They are used for everything from writing an email to writing a book.

The advantages of qwerty keyboards are:
* they use a simple, old-fashioned technology with little that can go wrong;
* people feel comfortable using them.

Disadvantages are:
* qwerty keyboards are slow compared with some more automated input devices such as bar code readers;
* keyboards for public use are susceptible to vandalism.

SAQ

1 We said above that data input is slow using a keyboard compared with other ways of inputting data. What makes this method of data input slow?

Question

1 A timber yard has a desk where customers go on arrival so that they can order the timber that they need. The receptionist has a qwerty keyboard. Describe why a qwerty keyboard would be needed and what it would be used to input.

Extension

Investigate different layouts of keys on keyboards. For example, look at the Dvorak keyboard and keyboards designed for use with languages other than English.

Find out about keyboards that are qwerty keyboards but are not the normal rectangular design. These are sometimes called ergonomic keyboards.

Concept keyboards, unlike qwerty keyboards, allow the user to decide what each of the keys should stand for and they can be changed when necessary.

A concept keyboard looks like a flat sheet with pressure pads all over it. If a sheet of paper sometimes called an overlay is placed on top showing different symbols (Figure 2.4) then the computer can be programmed to show that particular symbol when the key is pressed. If the program is changed then the same pad can stand for different symbols.

Concept keyboards can be used when the normal symbols are inappropriate or when the person who is to use it would find difficulty in using an ordinary keyboard.

An advantage is that the number of different symbols can be very restricted, but this can also be a disadvantage because it makes it difficult to produce any input outside a very limited group of inputs.

Figure 2.4 An overlay sheet for a concept keyboard in a fast-food restaurant. The sheet is laid on a fixed grid of pressure pads. Each pressure pad is linked to a computer and programmed with whatever data the user wants; in this case a food or drink item (and its price) from a set menu.

Question

2 Find out about the use of concept keyboards in your school. Alternatively, find a retail outlet (fast-food outlets are good places to start) which uses concept keyboards at the counter.
   a Why is this a good type of input device to use?
   b What outputs are generated by the inputs?

 SAQ

2 A concept keyboard is on the desk in the timber yard. It allows the user to input measurements and amounts of timber quickly.
   a What features will a keyboard that could be used for this purpose have?
   b Why will it still be necessary to have a qwerty keyboard? How can the concept keyboard allow the user to input addresses for delivery? Is this better than the qwerty keyboard?

Most qwerty keyboards have a section on the right with a group of keys representing the digits from 0 to 9 arranged in a rectangle. This is a **numeric keypad** (Figure 2.5). It becomes more distinct if it does not have the rest of the keyboard attached to it.

numeric keypad

Figure 2.5 On most qwerty keyboards there is a numeric keypad on the far right.

Numeric keypads are used by shoppers to input their PIN numbers when they pay for something by card. They are used as part of the keypad on ATM machines. They are used on digital locking mechanisms to control entry to rooms, houses or offices so that physical keys do not have to be used. They are used instead of keys on room safes in hotels or on lockers. The most common use, of course, is on a mobile phone.

Numeric keypads are small, easy to use and language independent. They are also easy to cover up when you don't want anyone else to see what is being input. A disadvantage is that inputting symbols other than digits is difficult, which limits the ways you can use them – typing a text message on even the best mobile phone keypad is slower than using a qwerty keyboard.

? SAQ

3   If I key in a telephone number on my mobile phone by copying the number in an advertisement in the newspaper, or I type in a text message, I am using a manual input method. When might I use a direct input method on my mobile phone?

Question

3   Numeric keypads are used as input devices on mobile phones. Explain how the keypad can be used to input symbols other than numbers.

Pointing device

A **mouse** is a device that allows the user to move pointer on the screen and to make choices by clic buttons on the body of the mouse. A typical mouse a small ball underneath (Figure 2.6). As the mouse pushed around on a desk, the ball rolls against the fla surface. The movement of the ball is detected and sen the computer, which works out how the mouse has bee moved and then moves the pointer to match.

A mouse is used with a desktop PC, particularly when a GUI is being used (Module 1, page 6). It is convenient because the PC will normally be on a desk, which means that there is a flat surface to use the mouse on.

The advantages of using mice as pointing devices are:
- they provide a fast method of input;
- they are intuitive to use because they involve pointing at things.

The disadvantages are:
- mice can be easily damaged or vandalised;
- some people, particularly if they have physical disabilities, find mice difficult to use;
- mice need a flat surface to be moved around on.

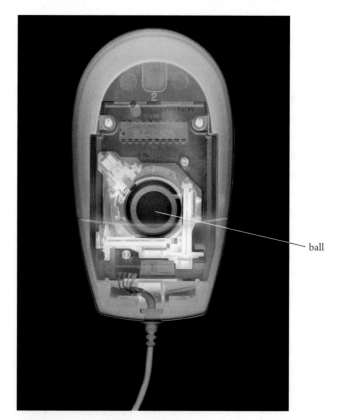

ball

Figure 2.6 A mechanical mouse.

Questions

4 There are other types of mouse apart from the mechanical one described here.

   a Find out about optical mice. Explain how an optical mouse works. Explain the advantages that an optical mouse has over a mechanical mouse.

   b Some mice do not need a wire to connect them to the computer. Explain how they work and what advantages they have.

5 If you need to select an icon or menu item shown on screen using a mouse, the mouse needs to do more than just sense how it's being moved around. What other features are needed to let you select particular things using a mouse?

? SAQ

4 The computer system used by the timber yard has a mouse to allow the user to input data. What sort of mouse would be sensible and what sort of data would be input?

A mouse is sometimes not a suitable way to control the pointer. A laptop computer is designed for use in places other than on a fixed surface. This means that there is often no surface to use the mouse on. A laptop is designed to have all the necessary peripherals in one case and a mouse would have to be carried separately.

Laptops may use a variation on a mouse for its pointing device. It is called a **touchpad** and is a flat area next to the keyboard (Figure 2.7). You simply touch the touchpad with a finger and the computer can tell where the finger is and in which direction it is moving. This movement can be applied to the movement of the pointer on the screen.

Most touchpads also have buttons that can be used like the buttons on a mouse. Alternatively, you might be able to tap on the pad with a finger to have the same effect.

touchpad

Figure 2.7 A laptop computer with a touchpad.

A touchpad's advantages are the same as those for a mouse, and they can also be integrated into the case of a laptop computer for easier transport. One disadvantage can be the small size of the touchpad relative to the laptop's screen.

Trackerballs are a little like upside-down mechanical mice (Figure 2.8). They have buttons like those on a mouse.

Figure 2.8 A trackerball.

The ball is rolled around directly by the user rather than being moved by the whole mouse being pushed. Trackerballs can be used in the same types of application that a mouse can be, but have the following advantages over a mouse:

- A trackerball is stationery and does not need a surface to be moved around on.
- It can be built into a machine like an information system and is not as likely to get damaged as a mouse.
- It can also be used by disabled people who may not have the freedom of movement necessary to use other pointing devices.

A disadvantage is that trackerballs can be difficult to use for some applications needing fine control.

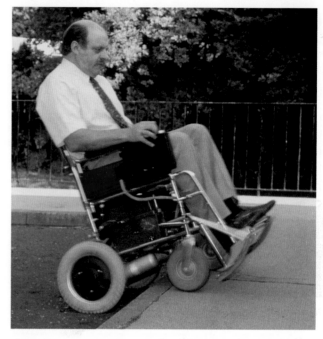

Figure 2.9 Joysticks are used in many practical applications, not just as a pointing device in a computer system. Here a man is using it to control his motorised wheelchair.

Question

6 The pointing devices discussed so far were designed for manipulating values on a screen. They are normally used with a GUI.

What other input device may be even more appropriate to use with a GUI?

SAQ

5 The owners of the timber yard have decided that a mouse is not an appropriate pointing device to use.

a Explain why a mouse is not appropriate.
b Assess touchpads and tracker balls as input devices in this instance.

A **joystick** can carry out the same tasks as a mouse as well as other functions such as controlling the movement of a motorised wheelchair (Figure 2.9).

As a pointing device, a joystick might move a character in a game or a spaceship or any other shape as a pointer. The joystick might have buttons with specific uses such as picking up an object in the game. Individual actions depend on how the joystick's software has been programmed. If the stick is pushed forward, the pointer will go forward; if it is pushed to the left, the pointer will go left, and so on.

Some laptops do not have a touchpad, but embed a very small joystick (a 'thumbstick') operated by a user's finger or thumb in the middle of the keyboard. A variant of these is sometimes used on mobile phone keypads.

Because of their advantages, joysticks are used in applications like the following:

- Joysticks are used to play many games because they give the user the impression of being in control. There is also a direct and immediate result of the player's actions which adds to the enjoyment of the game.
- They are used to control aircraft because of their simplicity in a very complex environment.
- Severely disabled people can use them to control motorised wheelchairs because they allow the user to give many different commands with very little physical movement.

The disadvantage of using a joystick as a pointing device is that it is more difficult to control the fine movement of the pointer on the screen than with a mouse.

SAQ

6 Describe a use for a joystick in a timber yard.

In a **touchscreen** input device, the options are shown on the screen and the user simply touches the screen where the option is showing (Figure 2.10). The touchscreen can determine where on the screen the user has touched and sends that information to the processor.

Figure 2.10 A touchscreen.

These screens are common in information systems in places like train stations because:
- they are difficult to vandalise compared with something like a mouse;
- they are largely weatherproof so can be in the open air like a station platform;
- they need no computer knowledge at all to be able to operate them.

A disadvantage is that disabled people can find them difficult to use.

Many touchscreens are basically on/off switches in that they rely on a particular area of the screen being touched; the input is simply whether or not that area has been touched. In this way the ticket machine inputs the type of ticket simply by interpreting the area of the screen that has been pressed.

More advanced touchscreens allow for more than a simple on/off type of input. A stylus can be used like a pen to write on the screen. The touchscreen software then interprets what has been written. The devices often carried by delivery people are examples. When the delivery is made the customer 'signs' the small screen to show that the package has been received.

 SAQ

7 List the advantages and disadvantages of using touchscreens as input devices.

Question

7 Touchscreens are often used as the input device attached to information systems like those at train stations, but they are used in many other situations, particularly where there are only a limited number of options to choose from.

a Investigate the use of touchscreens in places around where you live. Try to decide what makes it sensible to use a touchscreen in the examples that you find.

b Most touchscreen applications have two areas of the screen always reserved for two important commands. Try to discover what they are and decide why they are important.

Extension

Investigate the use of touchscreen technology on devices like mobile phones and portable game machines like the Nintendo DS.

A **graphics tablet** is like a very large touchpad (Figure 2.11). It senses the movement of an object moving over its surface and sends this information to the computer.

Figure 2.11 A graphics tablet can be used to 'draw' diagrams and illustrations.

Usually, a graphics tablet's active surface is treated as though it was the computer's screen – touching the top left of the tablet will move the pointer to the top left of the screen and touching the bottom right will move the pointer straight to the bottom right. Unlike a mouse or touchpad, there is no need to move the pointer across the screen: it moves straight to where the user touches the tablet.

Unlike touchpads, graphics tablets are usually used with a stylus rather than a fingertip. A **stylus** is a plastic pen-shaped device, but it doesn't actually draw anything. Instead, it lets the graphics tablet record its movements as accurately as possible, and can even tell the computer how hard you are pressing or which way up it was pointing – so you can 'rub out' what you've drawn, for example.

Graphics tablets are used for copying drawings on paper by allowing the user to trace over the top of the drawing. They are also used for creating original drawings and even writing, particularly for languages such as Chinese and Japanese. The ease of drawing and writing like this is the main advantage of using a graphics tablet.

A disadvantage of using a graphics tablet is that it can sometimes be difficult to relate the position and movement of the stylus on the tablet with the position and movement of the pointer on the screen.

A **light pen** is a device that can be used for 'drawing' directly on to a CRT screen (Figure 2.12).

Figure 2.12 Using a light pen.

The picture on a CRT monitor is created by electrons being aimed from the back onto the surface of the screen. A light pen does not shine a light but picks up the light from the screen. An electronic chip in the pen can tell the computer exactly when the light was picked up by the pen and the computer knows which part of the screen was being illuminated at the time. In this way

the computer can work out where the pen was pointing and can 'draw' on that part of the screen.

The advantage is that only the screen and the light pen need to be in the area of use so it can be used where there is little space. The disadvantages are that accuracy is poor and the light pen requires a wire to connect it to the computer, which makes it cumbersome.

Light pens are rarely seen these days, now that touchscreens and graphics tablets are widely available.

Inputting images: scanners and cameras

A **scanner** is a device that shines light at a drawing or a photograph and can interpret the reflected light so that the image can be stored in a computer system. Most scanners have a flat sheet of glass on which the **hard copy** (a photo or printed piece of paper) is placed (Figure 2.13). The advantage of scanning documents is that hard-copy material can be changed into a form that can be edited or stored on the computer system.

Figure 2.13 A flat bed scanner.

...ers are often used for three different types of

...ages from hard-copy material;

- optical character recognition (OCR) from hard-copy text (see page 22);
- optical mark reading (OMR) from specially prepared hard-copy forms (see page 22).

While scanners make it possible to put images of hard-copy photographs and printed illustrations into a computer, there may be a reduction in the quality of the image, and scanned diagrams can sometimes appear distorted. However, this reduction in quality depends on the technical specification of the scanner.

? SAQ

> 8 What are the advantages of scanning your class photograph rather than having a printed copy?

Digital cameras are used to take pictures in much the same way as a film camera (you may have studied how these work in your science lessons). However, instead of the image being caught on film it is caught by a series of sensors that are arranged in a grid (Figure 2.14). When all the individual pin-pricks of colour are put together they make a picture. These little areas of colour are called **pixels** ('picture elements'). The more pixels that are used, the better the quality of the picture.

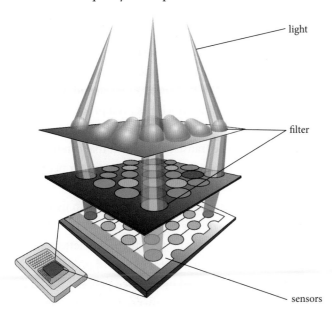

light

filter

sensors

Figure 2.14 How a digital camera works.

The camera records what each of the individual pixels has captured in storage, either in flash memory or on a removable media card (see Module 3 page 41). This card can be used to upload the picture into the computer; alternatively, most cameras can be connected to the computer with a cable and the images uploaded directly.

Once the image is in the computer it can be modified using software which allows the image to be changed in size or colour. It is even possible to combine images together so that they look like one image.

The images can also be manipulated and printed out on paper without the need of a separate computer by using a device called a 'photo printer', which has more than the usual four ink colours and so can print colours more accurately.

The advantages of digital cameras over film cameras are:

- the picture can be seen immediately and erased if it is not good enough;
- digital images can be manipulated more readily than those on film;
- the image can be used in other electronic documents.

One disadvantage of a digital camera is that its battery must be charged before it can be used to take pictures.

Question

> 8 'The camera never lies' – is this true? What effect does the possibility of image manipulation have on people in the photographs and those who are looking at them?

Extension

> Investigate the number and colour of printer inks which are found in different types of printer. Why will there be more colours in a photo printer than in an ordinary printer? What will the colours be?

Video cameras are used to take a series of images that can then be run together to produce the illusion of movement (Figure 2.15).

A video camera can be linked to a computer in order to feed the video directly into the computer. Once stored in the computer, the video can be edited directly

Figure 2.15 Girl using a video camera.

and incorporated into websites or stored on a portable storage medium.

Video cameras are used for leisure and also for security purposes. Video footage can also be taken using digital cameras and mobile phones.

Webcams are a special category of video camera that have no storage capacity but are connected directly to a computer (Figure 2.16). Laptops may have a webcam built in to the lid, just above the screen. Another type of webcam can be plugged into a desktop computer and used that way.

Webcams are often used to provide live video pictures when chatting with friends and family members using applications such as Skype or iChat.

They can also be used to provide pictures to accompany a meeting held by people who are talking to each other over the Internet. Such a meeting is called a **video conference**.

The live images provided by a webcam can be added to a website. For example, some webcams show street scenes; others might show wildlife habitats.

Webcams are dedicated devices so they can be left on permanently if necessary. This means that they can be used for remotely watching a property for security reasons or remotely monitoring elderly

webcam

Figure 2.16 Using a webcam.

people while allowing them to maintain their freedom. A disadvantage is that they need to be connected to a computer because they have no storage.

 SAQ

9 How might a timber yard use webcams to improve security inside and outside their building?

Inputting sound and music

Microphones can be used to allow a computer to convert sounds into data that it can handle. This can be used to allow a number of different applications including adding speech to a presentation which has been produced using a piece of presentation software. Microphones also allow people's speech to be translated into text that can then be used by a word processor. This can be useful for people with physical disabilities (Figure 2.17).

An advantage is that input is far easier than using a keyboard. Software on the computer can interpret the sounds of spoken words and turn them into letters and words in electronic form for use in a word processor. Microphones are also used by disabled people for whom the use of some more commonly used input devices is simply not possible.

A disadvantage is that the software used to translate the spoken word into words to be used in a word processor can be unreliable.

Figure 2.17 Microphones can be used with speech-to-text programs.

 SAQ

10 Who is most likely to use a microphone for speech-to-data in the timber yard business? State your reasons.

Question

9 Microphones can be used as an input to a processor which controls a burglar alarm system in a car. The processor might be set to identify the sound of broken glass. This would be picked up by the microphone if someone broke a window in order to steal something, but what about a bottle being smashed outside the car? How can the processor–microphone combination recognise that this is not damage to the car?

A music or **MIDI keyboard** can act as an input device (Figure 2.18). It needs to be connected to the computer system using a MIDI interface – a special type of interface which translates the signal coming from the keyboard into electronic data that the computer can handle. For example, when a key is pressed on the keyboard, the MIDI turns that input into the pitch, duration and so on of the note, which can be used to reproduce the note electronically.

Figure 2.18 Using a music keyboard to input music via MIDI.

The disadvantage of this form of input is that the user needs to have musical ability. However, storing MIDI data this way takes less space than storing sound samples. This technology is widely used for digitally recording and editing music. It also lets one musician play many instruments on the same recording.

Extension

Other types of MIDI devices are available. Investigate the possibilities and compare the qualities of each. A starting point would be to look at the Yamaha WX5 which allows synthetic wind instrument control.

2a, b **Remote controls**

A **remote control** is a small, handheld device which can be used to operate equipment such as a TV or stereo (Figure 2.19). It has a number of buttons. When a button is pressed, the remote control sends a signal to the equipment. Each signal contains a code; there are enough different codes to allow all the buttons to have their own code so that the equipment knows what to do. Remote controls are used to control home entertainment systems and satellite boxes.

An advantage is convenience – for example, you do not need to stand up to change TV channel. A disadvantage is that the signal can interfere with other equipment and can be blocked by objects between the remote control and the equipment it controls.

Figure 2.19 Using a remote control.

Question

10 A recent radio play in the 'Torchwood' science fiction series featured a universal remote controller. It belonged to someone from the future who lived in a society where everyone had one of these devices and they could be used to control any mechanical device.

How close are we to this being a reality? Is it something that we should be looking forward to? Can you see problems arising if they were to become a reality?

Extension

Remote controls are commonly used to lock and unlock cars. This type of remote control differs from that used to control a TV in two specific ways. Investigate how it differs.

A garage door can be opened and closed automatically using a remote control inside a car. Investigate how this differs from other remote controls.

2a,b Direct input systems

So far in this module, we have looked at input devices that are used by people to enter data directly, or **manual input devices**.

We are now going to turn to devices and methods that enable data to be entered directly, without human intervention. These **direct input** or **direct data entry**

methods are used when large amounts of similar data need to be entered, often in commercial or business applications.

OCR and OMR

We said above that scanners can be used for three different types of input:

- images from hard-copy material;
- OCR from hard-copy text;
- OMR from specially prepared hard-copy forms.

We looked at the first input method above. We now focus on the second and third input methods possible using a scanner.

If a scanned image contains text, you can use software to turn it into text that can be used by a word processor. This is known as optical character recognition (**OCR**).

OCR software compares the shape of each character with the shapes that it knows and, when it is matched, the computer stores the fact that it is a letter R, for example (Figure 2.20). This can make the input of data from hard-copy documents much quicker than retyping them. It is also useful for blind people, who can put a typed document on to the scanner and then have the computer read it aloud. OCR software can also be used to read data from passports or identity cards directly into the computer.

One disadvantage is that the text produced is not always reliable, particularly if the hard-copy original is unclear or has smudged text.

A scanner can also be used to scan a sheet of paper looking for marks on the paper, such as answers to multiple-choice exam questions or even votes in an election. This is known as optical mark recognition or optical mark reading (**OMR**). OMR scanning aims to find the marks on the paper; it is not interested in their shape, only where they are.

The answer to question 1 in Figure 2.21 is E, so the shading in should be in the position labelled E. The scanner will record the coordinates on the paper of where the mark has been made. The computer knows the coordinates of the correct response and will award a mark if the two sets of coordinates match.

The advantage of this method of input is that it is extremely fast because there is only a small amount of data on a sheet and it is far more accurate than other

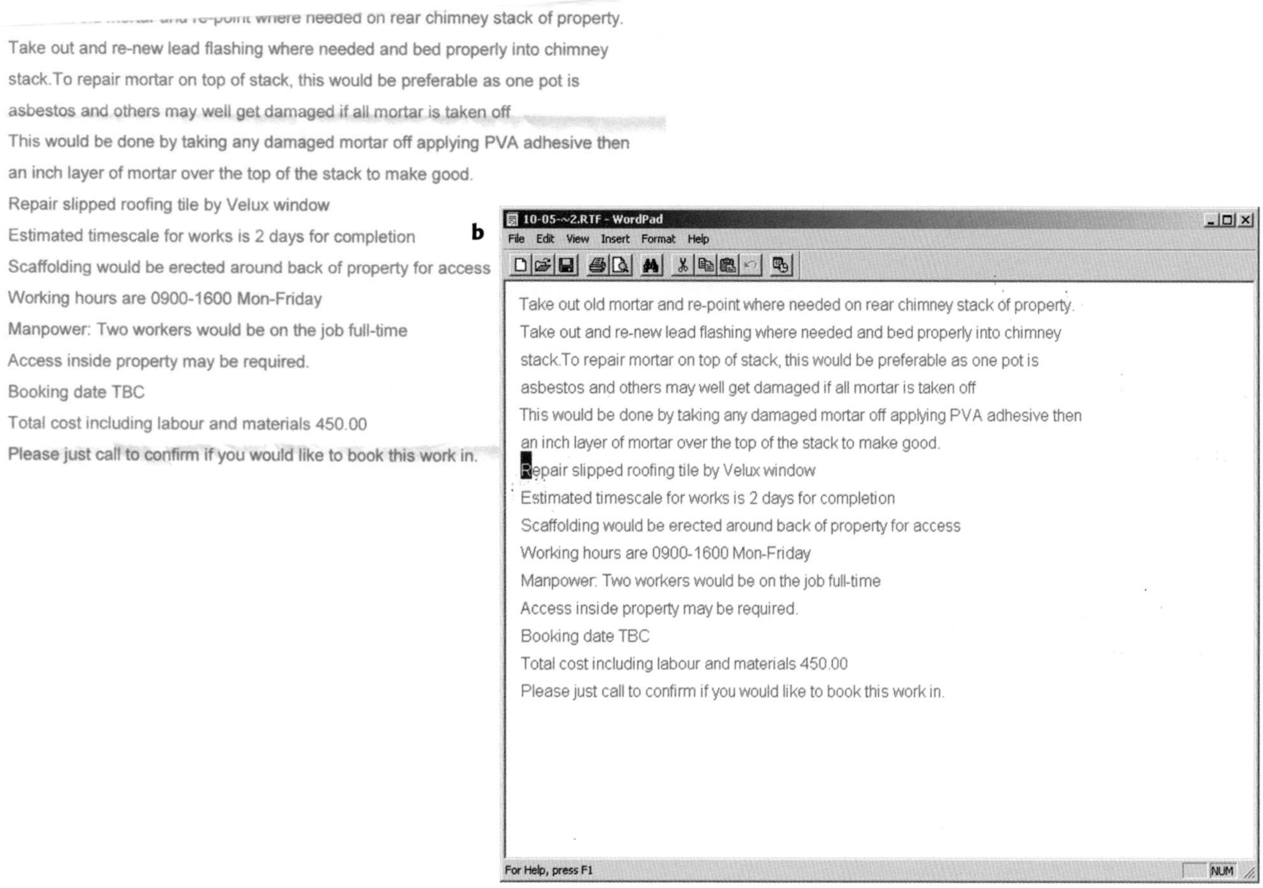
... and re-point where needed on rear chimney stack of property.
Take out and re-new lead flashing where needed and bed properly into chimney stack.To repair mortar on top of stack, this would be preferable as one pot is asbestos and others may well get damaged if all mortar is taken off
This would be done by taking any damaged mortar off applying PVA adhesive then an inch layer of mortar over the top of the stack to make good.
Repair slipped roofing tile by Velux window
Estimated timescale for works is 2 days for completion
Scaffolding would be erected around back of property for access
Working hours are 0900-1600 Mon-Friday
Manpower: Two workers would be on the job full-time
Access inside property may be required.
Booking date TBC
Total cost including labour and materials 450.00
Please just call to confirm if you would like to book this work in.

b

10-05-~2.RTF - WordPad
File Edit View Insert Format Help

Take out old mortar and re-point where needed on rear chimney stack of property.
Take out and re-new lead flashing where needed and bed properly into chimney stack.To repair mortar on top of stack, this would be preferable as one pot is asbestos and others may well get damaged if all mortar is taken off
This would be done by taking any damaged mortar off applying PVA adhesive then an inch layer of mortar over the top of the stack to make good.
Repair slipped roofing tile by Velux window
Estimated timescale for works is 2 days for completion
Scaffolding would be erected around back of property for access
Working hours are 0900-1600 Mon-Friday
Manpower: Two workers would be on the job full-time
Access inside property may be required.
Booking date TBC
Total cost including labour and materials 450.00
Please just call to confirm if you would like to book this work in.

For Help, press F1
NUM

Figure 2.20 Using OCR software. **a** Scan of original text. **b** Resulting editable text.

methods for this type of data. The disadvantages are that the sheets will not be read accurately unless they are properly lined up, and that dirty marks on the paper might be misinterpreted by the system as marks to be input. Many school registers use this sort of data capture.

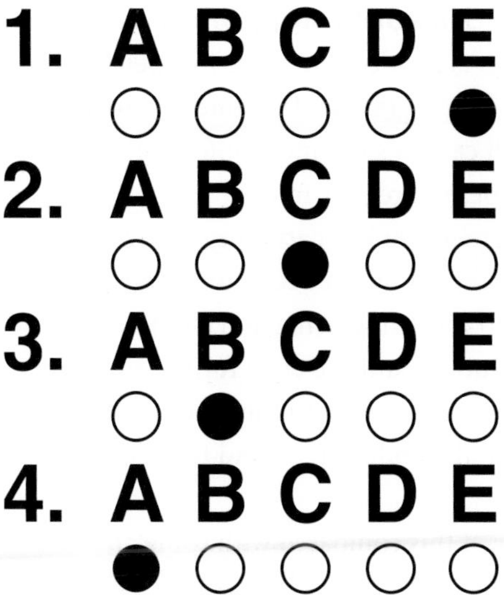

Figure 2.21 A multiple-choice answer sheet for OMR.

MICR

MICR stands for 'magnetic ink character recognition'. The magnetic ink helps the reader to 'see' the shapes of the different characters clearly. The special shape of the characters also helps to improve accuracy. The characters could be written in any shape that the computer is programmed to recognise but these particular shapes are used so that the characters can be read by human beings as well. This particular quality of being both human and machine readable is the main characteristic of MICR characters. If an exam question asks where they are used it is not good enough to say 'On cheques' because there are lots of other things on cheques as well. It is important that you state 'For the account numbers on the bottom of bank cheques'. The important thing is that it is the account numbers which are in MICR. There are very few uses for MICR; one other is that it is used to print the passport number on passports of some countries.

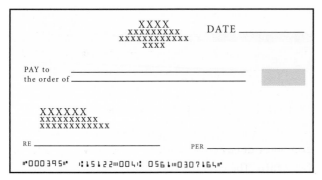

Figure 2.22 The numbers on the bottom of a cheque are printed using magnetic ink so that they can be read by a special reader even if they have been written over.

 SAQ

11 Describe each of the following input methods. Give an application where each is used, justifying your choice in each case.

   a OCR

   b OMR

   c MICR

Bar code readers

A **bar code** is a set of short parallel lines in contrasting colours, often black and white. The dark lines are thick, medium or thin. If they are taken in pairs of dark and pairs of light lines they can stand for the digits 0 to 9. These can then be read as a code number.

Figure 2.23 A typical bar code. Supermarket tills read bar codes like this one to register the price of a product.

Bar codes are read by devices that shine a laser at them and then read the reflection to tell how thick the lines are.

One advantage of using a bar code for data entry is that it is faster than using a keyboard. It is also more accurate because a human can make mistakes. One possible disadvantage is that it can be difficult for a shop to change details of products quickly if bar codes printed on the items include price information, for example.

Bar codes are sometimes used in libraries to identify both books and members (bar codes may be printed on membership cards). They are used on passports to represent the passport number, and on train tickets to hold information about date of travel and route to be taken.

A sensible use of bar codes is to represent something that does not change, like a person's name on a passport.

Extension

Try to find out the difference between the Universal Product Code and the European Article Number. These are not the only bar code systems in use but they are common ones. This exercise should give you more idea of how bar codes represent values.

When an item is passed over a laser scanner in a shop it will make a beeping sound to tell the shop worker that the code has been read properly. How does it know?

Magnetic stripe readers

On credit cards, library cards and hotel room card keys you may see a black **magnetic stripe**. The black stripe is magnetisable. It is divided into three independent strips which can be programmed to store different types of information. It cannot store much information, but many tasks do not require very much.

Imagine a hotel room key card (Figure 2.24). When the guest checks in, the receptionist writes information onto the stripe using a machine. The information includes a unique code for the room so, when the user puts the card into the reader on the hotel-room door, the code is read and the door is unlocked.

An advantage of this compared with using an ordinary key is that if the card is lost there is no way of identifying which room it is coded to open because

Figure 2.24 The magnetic stripe on the back of a hotel room card key is programmed with a code that will unlock the door.

all the cards look the same. Another advantage is that it is not so serious if the guest leaves without returning the key.

A disadvantage is that the information can easily be read or altered by using a small device that can be bought over the Internet.

Questions

11 There is room for three sets of information on the stripe.

   a What other information might the hotel set the card up to record?

   b Is this reasonable to do or does it clash with the rights to privacy of the customer?

12 Some colleges issue cards to their students. The students then use the cards to gain access to the different areas of the college.

   a What are the advantages to the college and to the individual students in doing this?

   b What disadvantages are there?

   c What other information might the college be able to learn from the use of these cards?

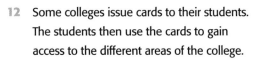

Chip-and-PIN readers

Credit and debit cards have always had a magnetic stripe on the back in order to store information that needed to be kept secret in order to maintain the integrity of the card and the account. The information was used to stop people using the account who should not do so. However, the relatively ready availability of devices that can read and alter the information on the magnetic stripes meant that a more complex technology was needed.

To make credit and debit cards more secure, they now include a small circuit with a number of computer devices all stored on a thin sliver of silicon, i.e. a **chip**. The chip can be seen on the surface of the card (Figure 2.25). This makes the information held very much more secure than it used to be on the stripe.

Figure 2.25 Front and back of a credit card, showing the chip (on the front), and the magnetic stripe (on the back).

When making a payment using a chip-and-PIN card, the user places the card in an input device called a **chip-and-PIN reader**, which reads the information stored in the chip (Figure 2.26). The most important piece of information in the chip is the **PIN** (personal identification number), which is a four-digit code that the user must know to use the card. The user types the PIN on the numeric keypad attached to the reader. The entered PIN is checked against the PIN stored on the card's chip, and if the two match the payment goes through.

The advantages of this technology is that the information held is secure because the chip is difficult to read. The disadvantage is that people tend to be careless when using their PIN – if other people can see it they would be able to use the card if they stole it.

Figure 2.26 Using a chip-and-PIN reader.

Chip-and-PIN readers are most used when buying goods in shops, but they can be used anywhere that the original magnetic stripe technology could be used.

Sensors

A **sensor** is a device which collects data. A keyboard does nothing until someone presses a key, but a sensor is collecting data all the time.

There are lots of different types of sensor, but most have something in common. They measure some physical property that can have any value (within limits), whether temperature, pressure or whatever. This sort of measurement is called **analogue data**, and computers cannot use data like this. They need to have data presented as a limited number of different values; this is called **digital data**.

Imagine a sensor is measuring the temperature of a room. The actual temperature may be 18.63547... °C. When this is sent to the computer, it may be sent as 18.6 °C. The data has been changed into digital data which the computer can use. This conversion is carried out by an **analogue-to-digital converter**. Module 5 will look in more detail at analogue and digital data and how they are converted from one to the other.

There are many different types of sensor, but you will study three types in this section: temperature, pressure and light.

For all of these sensors, it is important to realise that the sensor does not make the decision.

The advantages of using sensors as devices to collect data are:

- they are more reliable than a human being because a human may forget to take readings;
- a human may take inaccurate readings;
- it is not possible for a human to go to some places where readings need to be taken, like the inside of a reaction vessel.

A disadvantage of using sensors is that they power source. If there is a power cut or th they will stop working.

Temperature sensors read the temperature of surroundings and send the readings to the processor. The processor may then do something according to the input. For example, think about how an automatic washing machine works (Figure 2.27).

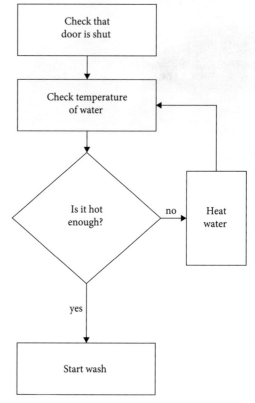

Figure 2.27 Using a temperature sensor in a washing machine.

When a washing machine is turned on to do the wash, the tub will fill with water. The processor in control of the wash cycle will need to ensure that the water is hot enough to do the wash. If it is not hot enough, the processor will turn on the heating element until the temperature sensor reports that the water is hot enough. If the water is too hot then the processor may let in some cold water to cool the water down until the temperature sensor reports that the water is cool enough.

Note that this device is called a 'temperature sensor'. It is not called a 'heat sensor', because heat is not a measurement. It is not called a 'thermometer' because that is something designed for human beings to look at.

Temperature sensors are also used in many other applications including:

- regulating the temperature of a room in a centrally heated or air-conditioned house;
- controlling temperatures in greenhouses (Figure 2.28);
- controlling the heat in reaction vessels in a scientific experiment.

Figure 2.28 Temperature sensors are used in systems that control the temperature in a commercial greenhouse.

SAQ

12 Explain what is wrong with this information.

'A thermometer is used to control the temperature in a fish tank. The temperature is measured by the thermometer which then decides whether the water is warm enough or whether it needs to turn on the heater to warm the water. A thermometer is used because a temperature sensor is electrical and cannot be used in water.'

Pressure sensors measure pressures and send the results to the processor where the decision is taken as to what to do.

A pressure pad could be used under the carpet in a house as part of a burglar alarm system. If something presses on the pad and that makes a contact which sets the alarm off then it is not a sensor. It is just a switch.

However, if measurements of the pressure are sent to a processor then a decision can be made. The processor can decide whether it is enough pressure to indicate a human being or whether it is the cat and so the alarm should not go off (Figure 2.29). If the processor can make a decision like this then the device that reads the pressure is a sensor.

Figure 2.29 Using a pressure sensor in a burglar alarm system.

Pressure sensors can be used in a wide variety of applications. They can be used to indicate the pressure that a robotic hand is exerting or the pressure in a reaction vessel in a chemical factory.

Light sensors measure the amount of light falling on them.

This could be used for something simple like a sensor in a car to decide whether or not to turn the headlights on because it is getting dark. Or in a burglar alarm system, if a beam of light is shone onto a light sensor then someone walking through the beam will reduce the light hitting the sensor. This information sent to a processor would indicate to it that there was something moving in the room.

A light sensor could be used for something very much more complex, like a robot truck in a factory which must follow a particular route (Figure 2.30). If the route is painted in white paint on the floor then a light shining on the floor from under the truck will cause light to be reflected from the white paint. If the

Figure 2.30 This robot truck uses a light sensor to follow a route through the factory.

truck has light sensors underneath then it will be able to send data about the amount of light reflected to the processor responsible for the truck. The processor will be able to guide the truck to follow the white paint.

Question

13 Some school geography departments record the weather in their area using an automatic weather station. How could the three types of sensor mentioned in this section be used to record the weather? Find out if your own school has a weather station like this.

Extension

Consider some other types of sensor and what they could be used for. Try to work out how sensors could be used for some other applications.

Some cars have automatic windscreen wipers. How does the processor know when there is water on the screen?

Output devices and their uses

We now turn to output devices and their uses, such as monitors, printers and control devices.

2c,d Monitors

A **monitor** is a device that displays information from the computer on a screen.

The advantage of using a monitor over other forms of output is that the output is immediate. The disadvantage is that it does not last – when the output is changed the previous output is lost from the screen.

There are two main types of monitor:

- CRT monitors (CRT stands for 'cathode ray tube');
- TFT monitors (TFT stands for 'thin film transistor').

CRT monitors are generally the cheapest form of monitor. They are also the oldest type and are extremely bulky (Figure 2.31). They tend to be about the same distance from back to front as they are wide across the screen. This means that they are sometimes very difficult to put on a desk.

CRT monitor

TFT monitor

Figure 2.31 These screens have a similar size display area, but the TFT monitor is far thinner and lighter than the CRT monitor.

CRT monitors make the picture appear by scanning a beam of electrons very quickly across the screen. By doing this many times every second, the electrons light up the areas of the screen that need to be bright, as you saw in the description about using light pens in the section on input devices. This is a good example of how closely related input and output devices are.

One advantage of CRT monitors is that you do not have to be directly in front of the screen to be able to see what is on it. This means that they can be used where many people need to be looking at the same screen at the same time. Another advantage is that CRTs can display a huge range of colours.

The main disadvantage of CRTs is that they are so bulky. They can be difficult to move or to mount on a wall because they are so heavy. However, they have been superseded almost entirely by TFT monitors.

TFT monitors use a different technology to CRT monitors. TFT monitors don't use a beam of electrons. Instead, they have a white light behind the screen that is blocked by tiny coloured windows. When the window is opened, light shines out. By opening and closing these tiny windows many times each second, the monitor makes a sharp, coloured, moving image. This technology means that the units can be very thin (Figure 2.31).

Because they are so much smaller and lighter than CRT monitors, TFT monitors can be easily and safely wall mounted. If they need to be placed on a desk, they take up very little space. TFT monitors are used in laptop computers and mobile phones.

Another advantage is that, because of the technology that is used to produce the picture, there is far less glare on the screen which makes them more restful on the eye. The image on TFT monitors can also be crisper and so better for word processing and similar work (they can cause less eye strain).

One disadvantage of TFT monitors used to be that you needed to be almost directly in front of the screen to be able to use it properly. If looked at from the side the picture tended to lose contrast and some of the colours altered. This meant that it was difficult to arrange for a group of people to be able to see the screen at the same time. However, these problems have largely been solved. Output to a laptop screen is small and should be viewed from a narrow angle to get the best effect. People who need to use computer files for training or presentation purposes need a better way of showing the information.

Also, TFT monitors cannot display the range of colours possible on CRT monitors.

Multimedia projectors are devices that can project an image from a computer onto as large a surface as is necessary (Figure 2.32). The only limit to the size of the projection is the power or brightness of the light produced by the projector. In all other respects the device is the same as an ordinary monitor screen.

Figure 2.32 Using a multimedia projector.

Projectors can also use television signals as their input or be linked to DVD players to produce a cinema-like effect. They are often used in public areas like hotels for showing football matches to customers. A projector can be fixed into the ceiling of the room if it is going to be used often. Alternatively the device can be totally portable. A disadvantage is the fact that it relies on a powerful and expensive bulb to provide the pictures. These bulbs are fragile, particularly if the projector is moved while it is still hot.

Questions

14 How does a projector show black? What effect does this have on other colours? What is the effect on a projector of a bright summer day?

15 Projectors and monitors have different resolutions. Find out about resolution. What sorts of applications are appropriate for the different resolutions?

16 Some classrooms in your school may have interactive whiteboards. Find out how they work. Which input and output devices from this section do they most resemble?

a

b

Printers and plotters

Printers and plotters are output devices which produce characters and/or graphics on paper or other materials.

You will learn about three types of printer here: laser printers, inkjet printers and dot matrix printers (Figure 2.33).

Laser printers work by using a laser to 'draw' the required outputs onto a drum (Figure 2.34). This puts a positive electric charge on those parts of the drum which have been hit by the laser. An ink powder (called toner) is then sprayed on to the drum and it sticks where there is an electric charge. This drum is then pressed against a piece of paper and the ink is transferred to the paper. The paper is then heated by a 'fuser' so that the toner binds to the paper, producing a printed copy. If there are four drums with four different colours of toner then coloured printouts can be produced.

Laser printers are used when quality and speed of output is important. They are used in schools and businesses particularly for communications with outside agencies because the quality of print makes a good impression.

One disadvantage of using laser printers is that the toner is toxic (poisonous) and the cartridges that it comes in must be disposed of carefully. Another disadvantage is that the first copy takes a long time to print. Subsequent copies are produced quickly. Consequently in a school a laser printer would be useful for producing large quantities of a newsletter, but would be less useful if producing single copies of a student's project work.

Figure 2.33 Different kinds of printer: **a** laser printer, **b** inkjet printer, **c** dot matrix printer.

Another issue with laser printers is that the reproduction of colour is not as precise as it is with an inkjet printer.

Laser printers tend to be more expensive to buy than other types of printer but other factors may make them cheaper in the long run.

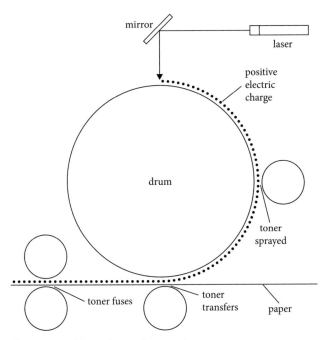

Figure 2.34 How a laser printer works.

Inkjet printers work by squirting ink at the page out of different nozzles for different coloured ink (Figure 2.35). A stepper motor advances the paper while the printhead with the nozzles scans across.

The advantages of inkjet printers are the high-quality output they produce and the fact that they are cheap to buy,

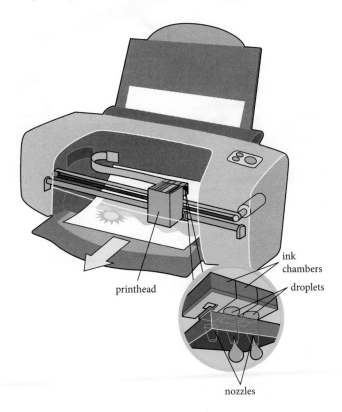

Figure 2.35 How an inkjet printer works.

making them affordable for family home use. The speed with which a page can be produced also makes them useful for home use, perhaps for printing a project for school.

One disadvantage of inkjet printers is that they often use water-soluble ink, so if printouts get wet, the ink will run. This does not happen with printouts from laser printers. Another disadvantage is that they are often slow, especially if a lot of copies of the same document are needed.

Inkjet printers are cheap and plentiful, and they are light and relatively small. For these reasons they are commonly used in home computer systems and small offices where most printing is for single copy outputs.

Inkjet printers are often used in machines that print out photographs directly from digital cameras. These may have some basic photo-handling software so that a limited amount of image manipulation can be done before printing.

Extension

The next generation of printers are 3-D printers. Some of these use layers of ink to build up a 3-D representation of an object; others use materials like glue and glass rather than ink.

Investigate 3-D printers. Starting points might be the websites for RepRap (http://www.reprap.co.uk) or CandyFab (http://candyfab.org).

Dot matrix printers use a set of pins to press an inked ribbon against the paper (Figure 2.36). Where the pin hits against the paper a coloured dot is left. These dots can be arranged in patterns to produce the required output on the paper. If different coloured ribbons are used then coloured printing can be produced.

The fact that they press against the paper means that if two- or three-part stationery (multi-part stationary) is used then more than one copy can be produced at a time. This is useful in a shop where they need to print a receipt for the customer and also keep a copy for their records.

Dot matrix printers are slower than other types because the method used in printing is mechanical. This also makes them very noisy.

An advantage of dot matrix printers is that they are robust and less likely to go wrong in dirty environments than other printers so they tend to be popular on production lines and in places like garages.

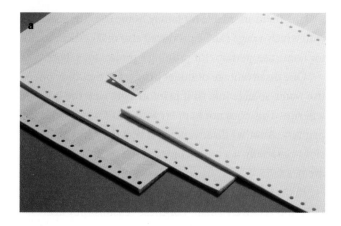

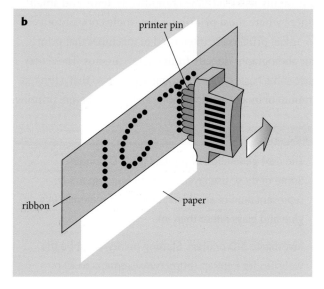

Figure 2.36 A dot matrix printer is useful when multi-part stationery needs to be printed. **a** Multi-part paper. **b** How a dot matrix printer works. Printer pins press on paper through an ink ribbon.

The disadvantage that they are noisy can sometimes be an advantage. In the control room of the nuclear power station at Heysham in the north of England there are lots of screens and printers and flashing warning lights. The most critical machine in there though is a dot matrix printer which is placed next to the chief technician's chair. It is this printer which will report any really dangerous problem that might arise. The reason is that the noise it makes is so different from everything else in the room that it would immediately attract everybody's attention.

Plotters are, by contrast, fundamentally line-drawing devices. They don't deal with dots at all but rather with lines of various lengths and colours. Rather than covering the page in strips, working steadily from top to bottom, a plotter will drive its pen around the page in curves or lines. It may go up and down and across the page many times until the output is complete.

Flatbed plotters (Figure 2.37) have the paper lying flat under the pens. The pen itself is attached to a motor in a very similar way to the print head of an inkjet printer. But instead of just going back and forth with its ink nozzles firing at the right time, the motors in the plotter can drive the pen across the page at any angle for any distance, curving and returning. This makes plotters ideal for creating clean, sharp blueprints for engineering or architecture.

In a **drum plotter**, the paper lies on a drum that spins to drive the paper under the pen while the pen itself moves across the drum – very similar in principle to the flatbed plotter but it takes up less space.

Whereas printers are great for solid blocks of colour, plotters are great for smooth lines, especially on large pieces of paper. Plotters are rarer these days because printers' resolutions are so high, but are still found in some niches (very large sheets of paper and applications where a different tool is used rather than a pen, such as vinyl cutting for sign making).

Figure 2.37 An example of a flatbed plotter.

 SAQ

13 Describe each of the following print devices. Give an application where each may be used, justifying your choices.
   a Dot matrix printer
   b Inkjet printer
   c Laser printer
   d Plotter

17 Printers can produce output on many materials other than paper. Investigate the use of other materials and the problems that might arise because of their use. Here are two suggestions to get you started.

   a Try to find out how a street vendor at a tourist attraction can offer to print your photograph with the attraction in the background, on a tee-shirt.

   b How can the graphics on the side of a business van be produced?

Speakers

Many pieces of software and different applications require the user to hear sounds, often connected with what is on the screen, such as a video explaining how volcanoes erupt. The sound of the eruption adds to the realism of the video and lets a narrator explain what is happening while the user is watching.

Any multimedia application will need the use of sound as part of the presentation. Similarly, a user might want to listen to music while working on the computer. To allow the user to hear sounds or music the system will need to have **speakers** (Figure 2.38).

Figure 2.38 Typical desktop speakers used with a computer.

Another important use of speakers is as an output device for some disabled people, particularly blind people who would not be able to see the screen. The

speakers allow special software (a screen reader) to describe aloud what is shown on the screen.

Headphones are personal speakers, and are often used in environments where other people should not hear the sounds produced. This might be because it would disturb their concentration or because the output is confidential.

Speakers would be used for a sales presentation to a group of customers but headphones would be necessary in a classroom where each of the students is engaged on different work and the noise from so many different speakers would be intrusive.

Question

18 One of the advantages listed for both microphones and speakers was that they allow input to and output from a computer system for blind people.

Investigate other input and output devices which are designed for use by blind people.

Extend the enquiry to cover devices designed specifically to help people with other disabilities.

Control devices

In this module, input devices have been discussed first and output devices afterwards. There is a certain logic to this as you would expect to provide input before getting any output.

However, it is also important to understand the links between certain types of input and output devices. We have just been talking about speakers and headphones as output devices; they naturally pair up with a microphone as an input device.

The next type of output device is an actuator. Actuators are used in control applications and match up with sensors as input devices because both sensors and actuators are automatic devices which do not need any human involvment.

Earlier you saw how sensors collect data automatically as input. This section is about control devices, which work in parallel with sensors. **Control devices** are used to change some physical value in response to a command from a computer.

Sensors and control devices together with the controlling computer make up a **control application**. You will look at many examples of control applications in Module 7.

Think for a moment about how a computer might control turning on a light (Figure 2.39). The computer can produce an electrical signal, but this would not be able to turn the light on – a switch is needed to do that. Instead, the computer signal might be sent to a device that can turn the signal into movement. If a light switch is attached, the device can switch it on or off. The device that turns the computer signal into movement is called an **actuator**.

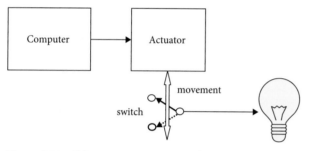

Figure 2.39 Using a computer to control turning on a light.

Heaters can be controlled by actuators. They are used in central heating systems and to ensure that greenhouses do not fall below a certain preset temperature.

Motors can be used by a computer processor to control elements of many household devices from washing machines to DVD players to air conditioners. If a device follows a set of specific rules, it can be controlled by a processor. Similarly, if a device uses motors to carry out actions, those motors can be controlled by a processor.

In industry, the robots on a production line are controlled by many small motors, each controlled by a processor that works out the required actions.

In a computer system, motors are essential for pushing paper through a printer, spinning the disk in a hard disk drive and moving the read–write head to the correct position. All of these motors and many more are controlled by the processor.

Buzzers or beepers make a single sound and are often used to inform a user that a particular thing has happened. For example, when the time is up on a microwave, the microwave may make a beeping noise.

Buzzers are usually used in a quiet environment because they will then be heard clearly. However, using a buzzer to tell a mechanic that a device has finished checking exhaust fumes from a car would not be helpful because the environment is likely to be very noisy.

Many devices use **lights** and **lamps** as sig[...] user. If the device is controlled by a processo[...] light can be considered to be an output devi[...] of lights as output devices might be:

- lights in a house that are computer controlled to give the impression that someone is at home;
- lights in a greenhouse to persuade plants that there is more daylight than there really is in order to speed up the growing process.

Case study: sensors and control devices working together

Throughout this module, input and output devices have been mentioned as working together. For example, the input of a mouse's movement results in a change displayed on a monitor screen. This section looks in more detail at an example where sensors and control devices work together – that of a washing machine washing a load:

- The washing machine is switched on.
- The first action would be for the processor to check that the door is properly shut. To do this a signal from a pressure sensor attached to the door catch is read.
- If the signal shows that the catch is not fastened properly, the processor uses a buzzer to raise an alarm. It also lights a particular light on the front of the machine which indicates that the door is not properly shut.
- If the door is shut, the processor uses an actuator to open a valve to let water in. A temperature sensor continually measures the temperature of the water in the tub. The processor makes decisions about the water temperature and uses valves to regulate the flow of hot and cold water. It also controls the heater to get the temperature correct.
- The processor uses the motor of the machine to turn the tub and begin the wash cycle.
- When the wash cycle is complete, the processor uses an actuator to open another valve to let the water out.
- The processor then turns on a light on the front of the machine to show that the wash cycle is complete.

Question

19 The example of the washing machine shows how sensors and control devices can be used in a household application. A number of stages have been left out.

Work through the example and try to identify the other necessary stages to allow the machine to do the wash properly. How can sensors and control devices be used to carry out these other important stages?

It may help your understanding if you draw the stages as a flowchart as in Figure 2.27, which is reproduced here.

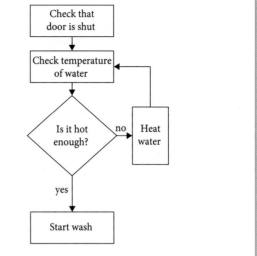

Figure 2.27 Using a temperature sensor in a washing machine.

Summary

You need to recognise the following input devices and say where they are used:
- manual input devices (used by people to enter data):
  - keyboards and keypads
  - pointing devices
  - scanners
  - digital cameras, video cameras and webcams
  - microphones and music keyboards
  - remote controls;
- direct input systems (used to enter data directly, without human intervention):
  - OCR systems
  - OMR systems
  - MICR readers
  - bar code readers
  - magnetic stripe readers
  - chip-and-PIN readers;
- sensors, e.g. for temperature, pressure and light, that collect data automatically.

You need to recognise the following output devices and say where they are used:
- CRT and TFT monitors, and multimedia projectors;
- laser, inkjet and dot matrix printers, and plotters;
- speakers;
- control devices.

3

Storage devices and media

When you have finished this module, you will be able to:

- understand the difference between main memory and backing storage
- describe common storage media and associated devices
- identify uses for backing storage devices
- identify advantages and disadvantages of each type of backing storage
- understand the term 'backup' and the need for backing up data.

Overview

Storage devices are peripheral devices that are used to hold data even when the computer is turned off. The **storage medium** is the part that holds the data while the **storage device** is the machine that lets you store data on the medium and read data from it (Figure 3.1).

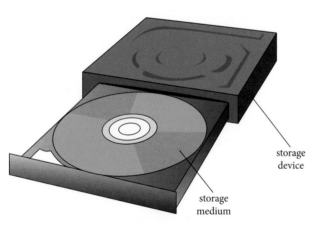

storage device

storage medium

Figure 3.1 The CD-RW disk is the *medium* because this is what has all the data on it. The CD-RW drive – the machine that the disk is put into and that allows the computer to read things from it – is the *device*.

In this module you will look first at the differences between main memory and backing storage.

You will then move on to look at the different storage devices and media, and their advantages and disadvantages.

Finally, you will consider how a backup system might be developed.

But first, a word of warning. The term 'backing storage device' simply means some device outside the main computer that can be used to store data. A 'backup copy' sounds as though it is the same thing, but it isn't. A backup is a copy of data used to keep the data safe and can be in the same computer and even the same disk. Be careful to treat the two things differently.

Reminder: bits, bytes ...

In Module 1, you saw how computers store and process data using binary numbers. For example, a computer might store the letter B as 10000011.

A single unit in binary is called a **bit**.

Computer memory and backing storage are both measured in **bytes**. One byte is usually made up of eight bits (this has become the unofficial standard). Because the capacity of both memory and backing storage is measured in thousands of bytes, prefixes are used. Table 3.1 shows how the units relate to each other.

Table 3.1 Common units for measuring the size of memory or backing storage.

Unit	Abbreviation	Size
kilobyte	kB	1 kB = 1024 bytes
megabyte	MB	1 MB = 1024 kB
gigabyte	GB	1 GB = 1024 MB
terabyte	TB	1 TB = 1024 GB

SAQ

1   Use a calculator to work out how many megabytes there are in a terabyte.

Main memory and backing storage are different

In Module 1 you looked at the two types of main memory, RAM and ROM.

Memory and storage are two different things:

- The computer processor can only use data or software in the memory. But the memory is not large enough to store all the data and software required by the user. In addition to this, the content of RAM is lost when the computer is turned off and the content of ROM can't be changed. Therefore, there is nowhere in the memory where data can both be stored long term and be changeable.

- Data that is stored in backing storage is, on the other hand, usually changeable and can be stored long term.

Most computer systems need to store data for long periods of time but they also need to be able to use it. This means that there will be a need for both storage and memory. The only systems that do not need backing storage are those systems that are embedded in things like washing machines and always do the same things so the instructions do not need altering and there is no point in storing details of the last wash program that was done.

As the processor can only use data and instructions that are in the memory, anything that is stored outside the memory will have an added stage of being copied into the memory which will slow down its processing.

Question

1   Explain why access speeds to data held in memory and data held on backing storage are different.

Common storage media and devices

There are three different types of storage device, and each type stores the data in a different way:

- **Magnetic storage media** hold the data magnetically. Tiny areas on the surface of the media can be magnetised in different ways and these store bits (see above) in codes that represent characters. If the device can read the medium then the tiny magnetised areas can be turned back into codes which the computer can use.

- **Optical storage media** store data on their surface by little 'pits' burnt by a laser into the surface. The laser can then be shone onto the surface more gently and, where it hits the pits, the reflection is different to that coming from a flat surface. These differences can be used to store codes for characters.

- **Solid-state storage** is different to the other two because it has no moving parts and fits directly into the computer. The device and the medium are the same thing.

Extension

Rewritable optical storage media store data on their surface in a different way to that described above. Investigate this.

Find out how solid-state storage works. A good place to start is http://electronics.howstuffworks.com/flash-memory.htm

Magnetic storage media

A **fixed hard disk** is the main storage on most personal computers. The data is stored on one or more disks.

Each disk has a device called a **read/write head**. This can write data onto the disk so that it can be stored and can read data from the disk when it needs to be used.

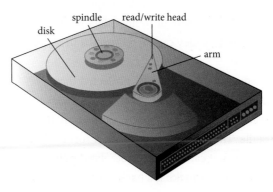

Figure 3.2   A hard disk.

Fixed hard disks are used as the main storage because:

- they can store very large amounts of data;
- access to the data is fast;
- there is no limit to the number of times they can delete data and then reuse the medium.

A disadvantage is that fixed hard disks are fragile, although they have been made more robust than they used to be. They are also stored inside the computer's case which gives added protection. However, data held on them should be backed up to ensure its safety.

Fixed hard disks are used to store three types of data:

1 the operating system of the computer;
2 the user's applications;
3 the user's data, including any work that the user has done on the computer and any files like videos and music that have been downloaded.

These three types of data are all stored on the hard disk and then sent to the computer's memory when they need to be used.

The data is organised on the disk so that **direct access** to it is possible. The disk has an index on its surface. If the user sends an instruction to read a particular file of data, the read/write head will look in the index to find out where it is and then go straight to that part of the disk. This is called **direct access to data** and means that there is no need to read through the whole disk to find just one piece of data – which speeds up the process considerably. Direct access to data is important when it is necessary to access data quickly.

Portable hard disks are very like fixed hard disks and use the same technology. The only difference is that they are not connected inside the computer case and will usually have a different type of interface to the computer. They can be easily connected to the computer to either have the data read off them or to have data written onto them. After this they can be removed and taken somewhere else.

They need to be more carefully protected than a fixed hard disk because they are likely to get knocked as they are moved about. Despite the protection, they are still fragile. They cost more than other forms of portable storage but can hold far more data so they are particularly useful for making a backup of all the data in a system.

Figure 3.3 A portable hard disk.

 SAQ

2 What does the disk drive use to find a particular file on the hard disk?

Magnetic tapes store data in a similar way to how data is stored on magnetic disks. The only difference is that the data is stored in a long line on the tape rather than being scattered over the surface of a disk.

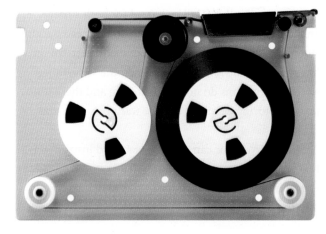

Figure 3.4 Inside of a 250 MB data cartridge showing the magnetic tape.

The tape is read and written to a read/write head similar to those used on magnetic disks. However, in the disk device the read/write head moves to the correct position to access the data. In a magnetic tape reader, the read/write head stays still and the tape moves past it. This means that data that is at the far end of the tape will take a long time to get to because all the other data will have to be read first. This sort of storage is called

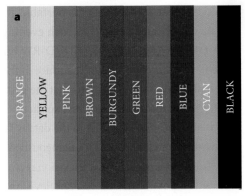
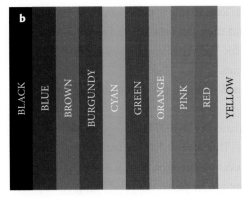

Figure 3.5 The difference between **a** serial and **b** sequential storage. In **a**, the colours (data) are in a random order so the read/write head has to move along the tape until it finds the requested colour. In **b**, the colours (data) are stored in alphabetical order, which means the read/write head can fastforward to the correct part of the tape.

serial storage. Serial storage means that the data is stored one piece after the other (Figure 3.5a).

If the data is arranged in some sort of order, perhaps alphabetical order, this would speed up finding a particular data item because the device could fast-forward through the unwanted bits. This form of storage is called **sequential storage** (Figure 3.5b). It gives faster access to data than serial storage, but is still very slow compared with the direct access to data on hard disks.

Magnetic tapes are used where there is a need to store large amounts of data and where the speed of access is not important – for example, for storing backups where a lot of data needs to be stored. Tape storage is also cheaper than disk storage and is less likely to be corrupted.

Sometimes the sequential way that data is stored on a tape is very useful. For example, the payroll for a large company is processed once a week. It is important that everyone gets paid. If the data is stored on a tape then everyone's data has to be read and there is no danger of missing someone out. The same is true of utility bills. These need to be sent to every customer on particular dates. (You will learn more about these and other examples in Module 7.)

Optical storage media

A **CD** (short for 'compact disk') can hold quite large files but is limited to about 1 GB. This makes CDs ideal for holding data like music files. However, when the file becomes larger, as for a movie, they are too small.

For larger files it is necessary to use a **DVD** (short for 'digital versatile disk'). DVDs can hold 5–10 GB of data.

Both CD drives and DVD drives use a laser to read and to write the data, but a DVD drive uses a more precise laser. Because of this, the data on DVD media can be closer together and therefore more data can be squeezed onto the surface.

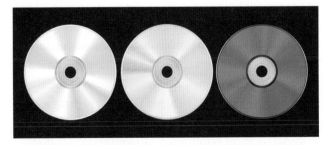

Figure 3.6 Left to right: CD, DVD and Blu-ray™. CD-ROMs, CD-RWs, DVD-Rs and Blu-rays look similar but hold different amounts of data. Also, some can be written to (recorded on) whereas others cannot.

Throughout this section on optical backing storage, it is vital to distinguish between disks that can be written to and those that cannot. A good principle is never to use 'CD' or 'DVD' on their own; they should always have some letters after them to say what type they are. The main types are as follows:

- ROM stands for 'Read-Only Memory' – these cannot be written to, only read from.

- R stands for 'Recordable' – these can be written to just once and then can only be read from.
- RW stands for 'ReWritable' – these can be written to multiple times.

So, what are the different types of optical storage media used for?

CD-ROMs and **DVD-ROMs** cannot be written to, only read from. This means that the contents of the CD or DVD can never be changed. This is a big advantage if the contents need to be protected from being corrupted in some way. Examples include using them to sell music or movies. Software companies use them to distribute software and data files, and publishers to distribute reference material like encyclopedias.

This form of storage is robust because the media are not easy to damage and yet they store large amounts of data and are fairly cheap. They also have the advantage of protecting the data that is stored on them, because it cannot be changed.

What is an advantage at some times is a disadvantage at others. When you no longer like the music or have watched the film as often as you want to, it would be nice to change the contents but it is not possible.

CD-Rs and **DVD-Rs** can be written to just once, but after that the contents can no longer be changed. They can be used to store music or movies, or to make a copy of files at a particular time – for example, for an archive. However, once they have been recorded on, no further changes can be made to the data, which makes them less useful for making regular backups of files because every time a backup was needed a new disk would have to be used.

The advantage of CD-Rs and DVD-Rs is that the user can write what they want on to them and then the material on them is protected. Disadvantages are that they can be used only once and not all CD/DVD devices (e.g. music CD players) can play them.

CD-RWs and **DVD-RWs** are ideal for moving files from one computer to another, perhaps taking work into school that you have been doing on your computer at home. They are not easy to damage and can store large amounts of data. Because they are rewriteable, they can be used over and over again. This quality also makes them ideal for taking backups of the files on a system.

If a business decides that it is sensible to back up all the files on their system each evening in a form that can be removed from the building overnight, a DVD-RW would be ideal. It is robust, it is portable, it can hold a lot of data and it can be rewritten each evening.

A **DVD-RAM** is very like a DVD-RW but the data is stored in a different way on the surface of the disk. The different form of storage means that the surface can be written to far more often than the surface of a DVD-RW can. It also means that access to the data is faster. Reading and writing can take place simultaneously: if a DVD-RAM were used as the storage in a television recording machine it would be possible to record one television programme while watching a different one from the disk at the same time. This means that they can be used in household recorders for recording and watching TV programmes and can also be used as a subsidiary system to support the memory of a computer. Despite being more expensive than other forms of DVD, they have a greater capacity, though they cannot be used in an ordinary DVD player.

HD-DVD (short for 'high-definition DVD') was an attempt to put more data onto a DVD. The idea was to use it with high-definition video and computer games. However, in 2008, the format was dropped when the last major manufacturer withdrew its support for the format. The way was left open for the rival version, which is known as Blu-ray™.

Blu-ray disks have much larger storage capacities than other optical storage media (25–50 GB) while at the same time they are able to cope with high-speed transfers. These two advantages mean that it is now possible to record and play back hours of high-definition video. The disadvantage is the cost, which is much higher than that of standard DVDs.

 SAQ

3   Is it a good idea for a small company to use DVD-Rs for backing up every day?
Give a reason for your answer.

 Question

3   a   Name eight different types of optical storage.
    b   Explain the difference between the ROM, R and RW descriptions. When would each be used?

The difference between HD-DVD and Blu-ray devices is in the type of laser used. Different lasers use different parts of the available wavelength of light. The shorter the wavelength used, the more data can be squeezed onto the disk surface.

Investigate this and try to explain why this type of disk is called 'Blu-ray'.

Solid-state storage

Solid-state storage devices have no moving parts. This makes them more robust than other types of storage. They use similar technology to RAM and ROM memory chips, but don't need electricity to maintain the data. They are small and extremely portable, and can store large volumes of data. They are also straightforward to use since many of them are designed to fit straight into a computer port.

Figure 3.7 Examples of solid-state storage.

Memory sticks and **pen drives** (two names for the same thing) are small, with a lot of storage space. They are ideal for storing data and software that needs to be transported from one computer to another. They can be used for backups of the main files on a computer system.

Flash memory cards are similar to memory sticks as they are a form of portable memory. The distinctive difference is in their shape and the way that they connect to the parent device. A memory stick or pen drive fits into the USB port in a computer while a memory card gets its name from the fact that the device is flat and looks like a card. Because of this it is not sensible for the connector to be a USB, but the card slots into a port which is a different shape.

Flash memory cards are used in small electronic devices that need large volumes of storage, such as digital cameras to store photographs, mobile phones to store photographs, telephone numbers and other data, and MP3 players to store music files. They can be slotted into a computer case so that their contents can be downloaded quickly.

Solid-state devices have two main disadvantages. First, they are more expensive than other forms of secondary storage (although their price will reduce significantly in the future, making them attractive as backing storage). Secondly, their lifespan is more limited because of (as they need to be as small as possible) their lightweight protective cover.

Comparing different storage media

While the advantages and disadvantages of each type of storage medium are listed above, it can also be useful to compare them using these five particular qualities:

- volume of data held (Table 3.2);
- speed of data access (Table 3.3);
- portability (Table 3.4) – this is based on size and weight, and how easy it is to remove the media from the computer;
- robustness (Table 3.5) – how easy it is to damage the media or device, and whether it is easy to lose the contents;
- cost (Table 3.6).

First, note that it is not possible to state the exact storage capacity for each type of device for two reasons:

- The media are not fixed and are often available in a range of different sizes and types. For example, the amount of storage on a magnetic tape depends on how long the tape is and the particular tape technology used.
- The capacities are changing on a regular basis, and so by the time this book is published all the numbers involved are likely to have changed.

Second, note that the cost of a device includes a number of factors. The obvious one, which we focus on here, is the cost of buying it in the first place. However, there are other costs, such as the cost of the CD-RW that has to be put into the drive, or the cost related to the time taken by an employee to do something. An example of this might be having to change a large number of CDs in the drive to make a full backup of a large system; if a portable hard drive were used instead then the whole backup would fit on the drive. One measure of cost for storage devices is the cost for each gigabyte of data stored. However, because this is so variable the charts do not include this. The important thing is to be aware that there is more to 'cost' than the price of the device.

Because of these and similar issues, there are no actual values given in the tables. However, barring any technological breakthroughs, the pattern in each chart should remain the same.

Table 3.2 Comparing the volume of data held by various storage media/devices.

Very large storage capacity	Fixed hard disks Portable hard disks Magnetic tapes
Large storage capacity	Memory sticks/pen drives Flash memory cards Blu-ray/HD DVD DVD-ROM DVD-R, DVD-RW, DVD-RAM
Limited storage capacity	CDs

Table 3.3 Comparing speed of data access.

Very fast access to data	Flash memory cards Memory sticks and pen drives
Fast access to data	Fixed hard disks Portable hard disks All CDs, DVDs, Blu-ray
Slow access to data	Magnetic tape

Table 3.4 Comparing portability.

Very portable	Flash memory cards Memory sticks/pen drives All the CDs and DVDs
Less portable because of size	Portable hard disks While some tapes are small, others are large
Not portable	Fixed hard disks

Table 3.5 Comparing robustness.

Very robust	Memory sticks, pen drives Flash memory cards
Robust but might damage in some circumstances	CD-ROM, DVD-ROM CD-R, DVD-R HD-DVD, Blu-ray
Robust but may lose data if wrongly used	CD-RW, DVD-RW, DVD-RAM BD-RE (rewritable Blu-ray) Portable hard drive Magnetic tape
Very fragile if moved	Fixed hard drive

Table 3.6 Comparing cost.

Low cost	CDs, DVDs HD-DVD/Blu-ray
Medium cost	DVD-RAM Memory sticks, pen drives Flash memory cards
Expensive	Magnetic tape Portable hard drives Fixed hard drives

Questions

4 Make a list of the storage devices that you use at home and at school. What do you use them for? List the individual advantages and disadvantages that are important for what you use them for. Do you use any types of storage that are not mentioned above?

5 One type of storage device not described here is a minidisk. Find out how a minidisk works. What is it used for? What are the advantages and disadvantages of minidisks?

6 Try to look into the future. What sorts of storage device might there be in 10 years' time? Will we have memory chips implanted beneath our skin so that, for instance, if we get taken to hospital a reader can immediately tell the doctors our full medical history? What other things could a form of storage like this be used for?

Data backups

If a computer is being used to store data and something goes wrong with the computer, the data might be lost. If you are working on some data and accidentally delete something, you might find that what you deleted was important and should not have been deleted. If a virus attacks your computer and deletes some of your data you may lose very important work.

For all these reasons and more, it is sensible to make a copy of any data you have on a computer just in case something happens. Such a copy is called a **backup**.

Sometimes it is good enough to make a backup copy on the hard disk of the computer. This would be good enough if the original copy was accidentally deleted because there would be another copy that could be used instead. But what if the hard disk was damaged so that all the data was lost? The original would be lost and so would the backup.

For this reason it is sensible to have copies on different storage devices that can be kept separate from the computer. If something terrible happens to the computer, there will still be a copy of the data.

Imagine a business that had all its customer records stored on a computer system. If the computer was stolen it would be annoying but the business could probably claim for a new computer from its insurance company. But what about the customer records? Without those the business might not be able to carry on.

Backups of important data like this need to be stored on media away from the computer so that it is safe.

Case study: Developing a backup procedure

Background: Introducing Cottonwoods Ltd

Cottonwoods Ltd is a small firm of 25 employees which specialises in selling cotton products on the internet. The firm has a number of regular customers but also sells to buyers who place individual orders after seeing details of products on the firm's website.

Figure 3.8 Cottonwoods Ltd office. Most employees work at desks on computers.

All accounts are done on the firm's computer, and records of transactions and payments are stored on the computer. Customer details are also stored, particularly for customers who buy products on a regular basis – this amounts to several thousand records. Records of suppliers – there are under 100 – are also stored, together with the products that they supply and payments made to them.

The firm chose to use a fixed hard disk for storing most of the data needed on the system because it allows a very large volume of data to be stored. Access to the data is also very fast so that, if a customer rings up with an enquiry, the person who answers the call can bring the customer record up on the screen very quickly.

The website will be stored on a hard drive in a computer owned by a different company, which Cottonwoods has employed to publish their site on the Internet. The website will not be accessed by Cottonwoods' workers very often but will (hopefully) be visited often by customers, and needs to be available quickly.

Question

8 The firm is worried that if something happens to the data stored on the computer they will not be able to continue in business.
Discuss how they can protect against a loss of data being too catastrophic for the firm.

Figure 3.9 Potential customers looking at the Cottonwoods Ltd website.

What needs to be backed up? How?

All the firm's files need to be backed up, but how does the firm make sure that no files are forgotten or missed because of a mistake, the wrong files aren't backed up, or that the right files aren't sent to the wrong destination? A procedure to make sure that the backups are made correctly is called the **backup procedure** for the firm.

The backup procedure should include answers to these questions:

1 How often should the backups be made?
2 What media/device should be used for the backups?

3 Where are the backups going to be stored?
4 What can be done about changes made to the files?

Cottonwoods have many different types of file that need to be backed up. Here we look at the backup procedure for the customer and suppliers files.

1   How often should the backups be made?

The answer to this question depends on two things:
● How often does the data in the files change?
● How important is it?

The customer file will change every day as new orders come in. Making a backup of the file will mean it not being accessible very easily during the backup procedure so the firm decides to backup the customer file at the end of every day's business.

By contrast, the file of suppliers changes very rarely because the same suppliers are normally used. This means that the suppliers file may only be backed up once a month.

2   What media/device should be used for the backups?

The customer file is fairly large and the backup needs to be portable. It is being backed up regularly so the storage device needs to be alterable on a regular basis. For these reasons the firm has chosen to backup onto portable hard drives. They have two, which are used on alternate days.

3   Where are the backups going to be stored?

In case the computer is stolen or there is a fire in the building, the backups need to be stored off-site. One is stored in the company safe which is in another part of the building and the latest is taken home by the computer system manager after the backup has been made.

4   What can be done about changes made to the files?

The latest backup is an exact copy of the customer file when it is made. However, when orders come in during the day the customer file will change. It will now be different from the backup file, so if the system crashes and the file is lost the latest changes will also be lost.

The firm makes sure that any changes that happen to the file during the day are also stored on a file called the transaction file (or transaction log). This lists the changes since the last backup. This file will hardly ever be used; it will be cleared when the next backup is made. If something goes wrong with the customer file during the day, however, the changes on the transaction file can be applied to the backup and the customer file will be recreated complete with changes.

Question

9 Repeat the process of creating a backup procedure for some of the other types of file that the firm uses.

Extension

In reality, the whole system will be backed up each night because it is not worth backing up individual files differently. However, this probably does not apply to the website. Why? How is this backed up?

The ultimate backup procedure is to have a mirrored system. Explore what this would require and decide whether it is a sensible suggestion for Cottonwoods Ltd.

SAQ

5 a What is the name of the file that stores the day's changes?
 b Do you think a big company that makes lots of changes to its database might back up this file? How often each day might they do so?

Archiving files

The firm has found that the hard drive that is used to store all these files is getting very full because the files are so large. This is having a negative effect on the firm. It is taking longer to access data than it used to and the backup procedure is taking longer than it should.

The computer system manager has realised that most of the data stored in some of the files never changes. Many of the customers on the customer file no longer deal with the company. There are accounts from the date

that the company started. The only ones that are used are the ones from this year with occasional reference to last year's accounts.

The manager decides that copies of all these redundant files should be made and then the data can be removed from the hard drive. This will speed up access times and make more space available for the files that need it.

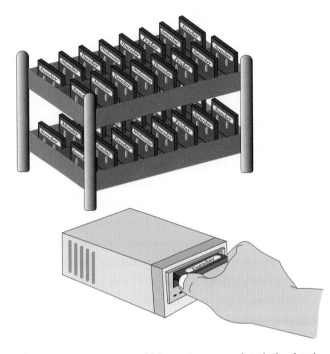

Figure 3.10 Computer archiving at Cottonwoods Ltd. The data is copied onto magnetic tape and stored within tape cartridges.

The redundant files are copied onto magnetic tape and stored off-site just in case they are ever needed. The copies that are on the hard drive are then removed. These files copied onto the tape are called the **archive**.

Archive files are useful for providing statistical information. They are also required by government agencies like the taxation authority who may want to look at past accounts.

Question

10 What would be a sensible backup procedure for the ICT department in your school?

 What would be a sensible backup procedure for a student with a computer at home?

 What are the differences in the procedures? What are the reasons for the differences?

Extension

Investigate the 'ancestral filing system' (or 'grandfather, father and son backup procedure').

Does it differ greatly from the description of the backup procedure for the customer file?

Under what conditions is it sensible to use the ancestral filing system?

Summary

- Memory consists of ROM and RAM. It is relatively small compared to the storage capacities of disks and tapes.
- Fixed hard disks are used for main storage.
- Portable hard disks and tapes are used for backup systems.
- Different types of optical storage are used in various applications:
  - CD-ROM and DVD-ROM are used for the sale and storage of software and encyclopedias;
  - CD-R and DVD-R are used for recording music and videos;
  - CD-RW and DVD-RW are used for backing up and transporting files;
  - Blu-ray media are used in video recorders and games consoles.
- Solid-state storage is small and easily transportable for relatively small files.
- A backup is a copy of material on the main computer storage, taken in case the main system is corrupted.

4 Computer networks

When you have finished this module, you will be able to:

- explain the use of browsers, email and an ISP
- describe the use of Wi-Fi and Bluetooth in networks
- define LAN, WLAN and WAN, and identify their characteristics
- identify some methods of communication over networks
- describe the use of various devices used on networks
- describe the advantages and disadvantages of using the Internet and intranets
- understand the use of IDs and passwords
- understand the problems of safety and security of data on networks
- understand the use of encryption and authentication techniques.

Overview

So far in this book, the focus has been on individual computers and the 'information' part of 'information and communications technology'. In this module you will see how computers can be linked together in a **network**, which enables them to communicate with each other and share information.

First, you will see how the computers in a small business can be connected in a small network and set up to access the Internet. Terms and technologies are introduced in this section and explained in more detail in the following sections.

Next, you will look briefly at how methods of communicating electronically were developed – essential if computers are to share information with each other.

You will then look in more detail at different types and sizes of network and the hardware needed to run them.

Finally, you will consider important issues arising from the widespread use of computer networks.

Setting up a home office network

Nabila and Rana have just been made redundant from their office jobs. They decide to work from home offering freelance secretarial help to local small businesses.

Nabila already has a PC and a printer, and has installed some office programs. She currently does not have access to the Internet from home. However, she knows from her previous job how much she used the Internet for research and communicating with others when doing her work.

Rana has decided to buy a laptop since there isn't enough space in her room to set up a desktop PC. She too would like to connect to the Internet.

At the moment, Nabila and Rana can each write letters using a word processor on their own computers. They can store details of customers using a database. They can use their computers individually to produce advertising material or create a presentation (see Module 7.1).

What they cannot do, however, is share information very easily. To do that, they need to save their work on a pen drive, walk to the other room, plug the pen drive into the other computer and copy the files across.

Figure 4.1 Individual computers are powerful tools by themselves, but linking them together so that they can communicate with each other and share information makes them even more powerful.

When Rana wants to print something she has to go into the other room, unplug the printer from Nabila's computer, then plug it into her laptop. Swapping the printer cable like this is not very satisfactory.

It would be useful if the computers could be linked together so that they could communicate with each other and share information and peripherals such as the printer.

When two or more computers are joined so that they can send information between each other, they are **networked**.

Connecting to the Internet

Because a lot of their work is likely to come from their customers via the Internet, Nabila and Rana decide that getting an Internet connection is a priority. They also agree that they will need to set up a wireless network so that Rana can use the Wi-Fi device built into her laptop.

To do this, Nabila contacts an **Internet service provider (ISP)** and sets up an account with them.

The ISP provides a wireless **router** which Nabila connects to the phone line and to her computer (Figure 4.2). The router enables Nabila's computer to access the Internet over the phone line. Because the router is a wireless one, Rana can share the connection via Wi-Fi.

Instead of a router, Nabila might use a **modem** to connect her computer to the Internet. A modem changes the digital signal from the computer into an analogue one which can be transmitted down telephone lines. When the message reaches the other end of the telephone line, another modem changes the signal back to a digital one for the computer at the other end to understand. However, modems are much slower than modern routers.

On her computer, Nabila sets up two pieces of software:
- a **browser** (Figure 4.3a), which she uses to find and look at information on the World Wide Web;
- an **email** program (Figure 4.3b), which she uses to send and receive messages over the Internet.

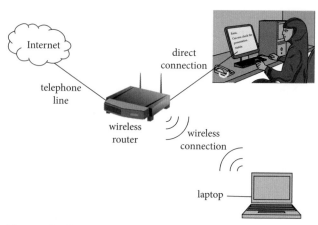

Figure 4.2 Using a router to enable a computer to access the Internet.

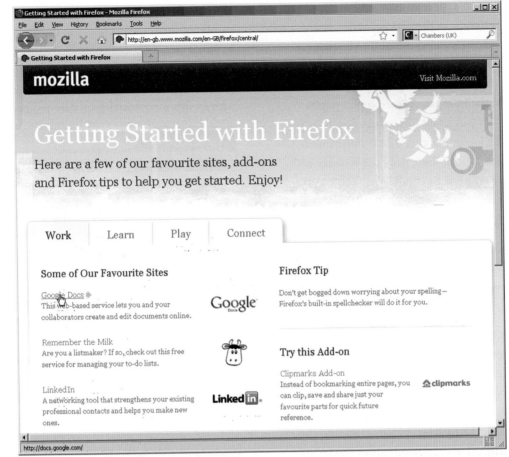

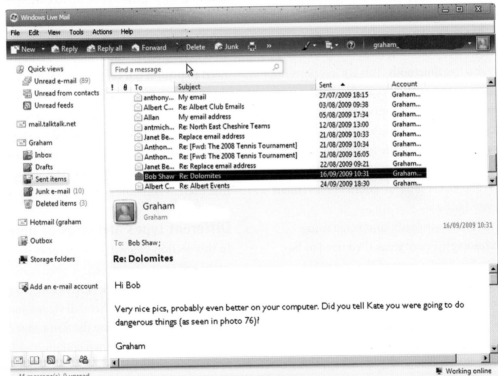

Figure 4.3   a Browser software enables you to find and look at information on the web. **b** Email software is for sending and receiving messages over the Internet.

A browser allows Nabila to ask for information in two ways. One is to type in the address of the data if she knows it. This address is called the **uniform resource locator** (URL). Each URL is unique.

The second way is to use the links that are available on many sites on the Internet. As the pointer passes over these links, it changes its appearance (see how the text under the hand in Figure 4.3a is underlined). When Nabila clicks one of these links the browser will immediately go to the location indicated.

 SAQ

1 a What hardware is needed to access the Internet?
  b What software is needed to access the Internet?

Using Wi-Fi and Bluetooth

The wireless router enables Nabila and Rana to set up a wireless local area network – a **WLAN**.

The WLAN uses **Wi-Fi** technology. Wi-Fi enabled devices can network with each other. Rana's laptop has a Wi-Fi network card which is capable of sending and receiving radio signals over relatively short distances. The transmission rate is high and Rana is not restricted by having to use her computer in specific locations within her home.

Rana's laptop also has **Bluetooth**. This is a less powerful form of wireless transmission than Wi-Fi. Bluetooth was developed to provide a wireless communication method between specific devices that are close together.

Rana can use Bluetooth to do the following:

- She can wirelessly connect and use a Bluetooth mouse, which allows her more freedom of movement than with a wired mouse.
- Some printers can be wirelessly connected using Bluetooth technology. Fewer wires then need to be used, which makes it safer around the computer (fewer wires to trip over).
- Rana's mobile phone has Bluetooth technology. This enables her to wirelessly synchronise contact details such as phone numbers between her laptop and the phone.
- Her games console uses Bluetooth technology. This allows her more freedom of movement in using the input device. It also allows two consoles to be connected so that she and Nabila can play two-player games.

All these uses of Bluetooth have two things in common. First, the range of the transmissions needs to be small. Secondly, the volume of data to be transmitted in a given amount of time is small. Both of these facts mean that there is no need for the more complex Wi-Fi with its more expensive hardware requirements.

Extension

What is the connection between Bluetooth and King Harald Batan of Denmark?

One use of Bluetooth with mobile phones is for using the phone with a hands-free device. Investigate other uses of Bluetooth with mobile phones.

4d Advantages and disadvantages of using networks

Networks are valuable because they allow hardware like printers to be shared, as well as the sharing of software and of files. For example, in a small business workers can all have access to the same customer file (which is stored centrally), and the part of the file they are working on will always be up to date. When they have completed their work they can save it for other people to see. They can send it electronically to other workers who may need the information. Perhaps they might need to print it out on the central office printer which everyone shares.

There are some disadvantages to using networks. One is that the security of the data being stored is reduced. Another disadvantage is that extra hardware is needed to allow the network to operate. This extra hardware means that there is something else that can go wrong.

4g,h Different types and sizes of network

In this section you will look in more detail at different types and sizes of network.

A **local area network** (**LAN**) consists of a number of computers and peripheral devices joined together over a small area. Because the size and scope of the network is limited, external communication media such as a telephone line are not needed. Similarly, outside influences (for example, who controls the communication medium, or interference with the medium by outside agencies like hackers) are not a problem.

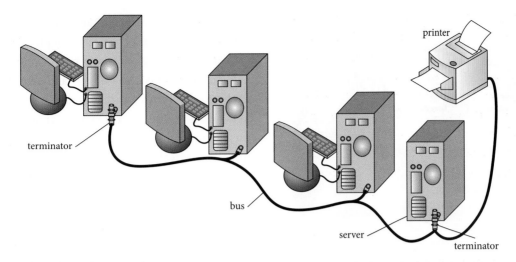

Figure 4.4 A bus network.

Typically in a LAN, hardware is connected by a cable. It can be connected together in different patterns. Two common patterns are a bus network and a star network.

In a **bus network** (Figure 4.4), the computers are all connected to a cable which is known as the bus. All the data is sent along this one cable. It needs special devices at the ends of the bus called **terminators** which absorb signals so that they don't get reflected back into the network and cause data corruption.

Bus networks are usually easy and cheap to install. There is little to go wrong, but if a fault occurs the whole network is likely to be affected. They have generally been superseded by star networks.

In a **star network** (Figure 4.5), each computer and peripheral is connected to a central hub or switch (see later) by its own cable.

Star networks are more difficult to install than bus networks because there is more cabling. However, if one of the cables fails, the rest of the network will continue to operate. But if a hub or switch fails, none of the devices connected to it will be able to communicate.

A LAN which uses radio waves rather than cables to transmit the data from machine to machine is called a wireless local area network (WLAN).

Computers fitted with a wireless network card can communicate with the nearest wireless access point,

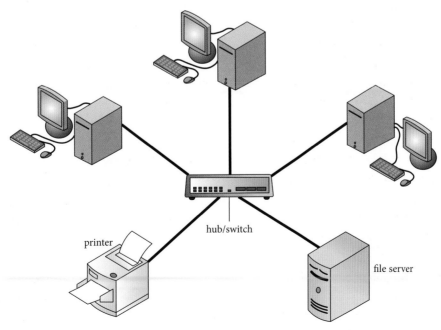

Figure 4.5 A star network.

Figure 4.6 A WLAN with several devices.

which could be your own wireless router (as in Rana and Nabila's case) or a public Wi-Fi access point. A network may have a number of access points (Figure 4.6).

A WLAN does not have any fixed wiring to the computers so a user can access the network from anywhere that is within range. This means that they can work from a convenient point rather than having to work near a network cable.

The main disadvantage of a WLAN is that other people can also access the network if they can get within range. This may not happen to a company because they will take the necessary precautions to stop unauthorised access. However, many home computer networks use WLAN technology and owners are less likely to take the necessary measures to protect their network. If you don't secure your own wireless router then your neighbours may be using it to access the Internet for free!

A **wide area network** (**WAN**) is a network which is spread over a larger geographical area than a LAN.

The ideas associated with LANs and WLANs of sharing data and making communications easier are still true with WANs. The difference is that because of the greater distances involved it is not possible to link the computers with cables or by radio.

A WAN normally uses communication media provided by a third party. An example would be a telephone company providing links via telephone cables or via broadband facilities.

Often, several LANs are linked up by a WAN. For example, a firm that has offices in London, Lahore and Colombo would probably use LANs in each of the offices. The company would then use telecommunication media to link the individual LANs together as a WAN (Figure 4.7).

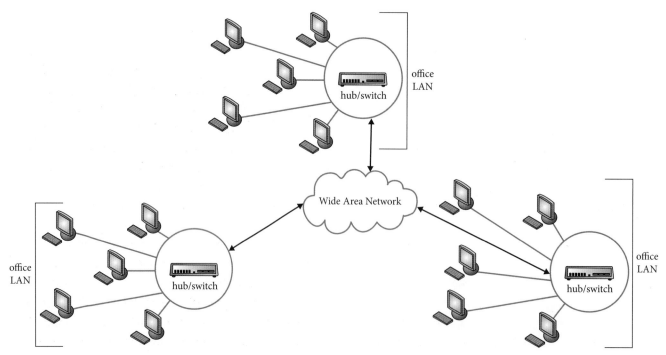

Figure 4.7 A WAN connecting several LANs.

SAQ

2 a Define the terms LAN, WLAN and WAN.

b What is the difference between a LAN and a WAN?

c Is the Internet a LAN or a WAN?

Question

1 Look back at the section describing how Nabila and Rana set up a home office network. Draw a diagram to show how the computers and other equipment might be connected. Are they using a bus network or a star network?

Communicating over networks

We have looked at networks and touched on how they can be used to share and send and receive information, but how is this achieved? Communication applications of various kinds are used which utilise the network to give different types of interface according to what we want to do.

A web browser is used to access web pages on the Internet. This allows us to see multimedia information from websites in any part of the world.

To communicate with a specific person there are several applications that can be used, the most common being **email** – electronic mail. The communicating computers must both have an email application on them, but the applications don't have to be the same kind. Messages can be composed, files attached, recipients chosen and the message sent from the email application. And of course the recipient can do the reverse – read the message, extract the attached file and see who sent the email.

But email isn't a real-time system; instant messaging is. An instant messaging application enables you to converse on-screen with another person who is logged on to the service, in real time. It is very similar to mobile phone texting.

If it is important to see and hear someone in a computer-enabled dialogue, then a **video conferencing** application together with a webcam and microphone attached to your PC make this possible. There are many variations on this theme: audio-only conferencing with

desktop images, video conferencing between several people rather than just one to one.

These are quite sophisticated applications of networks; a simple use of networks is the facsimile machine or **fax**. A fax machine (a simple computer nowadays) scans paper a line at a time and sends this over the telephone network to be received and reformed by the receiving fax machine. These were very popular in the past but tend to have been replaced by scanning combined with email.

The different methods of communication are looked at in more detail in Modules 7.1 and 7.2.

Network hardware

Network hardware enables communication across the network. It is different from the hardware of a computer system.

The **communication medium** is what allows the signals to be transmitted around the network. Typical media are cables and radio waves.

The medium chosen will depend on:

- the speed of transfer required;
- the distances that signals will need to travel around the network;
- how portable the hardware needs to be.

If users need access anywhere in the range of the network, then radio waves will be used on a wireless network.

If cable is used, then it will probably be twisted-pair cable or fibre-optic cable (Figure 4.8). Twisted-pair cable has two wires twisted together (usually four pairs of wires, the pairs twisted together), down which signals are sent. This form of medium reduces the amount of interference to signals. This interference is created by electromagnetic radiation coming from the signals themselves being sent through the wires and from outside influences. For this reason it is not sensible to lay a network cable next to an electrical cable or large electrical machinery.

Fibre-optic cables carry light signals down glass wires. This medium gives very high rates of transmission with little interference to the signal since electromagnetic radiation does not affect optical signals. The world's continents are all interconnected with undersea fibre-optic cables. Some fibres are used for the Internet.

orange–white/orange

green–white/green

blue–white/blue

brown–white/brown

b

Figure 4.8 **a** Twisted-pair cable. **b** Fibre-optic cables.

Extension

Investigate other media used for transmission of data around a network. Start by looking at different forms of cabling that can be used. Then extend your investigation to include infra-red and microwave transmissions.

Each computer on the network needs a **network interface card (NIC)** (Figure 4.9). This device allows the computer to use the communication medium to send and receive messages.

You might think of the NIC in a cable network as a socket that the network cable can be plugged into. Often an Ethernet NIC is now built into

a

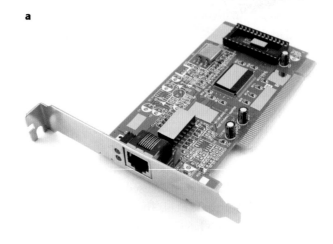

Question

2 Find examples of networks in your area. Your school is a good place to start as it may have a number of different networks. You might also consider networks in shops and offices and also in people's homes if there is more than one computer in a house.

What examples of networks that use cable of different types as the medium for data transmission did you find?

What examples of networks that use wireless transmission of data did you find?

What were the differences in the networks that meant that the different types of transmission media (cable or wireless) were used?

? SAQ

3 Why is the Internet so fast, even when accessing multimedia from another country many thousands of miles away?

b

Figure 4.9 Network interface card (NIC). **a** Card for a desktop. **b** Wireless card adaptor for a laptop.

the motherboard of a PC. (Ethernet is the most common standard which defines the wiring and signalling in a LAN.) In a wireless network the NIC provides the radio communication to the network access point.

You saw above that a star network has a central point to which all the signals from individual computers are sent. At this central point is a particular kind of network device, either a **hub** or a **switch**. The cables from all the computers on the network are plugged into this device.

Figure 4.10 Hubs and switches look similar but they handle signals differently.

Hubs and switches look the same (Figure 4.10). However, when signals are received from the network, hubs and switches treat the signals differently (Figure 4.11).

If a computer needs to send a signal to another computer on the network, the signal will be sent to the hub or switch.

If the device is a **hub**, then the signal will be sent to all the other devices that are connected to it (including back to the device that sent the signal in the first place!). This creates a lot of needless network traffic. If the hub can have 16 devices connected to it the amount of traffic will be 16 times greater than it needs to be. The message will be sent to all the devices on the network but only the device for which it was intended will accept it.

A message sent to a **switch** will have the address of the device to which it should be sent. The switch knows the addresses of the different devices on the network and only sends the message to the correct device.

Sometimes different networks need to be joined together. For example, at the head office of a particular firm, the workers in one office deal with the administration necessary to keep the firm's records; the computers in this office are arranged in a star network and have access to all the customer records. In another office, all the firm's accounts are dealt with by four workers whose computers are arranged on a bus network.

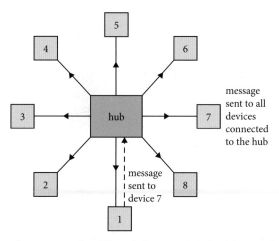

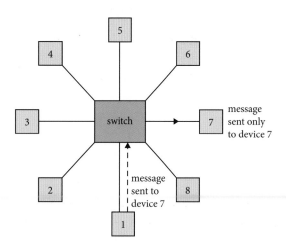

Figure 4.11 The difference between a hub and a switch.

Administration workers sometimes need to look at customer accounts in order to deal with customer queries. Workers in the accounts office sometimes need to look at a customer's record in order to read contact details.

This is a situation where two different types of network need to be joined together. The device which allows two dissimilar networks to send messages from one to the other is called a **bridge** (Figure 4.12).

A bridge can only connect networks that use the same rules for handling the messages. They can change the form of a message so that it is suitable for a different physical type of network like the star and bus network in this example. If the star network in the administration office uses a hub at its centre then all messages will be sent to all devices connected to it. This will include the bridge, so the bridge will have to be able to decide which messages should be passed on to the bus network and which should not.

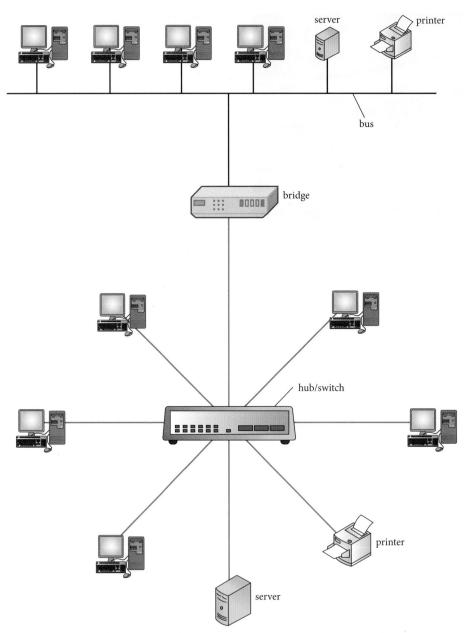

Figure 4.12 Using a bridge to join two networks together. In this example, a bus network is joined to a star network.

Figure 4.13 A wireless router and networking cable.

A **router** (Figure 4.13) behaves like a bridge, but looks just like a hub or switch. It provides a link between two or more networks. It differs because it is more 'intelligent':

- It can make decisions about whether a message should be passed between the networks.
- It can make the format of the message suitable for the new network.
- It can read the information about the message and decide not only where the message should be going but it can also decide the best route that can be taken for it to get there.
- A router is often used to provide a connection between a network and the Internet because of its ability to join together two unlike networks.

A LAN might be connected to other LANs or WANs or even to the Internet. The computers on the LAN could all have independent access to the other networks. However, it is more sensible to have a central access point for the whole network because of the control it gives over what is being accessed.

If Internet access is required, it is necessary to have an account with an Internet service provider (ISP).

If all the users on a LAN tried to use the ISP account at the same time, it would probably log off all but one. However, if all the traffic from the users is first sent to a server which can collect all the Internet requests and can then use a single ISP account to deal with all the requests, then the account will be used efficiently.

In this case, even though there are many users all using the Internet at the same time, the ISP allows it because it thinks there is only one user (the server). This server is called a **proxy server** (Figure 4.14) because it is a proxy for (that is, it stands in for) each of the users.

The proxy server has to remember who sent which message to the ISP. When responses are sent back, it must make sure that they are directed to the correct computer. It will also filter the material that can be allowed onto the network by using virus protection and will block attempts at access by unauthorised people (see Module 6).

Computers attached to the Internet often use a special sort of proxy server to protect them from hackers. This is a **firewall**, and it controls access in and out of the network. Again, you will learn more about firewalls in Module 6.

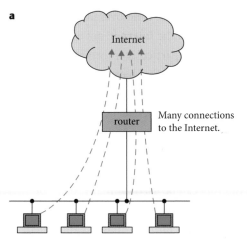

Many connections to the Internet.

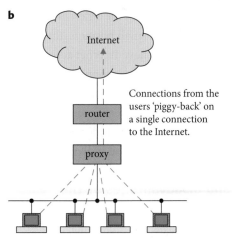

Connections from the users 'piggy-back' on a single connection to the Internet.

Figure 4.14 Connecting to the Internet. **a** Without a proxy server. **b** With a proxy server.

SAQ

4 a Which network device can find the best route for a message?

   b Which network device can connect dissimilar networks?

Question

3 You have seen a number of ways to connect devices to enable communication between them. Investigate the different uses for the different methods of data transmission. Consider the characteristics of different applications for which each would be useful.

4c Setting up a small network

You have seen that a network includes hardware to allow communication between computers and software that provides rules to allow the hardware to be used effectively. How might a network be put together in the first place?

The first stage in setting up a network is to use the facts that you know about different communications media to decide what medium should be used on the network and the 'shape' that the network should have.

If connection to the Internet is required, then a decision must be made about the physical connection. Should individual machines be connected with separate accounts or should the LAN be connected through a proxy server?

These decisions will be different for different applications. For example, in a small business, the boss might not want the workers to have Internet access, though one computer will need to be connected in order to allow contact with suppliers using email. A school, however, might want all the computers in one classroom to have access to the Internet so that students can investigate and search for information individually.

4d Advantages and disadvantages of the Internet

Earlier you saw the advantages and disadvantages of using computers linked in a LAN. The advantages are that:

- users can share hardware, software and files;
- they can communicate with other people who are using the LAN.

Another point is that some maintenance can be carried out centrally instead of having to visit each machine separately. The person who looks after a school network will be grateful for this when they are having to install a new piece of software so that students can use it on all the machines.

The disadvantages are that privacy and security of data on the network is difficult to maintain because of multiple access to files.

When this is extended to WANs and to the Internet, the advantages and disadvantages change slightly.

First, if the network is over a great distance, there is obviously no advantage in sharing hardware because the distances involved make it impractical. However, files can still be shared. This raises a bigger problem than the security issues on a LAN. There is still the problem of unauthorised access to data on the LAN or individual computers, but now the data is open to attack from other sources.

It is one thing to allow a number of people in the same room to have access; this is a controlled environment. But when you access the Internet, it means that other people can access your own systems, making them more vulnerable.

Earlier in the module we mentioned how use of a firewall between a network system and the wider Internet could control inappropriate access to the system. This helps to ensure that data held on the system is safe.

Second, the Internet has a large amount of potentially useful information, particularly when research is being done. However, because there is no overall quality control of information on the Internet, not all the information is reliable. If particular information is needed, it is wise to use sites that have a good reputation, such as the BBC Bitesize website for revision (http://www.bbc.co.uk/schools/gcsebitesize/). An alternative check is to compare two or more sites and make sure that they give the same information before believing what is said.

Third, the Internet can be used for many forms of entertainment. From some websites it is possible to download music or videos for free. These might benefit the user, but not the musicians whose music is being

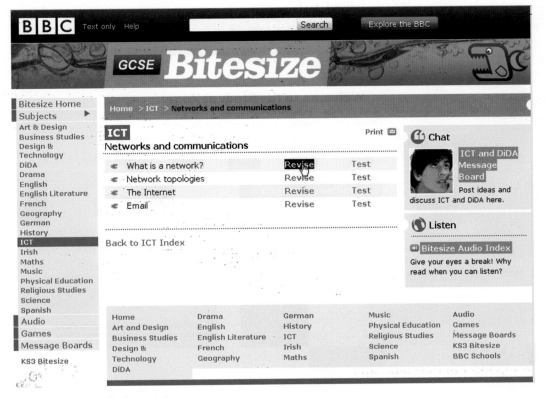

Figure 4.15 BBC Bitesize website.

downloaded. Bypassing music shops in this way means less business for the shops, which puts people out of work.

SAQ

5 What device is used to protect a school's network from unauthorised external access?

Question

4 A history teacher is to present a lecture to the parents of students at your school about the history of your area. The teacher wants to illustrate the lecture with slides about the points that are being made.

Search the Internet and try to find suitable material that you can give to the teacher so that they can then make a choice of what to use.

If the teacher is unsure about some of the facts that you find out, how can you convince them that the facts that you found are correct?

Intranets and the Internet

The Internet has benefits but also drawbacks. Because of this, some organisations have developed their own versions called intranets.

For example, a school might decide that open access to the Internet is not appropriate for all students, so develops an intranet. What would this intranet look like?

The school has a number of LANs which are connected together to form a WAN.

Students have access to various parts of the WAN. It includes an email service for teachers and for students. Students often use it for handing in homework which has been done on computer using resources made available on the WAN.

Teachers use the WAN to send messages to students about work and also about clubs and societies. The teacher in charge of the hockey team can send an email to all the players, marked urgent, telling them that the game this evening is cancelled. The science teacher can make information available to students in the form of web pages either taken from the Internet or created especially for the school WAN.

Students can access the WAN at school but also through their Internet connection from their home

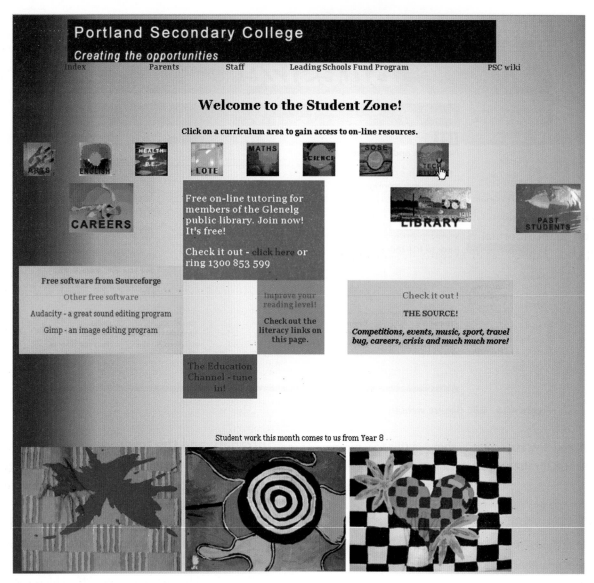

Figure 4.16 Page from a school intranet.

computer. To do this they will need a user ID and a password. The WAN is now a small version of the Internet – it even has pages of information which look like Internet pages because they are created in the same way.

Access to information on the WAN is via a web browser, just like on the Internet. A network used in this way is called an **intranet**.

Both intranets and the Internet have a large amount of information and can be used for communication. They both use browser software to allow a user to access information in web pages.

The main difference between an intranet and the Internet is size: an intranet is a small version of the Internet. In order to see and use the contents of an intranet you need to be known to the system and have logon details to identify yourself. The need for users to be known to the system and the consequent restriction on the number of people using it leads to a number of important differences between intranets and the Internet.

Advantages of intranets

1 Because the membership of the intranet is restricted, the views that are posted there are more

likely to be relevant (they will be about school or schoolwork).

2 The information on the intranet will be useful (information on the school intranet will be aimed at IGCSE level of understanding, not university level).

3 The information on the intranet will be reliable (information on the intranet will be correct and there will be no hoax sites).

4 There are fewer people using the intranet and there will be a limited amount of information on it. This will mean that communication and access to the information will be much faster; it will also be much easier to search for the required information.

5 Using the intranet is safer than using the Internet because the intranet does not have any inappropriate material on it and the people who are using it are all from within the school.

6 The intranet is less susceptible to hacking and viruses (see Module 6) because access to it is limited.

Disadvantages of intranets

1 Intranets are restricted so they have the disadvantage of not having the same volume of information as the Internet.

2 Intranets tend only to have one view whereas the Internet will provide different arguments from different people about a topic. (The science department may only have information about the beginning of the universe being due to the big bang because that is what is on the syllabus. There are many other theories about the start of the universe which would be featured on the Internet but not necessarily on the intranet.) Because of the need to control the size of the intranet it is necessary to be very selective about the information on it. This means that the information tends to reflect the views of the people who decide the information to be included, in this case the science teacher.

3 Communication on the intranet is fine as long as the people who you need to communicate with are also members of the organisation and hence have access to the intranet. This is very restricting and communication with others outside the organisation needs to be done by using the Internet.

Question

5 If your school has an intranet, why does it have one? If it does not, discuss whether or not your school would benefit from one.
In either case, describe what it can be used for by:
a teachers
b students.

4e Network security: user ID and password

The need to secure networks from unauthorised access has been mentioned several times in this module. This section looks at how this can be achieved.

Different people are allowed to use a network. Each person will have access to different parts of the network and will be able to access different files of information stored on the hard drive.

On a school network, some resources may be reserved for particular students. For example, a colour laser printer may only be available to students who are doing projects. Each student will have their own files and will not want other students to be able to access them. In order to ensure that only the correct students can access some of the resources, the network operating system needs to know who is logging on to a particular machine.

The **user ID** (or username) is like a name. It is used to identify the person to the computer. When a user ID is typed in, the operating system (OS) of the computer will look that user ID up in the table of IDs. When it is found, it tells the OS which hardware and software the user is allowed to have access to. It also tells the OS which files the user is allowed to see.

This is a fairly simple procedure but it is open to misuse. For example, someone else might identify themselves using a particular ID and then get access to resources that they should not have. User IDs are not intended to be secret or to be a complicated code – they are simply for identification. To stop the wrong person using the ID, the user is also expected to type in a secret code word which tells the OS that this really is the person.

Figure 4.17 Logging in to a network.

The code word used to prove to the OS that the person really is who they say they are is called a **password**. Because of the way they are used passwords must remain secret. When they are typed onto the screen, a series of symbols, normally * or •, fill in the space allocated for the password so that nobody can see it on the screen. The OS keeps the passwords associated with each user in the user ID table discussed earlier.

A password should be a non-dictionary word and should consist of digits as well as letters. Some of the letters should be lowercase and some uppercase. It should also be longer than six characters – the longer the more secure. Use anything that will make the password more difficult to guess.

Passwords should not be anything that is easily linked to the person whose password it is. Do not use the name of your dog or your date of birth for instance.

Passwords should be changed regularly. Many operating systems are set up to prompt the user to change their password on a regular basis, perhaps at the start of every month.

To sum up, the order of actions for the operating system when someone logs on is:

1 The OS looks up the user ID in the table of user IDs.
2 The OS is then given a list from the table of all the files and folders on the system which this user is allowed to have access to and the software and hardware they are allowed to use.
3 The OS then waits for the input of the password.

4 If the password matches the password held by the OS for that person, then they are given access to the things that the table says they are allowed to use. If it does not match, then a message is output to the screen warning of an inappropriate password.

> ### Question
>
> 6 Write down your user ID. Do not write down your password.
>
>   a Why is it reasonable to ask you to write down your user ID whereas it would not be fair to ask you to write down your password?
>
>   b What information is contained in your user ID and what is it used for by the system?
>
>   c What is your password used for by the system and how often do you change it? Why does the system ask you to input a new password twice?

Confidentiality and security of data

A stand-alone computer is only used by one person and is not connected to any others. This means that nobody except for the user can gain access to the data that is stored on the computer.

This does not make the data safe, of course. The user might make a mistake and delete some data which should have been saved. However, the data is safe from a malicious attack from someone outside the system. The problem of accidental deletion can be countered by taking regular backups.

Problems become more complicated when computers are linked together in networks. There are two types of problem that can arise:

- problems that arise because of a lack of confidentiality of the data;
- problems that affect the security of the data.

Confidentiality of data means 'How private is the data?' If a shop keeps records of its suppliers on one file and also keeps records of its customers on another file, there are two levels of confidentiality.

If someone manages to break into the suppliers file and reads the information, it does not really matter.

The owner of the shop might not want competitors to know who is supplying them with the goods on sale, but a look at the goods on the shelves will probably tell competitors that anyway. However, if the suppliers file includes details of the prices that the shop pays or the discounts that are given, it becomes rather more serious because this is sensitive commercial information.

The customer file is much more confidential. Customers will only have given their information to the shop on condition that it is protected and not inappropriately used. If a customer has just bought a new flat-screen television and this is shown on their record together with their address, it becomes dangerous for them if a potential burglar sees the data.

You have already seen in this module that user IDs and passwords can be effective in ensuring that only certain people have access to the network and hence to the files on the network. You have also seen how the operating system can give different access rights to different users. A further use for passwords is to protect individual files of data. This provides an extra level of security – an unauthorised person has to break one level of passwords to gain access to the system and then another to read the contents of a file.

The problem with this is that the data is there no matter how many passwords are created to protect it. A person skilled at breaking into computer systems will still be able to get through. If, however, the contents of the file are scrambled by using **encryption**, then even if the passwords are broken and the file is seen the attacker will not be able to understand what they see (Figure 4.18).

Questions

7 Investigate techniques of encryption.

The ancient Romans used a simple method of encryption. It consisted of two concentric rings with the letters of the alphabet on both. The inner ring could be spun around. As long as you knew the setting, a message could be encrypted or decrypted very quickly and easily.

Imagine the rings are set so that the letter on the inner ring is three ahead of the letter on the outer ring. Then A on the outer ring becomes D on the inner one, B becomes E, … and so on until W becomes Z, X becomes A, … and Z becomes C.

Then HELLO would become KHOOR.

To decipher the message the letters would be found on the inner ring and the new letter would be on the outer one.

Try to design your own encryption machine.

8 What are the weaknesses in the Romans' encryption method? Would it take long for an unauthorised person to break the encryption, particularly with the help of a computer?

Find out about some other forms of encryption.

Search for the name 'Sarah Flannery' on the Internet. She was just 16 years old when she won a prize for discovering a powerful form of encryption.

Try to discover your own encryption technique.

Figure 4.18 Encrypting data can help maintain confidentiality of information.

Two computers can be used for communication. Users can protect the data which is being sent, but how does one user know that the other really is who they say they are? It is necessary to have some way of identifying yourself in communications.

These methods of identification are called **authentication techniques**. Authorities have been set up to give electronic signatures to users of computers. These can be attached to messages and give an indication that the sender of the message is who they say they are.

Ordinary computer users are becoming more familiar with using authentication techniques with computer systems. An authentication system does not need to be complex – it is simply a way of making sure that you are who you say you are.

Consider a person who uses an ATM. The person must have with them something that has been issued by the correct authority that says who they are. In this case it is the plastic card issued to the user by their bank. This card is fed into the machine and it should then let them take out their money! But what happens if someone steals the card? There has to be something else to prove that they are who they say they are. In this case it is the password or PIN (personal identification number). Hopefully they are the only person who knows the PIN, so if they have the card

and they know the PIN then it is fairly certain that they are the right person.

Generally two items of identification are needed for authentication to gain access to a service.

Question

9 a How long is it going to be before the second piece of proof is going to be a person's thumb print? Would this make access to the client's money at the ATM more secure?

b Find out what information is needed to access a bank account online. The account holder cannot use a card at an ordinary computer, so what are the two pieces of information that are required?

c What other applications apart from banking use authentication techniques?

d What is the connection between this example and the idea of a user ID and a password?

Another way of ensuring that the information is kept confidential is to not store it on the computer system while the system is networked. This would involve storing the information on a removable storage device and removing it from the system before using the network. This means that even if the defences of the computer are breached the file is not there and hence the information cannot be stolen.

Security of data is concerned with keeping the data safe and uncorrupted. Part of this is obviously to restrict access to the data so that there is less chance of malicious damage to the data. Part of it is concerned with the recovery of data if it is damaged and this is done by using backup techniques as described in Module 3.

Question

10 Describe the difference between data security and data confidentiality.

Summary

- Browsers, email software and an ISP make communication over the Internet possible.
- Wi-Fi and Bluetooth are wireless forms of communication on a network.
- Fax, email and video conferencing are methods of communication.
- A LAN (local area network) is a small network. A WLAN (wireless LAN) is a small network that uses wireless communication.
- A WAN (wide area network) is a network over a large geographic area. It may include several LANs joined together.
- Network hardware devices include hubs, bridges, switches, proxy servers and routers.
- The Internet is open to all.
- Intranets are set up by organisations and access to them is strictly controlled.
- IDs, passwords and authentication techniques are used to identify users to networks.
- Data can be protected by passwords, firewalls and encryption techniques.

5 Data types

When you have finished this module, you will be able to:

- describe what is meant by field, record, file, key field, foreign key and primary key
- identify the need for different data types, and select the appropriate data types for given sets of data
- understand the need to validate and verify data entered into a system
- describe flat files and relational tables
- state the difference between analogue and digital data, and understand the need to convert from one to the other.

Overview

This module looks at how computers are used to store and manipulate data, and ways to ensure the data is correct and up to date.

We look at extracts from a school's student and teacher database files and how these are structured. We also define and describe some important features of the data.

The merits of flat and sequential files are considered.

Data types are important to the set-up of a database and help define the structure and input of data. Their use and different types are discussed.

Data types are also used in the validation of data. We go through some examples and then look at data verification.

The next section explains how files of data can be linked to each other with a relationship using keys.

Finally, we describe and compare analogue and digital data and the need to convert between them.

Files, records, fields and key fields

Schools and other organisations need to be able to keep information about many things – their students, their employees, their suppliers, their property and more. Clerks and accountants used to keep information such as this in large, hand-written books. To find information in them, keep them up to date and cross-reference between them was a very difficult, time-consuming and uncertain task. With the coming of the computer, it became possible to do all these things on a grand scale with speed and accuracy – as long as the data input was correct.

Here we look at how a school may build up the information about its students and teachers.

The 'student file' only includes a few of the students in the school and only a small amount of data about each of the students. In reality, there may be more than a thousand students and each student may have thirty or more pieces of information about them. It might take this whole book just to list all the data.

Figure 5.1 A clerk working at his desk.

Student file

ID number	Name	Gender	No. in family	Form tutor
18759	Noah Amu	M	6	Mr James
36729	Rose Thornton	F	4	Ms Arif
51734	Liene Faizan	F	7	Ms Sayer
51736	Omar Norton	M	3	Ms Arif

Definitions

The full set of data about all the students is called the **file** of data. To distinguish it from other files it is called the 'student file'.

The file is split into sets of data about a single thing, in this case, the students. These sets of data are called **records**. In the table above, each **row** of data is a record.

Each record contains many pieces of data. Each piece of data in a record is called an **item** of data and it is stored in a space called a **field**. Notice that all the records have the same type of data in any particular field but do not necessarily have the same items of data within the fields. Each of the columns in the diagram is a separate field.

Each of the records in a file must be distinguishable from all the other records so that we know that we are looking at the right set of data when we want to look something up. In the example above everyone has a different name so it seems we could use the person's name to distinguish one record from another. But can we be sure that there is only one person in the school called Noah Amu, or Rose Thornton? In the example we have introduced a field whose contents we can be sure is unique. We call it the **key field** and in this case it is the ID number. This is the only field which can be guaranteed to be different in all the records and it is used to identify the record.

The key field is sometimes called the 'key', the 'record key' or the 'primary key' – they all mean the same thing.

Example: the student file

Now we have defined some of the features of the student file, let us look at it in more detail:

- All the information about all the students in the school is in the student file.
- All the data about one student is in a row and is called a record – four records are shown.
- Each column is a field and contains information of the same type – 'ID number' is a field, and so is 'Form tutor'.

- Each piece of data is an item – it is the intersection of a row and a column. So 'Rose Thornton' is an item and '4' is an item. Each record in the table has five items shown, although in the full file there will be a lot more.
- The key field is 'ID number' because it is the only field that contains items that can never be the same as another item. It might be tempting to use 'Name' as the key because all the names in the example are different. However, it cannot be guaranteed that they are all different. In a large school it is quite likely that two students will have the same name. Think about your school. Do you have two students in your school with the same name?
- Some fields do not mean what they say. Noah is not an M! He is a male. We all know that M stands for male, so we are not trying to keep anything secret, it is just that M is easier to type in and takes up less space. This is an example of a coded field.

? SAQ

1. a What is the data item for ID number 36729 and field Form tutor?
   b What is the name of the female with seven people in her family?
   c How many students have less than five people in their family?
   d Which fields have data items in them with non-unique values?

Types of file

Notice that these records are in order of the key. This type of file is called a **sequential file** because the records are in sequence. Records are often stored in key order, either numerically or alphabetically, because this creates a file that is a lot easier to use and find things in.

If the file is in no particular order, or just in the order that the records were input, it is called a **serial file**. Serial files are not very useful because they make it difficult to find the record that you are looking for.

An alternative to converting a serial file to a sequential file to make it easier to read is to create an **index** and to allow the records to be stored randomly. The index will be in order and will indicate exactly where the record can be found, enabling rapid look-ups. This is called a **direct access file**.

Questions

1 a Consider the example student file. Try to expand the file by considering other information that the school would need to store about each of the students. Justify each of the fields that you decide are needed.

b Why would ~~~~~~~~~~~ possible for you to see ~~~~~~~~ our school?

~~~~~~~~~~~~~~~~~~~~~~ its ~~~~~~~~~~~~~~ will allow the use ~~~~~~~~ the point of sale. What ~~~~~~~~ would need to be included in ~~~~ file? What type of file would it need to be and why? What other fields would be necessary if the file is used:

a to supply the point-of-sale terminal with information

b to warn of low stock

c for automatic stock ordering?

File maintenance

Three types of maintenance are necessary in most files:

• Updates or amendments to a record. For example, the form tutor for each student may change at the end of the year. There is no need to key in all the other data again, it is simply a matter of changing that one item of data in each record.

• Insertions to the file. For example if a new student arrives during the school year, a new record will need to be inserted. If the file is stored sequentially this will mean rewriting large parts of the file in order to create a space to put the new record in. If the file is a

serial file then the new record can simply be put on the end of the file. If the file is a direct access file then it is only necessary to change the index.

• Deletions to the file. For example, if a student transferred to another school during the school year their record would need to be taken out of the file. Realistically, this record would be moved to another file – say the Transferred file, containing the records of all students transferred from the school.

 SAQ

2 What extra two fields would be required in the Transferred file?

Example: the teacher file

Here is an extract of the teacher file for the same school as the student file you have been considering so far.

Teacher file

Teacher	Form	Subject	Head of department?
Mr James	4AD	Maths	No
Ms Arif	3JU	ICT	Yes
Ms Sayer	6YD	Geography	No

Questions

3 Consider the three types of maintenance in the teacher file. Repeat this for some other applications, for example the stock file in a shop; the book file in a library; the booking file for an aircraft flight.

4 a Another field on the student file would be 'age'. What are the implications of this for updating the file? Is it ever sensible to store this information? Can you think of a more satisfactory alternative?

b A teacher gets married and changes her name. Explain how this would affect the updating of the teacher file.

Data types

Now we have seen what the student and teacher files consist of, let us consider the data that we put into the different fields. The data in each field looks consistent in terms of type and, to a certain extent, length: the ID number field contains data items that are numbers without decimal points and that are exactly five digits long; the Name field contains two alphabetic names separated by a space; the Gender field is a single alphabetic digit that is either M or F.

Any software that uses this data will expect these fields to be in a particular place in the file and the fields to have certain expected characteristics. Therefore, when we define the format of files we need to specify what type of data each field is going to hold – in other words we assign a **data type** to each field. We are constraining the data to be of a certain kind and range of values.

? SAQ

3 How many digits long do you think the 'No. in family' field is?

The implication for this is that once we have defined the data type for a field, we cannot go outside the bounds of it and try to input a different data type.

- We can't put in text where numbers are expected, for example, in the 'ID number' and 'No in family' fields.
- We can't put a six-digit number where a five-digit number is expected, for example, in the 'ID number' field.
- We can't put the letter X where X is not expected, for example, in the 'Gender' field where only M or F is allowed.
- We can't put numeric data where alphabetic data is expected; for example, 'Noah Amu2' would not be allowed in the 'Name' field.
- We can't put in more text than is expected; for example, a name of 80 characters would not be allowed in the 'Form tutor' field, even if it was all alphabetic (and assuming there was a character limit of, say, 20 characters).

? SAQ

4 Do you think the value 78.123 would be accepted in the 'ID number' field? Give a reason.

Applications that use databases can more easily search, sort and compare fields in different records if data types are kept uniform within a file.

The main data types that we can assign to a field and how they might be used are described below.

Numeric data types

Data that is made up of digits (0, 1, 2, …) is called numeric data. There are two main types of **numeric data**:

- **Integers** are whole numbers such as 16 or 256913; they do not contain decimals. Integers are used for counting things which have no fractional part (e.g. 23 washing machines, 7 people).
- **Real numbers** are numbers that have a decimal part, such as 12.5 or 3.141592654. They are used for things like a person's height, e.g. 1.76 metres.

The computer needs to know if a number is an integer because real numbers take up more storage space. If a database file has a million records, this can represent a lot of wasted space.

Question

5 A particular field holds integers.
Another field holds the answer when some arithmetic is carried out on the integer field.
  a What must be the data type of the second field?
  b Investigate whether this answer changes for different types of arithmetic.

Date data type

A date has a specific format. This often takes the form of three pairs of numbers separated by slashes, for example 27/04/09.

This is not the only form that a date can take. It may be necessary to store the year as the full four digits, as in 27/04/2009. This would make the storage space needed larger.

Extension

Investigate different ways of representing dates in a computer system.

What date is 01/02/03 in different parts of the world? For example, in the UK this date is the 1st of February 2003. What is it in the USA? What is it in Korea?

Consider cultures which use a different calendar, such as Israel or Iran.

Would the date be different if it was the date of birth for a patient of a doctor's surgery or the date that a particular event happened in a country's history?

How can an integer be used to represent a date? Find a piece of software which stores dates as integers.

Alphanumeric data type

Most data input to a computer consists of characters from the keyboard, such as B, x, @, 7, etc. This data has no hidden meaning (like the first two digits in a date must be between 1 and 31) and it is not going to be used in calculations, it just needs to be stored.

Data from the keyboard treated like this is called **text**. It is sometimes called **alphanumeric data** because it has mainly alphabetic characters and numeric characters.

Sometimes data looks as though it is numeric when it is not. To decide whether data is numeric, ask: 'Does the answer mean anything if two of these values are added together?' If the answer is 'Yes' then the data should be numeric. If the answer is 'No' it should be alphanumeric.

Question

6 Is a telephone number an integer?

Investigate the data type 'character'. How does a character data type differ from a text data type?

Logical data and Boolean data types

Some data can only be one of two characters. Data like this is called **Boolean data**. An example is Y or N for 'yes/no' type of data.

Sometimes data like this is used as the answer to a simple question like 'Is the data input bigger than 31?' This would either be 'Yes' or 'No'. If the data was meant to be the day of the month and the answer was 'Yes' then the computer would know that a mistake had been made. If the answer was 'No' then the computer would know that the data could be accepted. When Boolean data is used like this it is also called **logical data**.

Currency

Currency is a real number data type, but it is used so often that many software programs offer it as a distinct data type. It will be a number of digits followed by a point and then followed by two digits.

The difference between currency and real number data types is that real numbers can have any number of digits after the point whereas currency is forced to have two.

? SAQ

5 Are the following real numbers or currency?
  a $12.3
  b $12
  c $12.34
  d $12.345
  Try to justify all your answers.

Questions

7 Here is the record for Noah Amu from the school's student file looked at earlier.

ID number	18759
Name	Noah Amu
Gender	M
No. in family	6
Form tutor	Mr James

Consider the ID number. Is this an integer or is it alphanumeric?

State the data types that would be used for each of the five fields. Explain why you made each choice.

8 A stock file in a shop contains the following fields:

Bar code
Item name
Price
Number in stock
Whether on order or not
Date of last order
Supplier name
Supplier address
Supplier phone number
Percentage discount offered by supplier

For each field decide the data type to be used. Justify each choice.

Checking data entry

When data is entered to a system there are two ways that the data can be incorrect. The first is that the data has been collected incorrectly. If a person tells a researcher that their date of birth is 18th December 1997 when it was actually 18th November 1997, there is nothing that can be done to correct the data.

The second type of error is that the data was correctly given but that it has been incorrectly entered.

If the data is 18/11/1997 then if I press the wrong key and make a mistake on entering the data it could be entered as 18/13/1997. The system can be set up to

spot errors like this by giving it rules that the data must follow in order to be accepted.

When we set the data type for a field, we can also set rules about the format and range or length of the data.

In this case the computer was told that the second pair of digits must be between 1 and 12 otherwise there is an error. This is called **validation** and the test is called a **validation check**.

Figure 5.2 An artistic representation of a validation error.

There are a number of different validation checks that can be carried out:

- In this example, a length check can be done by counting the number of characters entered, it should be 10, so 1/11/1997 will show up as an error. It is the reason why you need to put a 0 in front of any day or month which only has one digit.
- A character check will make sure that the characters entered are the sort of characters that the computer was expecting. 18/Nov/1997 would be rejected because of the use of letters rather than digits.
- A format check checks that the data being input is in the right 'pattern', in this example it is expecting two digits, slash, two digits, slash, four digits so 18/1997/11 would be rejected.
- A presence check is used to make sure that some data has been entered. If the computer was expecting something to be entered in the space for date of birth and nothing is input it will state that an error has been made.

However, the data may pass the validation checks but still be wrong. If a mistake is made keying in the date and 18/10/1997 typed in, this is wrong, but the system will not spot a mistake because it has passed all the validation checks.

Mistakes like these are very difficult to spot. There are two methods which can be used. One is to compare the output on the screen with the original document to make sure that they match; the other is to input the data twice. It is highly unlikely that the same mistake will be made twice and consequently the system can compare the two inputs and warn the operator if the two versions do not match. This is known as **data verification**.

Question

9   Write down your address. Explain how each of the validation rules could be used to check for incorrect data entry.

Extension

Investigate other validation techniques. Explain the difference between a presence check and an existence check. How would an existence check relate to your input of your address?

Flat files and relational tables

In a **flat file** all the data for an application is stored in a single file. The data is structured with a row for each record and a column for each field. The earlier example in Question 8 of a stock file for a shop is an example of a flat file because it has all the data in one file.

Notice that a lot of the data will be repeated in many of the records. Every product that is supplied by 'A and B foods' (one of their suppliers) will include in its record the address, the phone number, and the discount offered by the supplier. If A and B foods supply the shop with 100 different products then those details are repeated 100 times. This makes the file much bigger than it should be and this, in turn, could decrease the speed of access to data in the file.

In the example of the school database, the data has been divided into two different files: the student file and the teacher file. It would have been possible to have put all the details in one file. If that had been done there would have had to have been fields for all of the details of the teacher in every student record. This would

have meant having the same details repeated in the file many times. It would also have been difficult to keep the confidential details of teachers secure because they would appear so often on the file.

Let us consider how the student file and the teacher file described here can be used to find the name of the form that a particular student belongs to. The database system would go through the following steps:

1   It would read through the student file until it found the correct student.
2   Once the correct student was found the form tutor of that student would be found in the record.
3   The teacher file is then searched for the name of the form tutor that was found in the student record.
4   Part of the record for that form tutor will be the name of the form that they look after. This is the student's form.

This process works because there is one field which is in both of the files. Not only that, but it is unique in the teacher file because each form can only have one form teacher.

Step 1 should mean that the computer will search for the ID number. That is difficult in this example as generally people in school do not know their ID numbers. In reality, the search will be done on the student's name. This means that we are using a field other than the key field to search for the record. When this happens the field that is used in the search is known as the **secondary key**.

Relationships

When two files are linked together it is possible to search both files for information when only one file is queried in the first place. This is very different from having everything stored in a single flat file. The normal work of a file is not affected. Finding data about students is still going to be done by looking at data in the student file. It is only when the search is for other data that is more obviously part of another file that the links within the files are used to access related pieces of information. When files are related to each other the name for the file changes to a **table** and because the tables are related they are called **relational tables**. Don't worry about this. For the sake of making things simpler to understand we shall continue to call them files, but remember that a table is another name for a file.

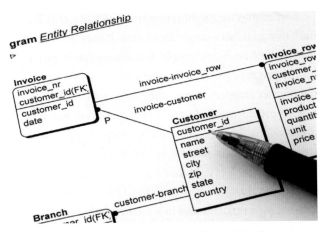

gram _Entity Relationship_

Figure 5.3 Artistic representation of a relational database.

Keys

We have seen before that each record must have a **primary key** so that it can be identified uniquely within the file. In this particular example the primary key of the student file is the ID number whereas the primary key of the teacher file is the teacher name.

Question

10 Explain why the subject field cannot be used as the primary key field for the teacher file. Explain why the form name cannot be used as a primary key in the teacher file. Why is the problem of uniqueness that we had with student names not true of the teacher name field?

The name of the teacher was used to provide a link between the student file and the teacher file. When this is done it is important that the field that provides the link is the key field in one of the files. In this case it was the teacher's name field. This is the key field in the teacher file and it also appears in the student file. A field in one file that is also the key field of another file is called a **foreign key**.

Question

11 What would happen if the linking field was not a key field?

Extension

A third file is going to be used which will link with the student and teacher files. This file will store details of the subjects that are taught in the school. Decide what fields would be a part of this file and what the foreign keys would be to link the files together.

Question

12 In Question 8 a stock file was described for a shop. Return to the list of fields that was stated and divide them into two related files (tables). One of the files should be suitable for use with the normal running of the shop and the other should be suitable for reordering supplies when necessary.

Which field would be the foreign key and why? What other fields will be necessary in the stock file if the computer is going to be able to work out whether new stock should be ordered? What other fields will be necessary in the supplier file if the computer is going to be able to order new supplies automatically?

(5e,f) ## Analogue and digital data

We can describe data as being in two different forms.

Analogue data is data that can have any value within a defined range. Any changes in the value of the data occur continuously rather than in discrete steps.

If I wanted to know how tall you were I could use an estimate just by looking at you and I would probably be accurate to within about 10 cm. This is a digital measure because I might say that your height was between 1.5 and 1.6 metres. If I was to use a metre rule and make you stand against a wall to take the measurement then I would probably get the accuracy to within 2 cm. I would be able to say that your height was between 1.53 and 1.57 metres. If I used a perpendicular to rule a line against the wall and then used the metre ruler I might get your height to the nearest cm. Now I am able to say that you are between 1.555 and 1.565 metres tall.

What about if I used a magnifying glass to measure you to the nearest mm, or I used a microscope to measure you to the nearest tenth or hundredth of a millimetre? I would still not have got your measurement exactly right.

In many measurements it is not possible to measure with complete accuracy. These are physical measurements like height or length or weight. Others would be temperature or pressure or intensity of light. In Module 2 we studied sensors and the way that they can be used to automatically take readings. Many of these sensors measure analogue data and produce analogue electrical signals.

The analogue electrical signal that is produced by a temperature sensor in a room during a day might look like this:

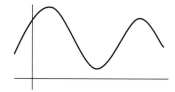

Extension

At any point in time on the graph, the temperature is represented by the magnitude of the voltage. The temperature range being sensed could be 0 °C to 35 °C and this might correspond to a voltage range of 0 V to 5 V. We might use the voltage produced to cause something to happen; for example, move the dial on a scale or vary the heat from a boiler.

a In the first example, where the dial on a scale is caused to move, what function is this describing?

b In the second example, do you think a high voltage will cause the boiler to increase or decrease the heat? What function is this describing?

Digital data is in the form of discrete patterns of 0s and 1s. We have seen in an earlier module that digital data is composed of bits which can be either 0 or 1 and that these bits are arranged into groups of usually eight called bytes. So a byte of data has 256 discrete values (there are 256 different combinations of 0s and 1s in eight bits from 00000000 to 11111111).

Sometimes we might represent something that has only two states as a single bit of data. It may be on or off, but not half-on. For example, if someone has stepped on the pressure pad in a burglar alarm system, they have either stepped on it or they have not (inside this type of pressure pad electrical contacts either touch or don't touch). A person cannot 'half step' on the pad. If we had eight alarm sensors in a house, these could be represented by a byte of data (one bit per sensor) which is stored in the alarm system. This data could be sent as a signal on a regular basis to a security company that looks after the house. Consider how this might work in a large company.

Similarly, a toggle switch is either on or off. Compare this to a dimmer switch: this is an analogue device – it can be varied anywhere between full on and off.

Conversion between analogue and digital data

A computer needs data to be in digital form to use it. Many of the measurements that are taken in the real world are analogue measurements, so before a computer can accept analogue data it must be converted into digital data. This is done by a device called an **analogue-to-digital converter** or A–D converter.

An A–D converter converts the analogue voltage from a sensor into a byte of digital data – or several bytes of data if more precision is required. It can do this at different intervals depending on what the data is for. In a burglar alarm or room thermostat, taking one sample every second would be adequate. A computer will convert music to digital data at speeds of 128 000 samples per second (kbps).

Computers are often used to control analogue devices. However, a computer cannot control analogue devices directly. A **digital-to-analogue converter** (D–A converter) is used to convert the discrete values of the digital data in the computer to analogue signals used by the analogue devices being controlled. This is the opposite of the A–D converter. In a pop concert, all the lights are computer controlled because the sequencing is so complex, but there must be banks of D–A converters to power the lights.

Figure 5.4 A light show at a pop concert. The sequence of lights is controlled by a computer but the lights themselves are powered by D–A converters that receive signals from the computer.

Summary

- A file holds all the data relevant to a situation. This file is divided into records of data that relate to a specific entity and each record comprises data items that are held in fields. Each record must have the same fields.
- Boolean, text, real, integer, date, currency are all data types. Data should be classified in this way so that the computer knows how to use it.
- Validation and verification are used for checking data input for errors.
- Files can be related to each other using primary keys and foreign keys.
- Analogue data is data that can have any value within a defined range. Any changes in the value of the data occur continuously rather than in discrete steps, as in digital data.
- Computers need analogue data to be converted to digital data before it can be used. Conversely, a computer needs its own digital data to be converted to analogue to control analogue equipment.

6

The effects of using ICT

When you have finished this module, you will be able to:

- describe the effects of microprocessor-controlled devices in the home
- describe the effects of ICT on patterns of work
- describe some capabilities and limitations of ICT
- describe how the Internet has changed and how it has affected the way we do things
- discuss issues of undesirability and unreliability of information on the Internet and identify security issues when transferring data
- explain what is meant by intellectual property and software copyright in particular
- describe what computer viruses and hacking are and some measures that can be taken against them
- describe how using ICT can affect our well-being in terms of health and safety and some of the things we can do about it.

Overview

In this module we look at how ICT has affected us.

We look at the use of microprocessors in the home, specifically how this has affected phones and the way we use them. The questions broaden this to consider the use of microprocessors in washing machines and leisure.

ICT has had a significant effect on jobs – we see how one family has been affected in terms of skill levels, types of employment, changes in employee numbers and training. We also see how teleworking has changed people's working lives.

There are some things computers are good at and some that they cannot do. Their capability is limited.

We look at several types of use and abuse of the Internet: how the Internet has become more interactive and how this has fuelled the introduction of blogs, wikis and media upload sites; whether we can trust information on the Internet, including dangers like phishing and pharming, and annoyances like spam; intellectual property and software copyright – how

can you use what you find?; hackers and how to defeat them; viruses – what they are and how to deal with them.

Finally, we look at how ICT and using it can affect our well-being. We identify some of the major health risks and offer some ways to prevent them; we look at some of the safety issues that present themselves in computer systems, from cables, to electrical supplies, to positioning devices, to false floors.

6d At home

'More computer processors were manufactured in 2007 and 2008 than in all the years up to and including 2006.'

'95% of processors that are manufactured do not go into computers.'

These two remarkable statements, gleaned from the Internet, raise the question: Where are they all?

Consider your home. Do you have a phone? Does it have a redial function? (Where does it remember the number that was dialled?) Does it have an address book of names and numbers? (Where are they stored, how does it dial automatically?) If it is a cell phone, how does it communicate with different ground stations when it is moved around?

There are many other questions that could be asked about modern phones but they all have the same answer: it has a small computer, complete with processor and memory chip, which is programmed to allow it to carry out these, and many other, functions.

Questions

1 Make a list of all the things in your house that have a processor in them. For each one decide what improvement is made by having a processor and whether the same tasks could be done by a device that is not processor controlled.

Find a device in your home that does not have a processor and describe how its uses could be improved by installing a properly programmed processor in it.

2 Ask someone who has retired about how they spent their leisure time as a child. Compare their responses to the way that you spend your leisure time.

Things you might want to consider: How much did they have in the home to play with? How often did they see their friends? How much information did they have access to?

Think about the way that you spend your leisure time – how much of your leisure time is reliant on computers or processor-controlled devices?

3 For many years the dream of a robot that could do all the housework has been just that – a dream. Have a look at http://world.honda.com/ASIMO/. How close to a housekeeping robot do you think we are? Think about the things that a robot might be able to do and those that it could not. Would people be comfortable around a robot? Would people trust a robot? What about problems of outsiders hacking into its systems?

Decide whether you think robots would be accepted.

Extension

There are two types of washing machine. One is controlled entirely by the user who must be present to control the system throughout the wash cycle. The other is processor controlled and requires no user involvement after it has been switched on. Describe the tasks that the human has to carry out in each case.

Console of a processor-controlled washing machine.

Consider the different hardware required by the processor-controlled machine. Describe what it is used for. Describe the processing which is carried out by the processor throughout the stages of the wash cycle. Describe the communication needed between the processor and the user of the machine.

6c At work

Ahmed worked in a steel mill. His was a very skilled job that took years to learn. He had to stand next to the great furnaces that were full of molten metal and decide when to add extra ingredients, like carbon to make carbon steel. He would also decide when to pour the molten metal off. He knew when these things should be done because of subtle changes in the colour of the metal in the furnace.

He was forced to retire when the steel mill introduced computer systems to do his job. The company is very happy with the new system because the computers get the timing right every time. This means that the finished steel is as perfect as it can be and the costs are lower because the system is automated,

Figure 6.1 Molten metal being poured into a mould in a steel mill.

which means that fewer people have to be employed. The sales are up because the quality of the steel is very high and it is cheaper.

However, there are no longer any people left who have the skills that Ahmed had. Soon, there will be nobody left who remembers that the job can be done by human beings simply by using their sight. What will happen if the machines can no longer do the job properly? This loss of skills is known as **de-skilling**.

Ahmed is happy in one way: his son was going to follow him as his apprentice in this very dangerous job. Ahmed is grateful that his son has instead got a job in the control room which controls the robots that manipulate the containers of molten metal. This job is not as skilled as Ahmed's used to be but still requires training to be able to do it. Ahmed's son is said to be **semi-skilled**.

Ahmed's daughter worked in the administration department but applied to go on a course about robotics when computer systems were introduced to her department and it was obvious that some of the workers would be made redundant. Having finished her course she is now one of the technicians servicing the robots in the mill. She changed her job by learning the skills necessary for another one and is said to be **re-skilled**.

The workers who are still employed in administration have had to learn to use the new technologies and their jobs have changed a lot. However, a positive benefit has been that jobs no longer have to be done at precise times, when other people are there, so the workers have the opportunity to plan their working hours around their family commitments.

The sales team no longer need to make so many visits to customers as most of their business can be conducted over the Internet by using various communication tools including **email** and **video conferencing** (see Module 7.2).

It is not only sales visits that are reduced. The sales team don't even need to visit their own company offices very often, so these workers can largely work from home – they are **teleworkers** (Figure 6.3).

Figure 6.3 A teleworker working from home.

Figure 6.2 Control room at a steel mill.

? **SAQ**

1 What are the essential hardware requirements for working at home if you are working as a salesperson?

Question

4　Discuss the advantages and disadvantages of being able to work from home rather than going in to work every day:

　a　for the worker

　b　for the company

　c　for society in general.

Question

5　There are two shops that sell food, general produce and household goods on the same street. Customers who go into either shop will be met by an assistant who greets them and asks what they need. The assistant will get their purchases from behind the counter and will keep a total of what they spend on a piece of paper.

This system has worked perfectly well in the two shops for many years, but the owner of one of the shops decides to introduce a computerised system into the shop. The system will use point-of-sale terminals reading bar codes on the products which shoppers select for themselves.

Investigate the answers to the following questions.

　a　What are the things that the shopper will notice when they go to the shop with the new system?

　b　Will all the shoppers from both shops be drawn to the one with the new system or can you recognise some reasons why some will still want to shop in the old-fashioned shop?

　c　What will be the effects on the workers in both shops? Don't forget to include all the people who work in the shops.

The introduction of new technology into businesses has changed many types of employment.

In the steel mill that Ahmed worked in, three people work in the payroll department. The management of the mill has decided to computerise the payroll system. This will have a big effect on the workers:

- Because the system is different, the business will only need two workers in the payroll department so someone will be made redundant.

- The two people who remain will need to go on training courses in order to be able to use the new system. They might be worried that they will find the new skills difficult to learn. This will cause them stress because they will be uncertain about their futures.

- The jobs that they have to do will change. They may be more interesting because the computers will do the tedious tasks, or perhaps their jobs will actually become more tedious because they simply have to look after the machines.

- They will have been on courses to be trained and hence they will have more knowledge. This makes them more qualified and hence they may be entitled to a higher rate of pay. Their extra qualification will make it easier for them to get another job if they need to change jobs.

- What about the need for people to be proud of what they do, to be proud of their job giving them a place in the society?

The important thing in all situations like these is to consider the good things about a change as well as the less positive things.

(6e, 7.2.j) Capabilities and limitations of ICT

However sophisticated technological devices become, there are always things that they cannot be expected to do.

If you programmed a computer perfectly then you would be able to input all the details of the football teams in the first division. All the statistics about the players and even things like the weather forecast could be taken into account. But you would never be able to get a computer to predict accurately the results of all the matches. This must be a good thing because otherwise is there any point in playing the games?

Why is it not possible? There are too many factors that will influence the outcome. Many of them will be random in nature: the bump on the pitch which the ball hit and bobbled over the keeper's outstretched hands; the sudden shower of rain which the visiting team's star striker particularly does not like and hence he has a poor game; the chanting of the home supporters which has upset the full back; and countless other factors.

A computer is programmed by a human being who simply cannot take all these things into account. There are too many variables.

Compare this to another game, chess. Here the game is all set on a simple 8 × 8 board and moves are predictable, whereas there is no way of knowing where the full back is going to kick the ball. There are a strict set of rules for each piece in chess, whereas there is no rule saying that the full back must stay in a certain part of the field, or only run diagonally across the pitch! The players in chess take turns to move, whereas the teams in football can keep the ball for long periods. The games also differ in many more ways than these obvious ones. As a result it is possible to make enough predictions in chess such that a computer can beat the world chess champion like in 1997 where Gary Kasparov was beaten by IBM's Deep Blue Supercomputer (http://www.research.ibm.com/deepblue/). But even with massive processing power the score was only 2 wins to 1, so the human was still able to win one game.

Figure 6.4 Artist's impression of Gary Kasparov versus the Supercomputer (it was not like this in real life).

What about something where there are no set rules? If you go to an art gallery, you will be able to make decisions for yourself about which pictures you like and which you do not. Computers cannot do this because the decisions are being based on things which are not really rules and so cannot be programmed.

Can a computer decide whether it likes one person more than another? No, because this is a decision based on feelings and opinions, broadly described as 'subjectivity'. Computers and their associated devices like processors and robots can do lots of wonderful things for us, but we must never imagine that they are capable of more than they actually are.

The Internet

The web used to be full of things like online encyclopedias where visitors could look up information and websites where people could visit to find things out. This type of use of the web is passive, although perfectly reasonable and still very widely used. It is known as **Web 1.0**.

People started developing interactive websites which are always open to updating instead of passive web sites that often didn't change for months at a time. They developed collaborative sites which anyone can change rather than encyclopedias that can only be looked at. The web suddenly became much more interactive, collaborative and community based, and to distinguish it from previous styles of use it is called **Web 2.0**. This section describes some of these new uses.

(6f, 7.1.b) Diaries, blogs and beyond

Before computers were so common, people would write in diaries. The diaries would contain their thoughts and experiences, and were sometimes private and sometimes for general consumption. People would write down what they had done that day and perhaps details of things that needed doing in the future. They would also write down the address and phone number of a new friend so that they could contact them. You might want to ask your grandmother if she kept a diary when she was a child.

The modern version of a diary is a **blog** (derived from 'web log'). They often have the same collection of thoughts and records of things that someone has done, but are produced for public or limited consumption on a website. They will be open to anyone, so you would

Figure 6.5 **a** An old-fashioned diary of pen and paper. **b** An electronic diary in the form of a blog on the internet.

have to be careful of what material you put on it and the material may be different in presentation. Instead of being just writing with a few pictures, a blog allows you to use video and sound (but note the warning in the section on copyright below).

Another difference is that a blog is like reading a diary from back to front because the most recent material is the first to appear on the screen. In a written diary, notes are made of people's addresses so that they can be written to. In a blog it would be common to have links to other blogs or even email addresses in order to contact friends.

Blogs are not just produced by individuals. Some businesses have blogs. Many radio and television programmes use them to continue stories that have been introduced on air. They are particularly popular with politicians, who find them useful for contacting younger people in the population to try to put their ideas across.

So far, we have considered a blog as a website that we control. Although blogs allow their readers to comment, what happens if we want to let other people add articles or posts to our website, or to change or add to what we have written? We need a different kind of site. We need a site that one person can create and post some information on but that lets other people come and look at that information and then change it, either because they disagree with something or they have extra information that may be useful. We now have a **wiki** – a site which visitors may alter or even add pages to using links. The most famous one is probably

Wikipedia – a free encyclopedia that anyone can contribute to.

The emphasis in recording personal information is changing from the rather secretive concept of the diary to a far more inclusive philosophy epitomised by blogs and wikis.

 SAQ

2 Encyclopedias and wikis are very different. Which of them gives the better, more accurate and reliable, information and why?

Extension

Try going to a website like http://pbwiki.com and see how easy it is to create a wiki.

Try to create a wiki which is accessible to the whole class and create a list of websites that are useful for revision or further research for each of the sections in the syllabus, or for other subjects that you are taking at your school.

Question

6 Find out about microblogging services like Twitter. Discuss in your group what the point of their service is and whether it is a sensible use of the Internet.

A **digital media uploading website** is precisely what it says: a website that will allow a visitor to upload files of information to it. Because it is now getting easier and easier to upload digital photos, audio and video files from school and home, these sites are becoming more popular. Perhaps the largest of all at the time of writing is the video sharing website YouTube. Other examples which you may have visited are Flickr, Photobucket and ImageShack.

Question

7   Discuss the uses of blogs and of social networking sites like Facebook, MySpace and Bebo. What are the good and bad points of these sites? Should they be controlled or would this ruin them?

What do you think of the arguments for freedom of speech? What about sites that encourage hatred or violence?

6g **Information – good and bad**

How much should we believe of what there is on the Internet? If I wanted to I could form a new society called 'The Grass is Red Society'. Hopefully nobody would believe what I put on the website even if they found it. Try going to the following site:

http://www.alaska.net/~clund/e_djublonskopf/ FlatHome.htm and think: do you believe what you can read here? Why not? It is on the Internet after all.

This is an extreme example but all the information that is presented to us when we search the Internet has been put on there by someone and we have few ways of checking whether or not they are reliable.

Much of the content of the Internet is undesirable to many people.

? SAQ

3   What would you do to verify the information in a wiki?

Question

8   What is acceptable to some cultures is not acceptable to others. Drinking alcohol is accepted in some places and yet it is illegal in others. The content of the Internet could be accessed by anyone anywhere.

If I am part of the culture which encourages alcohol use, do I have the right to extol the virtues on the Internet for people in other cultures to access? Do I have the right to set up an on-line shop to sell alcohol? Discuss these points.

Perhaps alcohol use is not important in your society. Perhaps the place of women is an issue, or the type of government you have.

It will become apparent that what is important in one society is not so important in another. The wider question is: just because I have access to the Internet and can place things on there, do I have the right to try to influence your culture?

There are other dangers on the Internet apart from potentially unreliable or undesirable content.

Phishing and **pharming** are methods used by **scammers** to gain valuable information that will then make it possible for them to access important files and even to steal your identity. Once the scammer has sufficient data about you, they may try a variety of fraudulent activities and all in your name: obtaining bank accounts, credit cards or government benefits.

A scammer sends you an email that appears to be from a trusted source, like a bank or an auction site, and directs you to log on to what looks like a valid website. The fake website asks for sensitive information like your credit card details or your date of birth. This is phishing and is often recognisable by looking at the address of the website you are being directed to – in most cases it won't have any relationship to the supposed source.

Pharming is a bit different. It also involves setting up a fake website to capture sensitive information but this time users get redirected to it from a legitimate website. Because the user started off in a legitimate website, they think all subsequent links are legitimate as well. Pharming is enabled by the scammers changing network addresses in various vulnerable places, such as on the client's computer, in a router or in a server that resolves network addresses (a DNS server).

Spam is a massive problem now and for the future of the Internet. Spam is unsolicited email, usually of a commercial nature – low-cost advertising for the sender but annoying and time-consuming for the receiver.

Individual spam emails are not a problem (unless you open it when it contains a virus) because they can just be deleted. However, if you receive hundreds of spam messages every day then it makes email unusable. There are three common methods for solving the problem of spam messages:

1   Let your email provider know about recipients that you are not willing to accept messages from. However, the list can be enormous and will never cover every sender's address, so much spam will still get through.
2   Have a list of senders whose emails are acceptable and don't let any other messages through.
3   Use software to filter the content of your emails. The software looks for things that are typical of spam messages, blocks those emails (or gives you the option) and then adds those senders to the blacklist so that their messages do not get through.

Figure 6.6   Example of a dialog box from a spam filter.

(6a)   **Software copyright**

If a person or a firm spends a lot of time producing something then they expect to benefit from all their efforts. This is easy to do if the thing that is being produced is something solid.

Imagine that an electronics company produces a new 3-D television system and puts the televisions on sale. If I want to use one then I have to buy it. The price that I have paid is probably far more than it took to make the set. Part of the reason is that I am also paying a share of what it cost the company to develop the product. Also, some money must go towards the people who first thought up the idea of 3-D television and how it could be done. I have paid some money for the solid 'box' of the set, some for the development and some for the initial idea. The solid bit is easy to understand but it is less obvious that you are paying the other two parts.

The research and development work is probably done in the company's laboratories and the scientists must be paid and the equipment that they use must be bought. The original ideas behind the 3-D technology are less easy to pin down. Someone, it could even have been you, had the original idea and registered that idea. If the company wants to use the idea and develop it then they need permission and will have to pay to use it. Ideas are difficult things to charge for because you cannot actually see them.

A film which is released on a DVD is another example. The DVD is the 'solid' bit and probably costs no more than a few cents. A company has had to put the film onto the DVD and then distribute it, which can be expensive and so the price of the DVD goes up. But somebody had to write the story, people had to act in it, someone had to compose the music for the film and so on. These extra bits that are not so obvious are what you are really paying for when you buy the DVD. You are paying for the ideas and skills of other people. This is known as their **intellectual property**.

Extension

Why is Google so successful? Google is a free service on the Internet. So where does it get its money? Where do all the adverts come from? Are the adverts the same for all users?

What is Ubuntu? Does it earn money? Where does it get its money from? What are the copyright issues here?

There is a law that protects books, music, art and other things that are written or recorded in some way – it is called **copyright law**. Copyright is an automatic right – it does not need applying for. If something is copyrighted, it means that the person who owns the copyright must be asked for permission to copy it, and will often expect to be paid for its use.

Software is a specific thing that is created and written on a computer just like a book or magazine article. As such it needs to be protected because it is so easy for people to copy it without paying for it. **Software copyright** is a way of protecting software from being used by a person that does not have permission. It applies to applications, websites, games and databases. Usually, with software, if the owner wants to be paid for its use then they will create a licence which defines the terms and conditions of its use, including the price.

Extension

Go to a website (for example http://arizona. diamondbacks.mlb.com) and work out the different parts of the content that the site's creators might have needed copyright permission to use.

Questions

11 Try to decide what the different types of costs are in producing a textbook like this one and who needs to be paid. If someone copied the text and sold it themselves, would they be doing anything wrong?

What if you had a school website and music is playing in the background? If you used some pictures in a project, would it make a difference where they came from or whether the project was for use in school or for your IGCSE assessment?

12 When someone buys a piece of software they buy the right to use it. Does this mean it can be used on a lot of machines or just one? Can one person use it or lots of people? Can copies of it be made?

Find out about the different types of license available when software is bought. What sort of licenses does the school have for its software?

Can you find any examples of free software? What about free versions of games that can be downloaded from the Internet?

6b Hacking

In Module 3 you looked at the procedure of backing up files of data in case they are corrupted or destroyed. This damage can be caused in many ways. One way is malicious damage caused by people who manage to get into computer systems that they have no right to access. People who do this are **hackers** and what they do is called **hacking**. Hackers have different reasons for doing what they do. Some gain access just to prove that a system is vulnerable. Some may want to steal some of the data to make money. Others want to alter or destroy the data for purely malicious reasons.

There are three main precautions that can be taken against hacking.

- Stop a hacker from getting into the system in the first place. Authentication (the use of user IDs and passwords; see Module 4) both to access the system and to access individual files is the primary barrier against hackers.
- Make the file unreadable for any hacker that does manage to get access to them by encrypting the data (see Module 4). If this is done then any hacker who manages to get past the passwords will not be able to understand anything they find, so no damage is done (unless they simply destroy the data).
- Have a copy in case hackers do manage to damage what they access. This is where the backup copies of the files are important.

Figure 6.7 An artistic representation of a hacker.

6b Viruses

A computer **virus** is a small piece of code which can be imported to a computer system and infect it without the user being aware. A true computer virus will try to copy itself (i.e. it is self-replicating) either in the host computer or to another computer by infecting further files. However, in the broader sense, there are many kinds of computer virus that work in different ways, such as Trojans, worms and spyware, and these are generally referred to as **malware**.

An infected file might do precisely what it is meant to, but at some point the virus will try to copy itself. It can attach itself to other files and be exported to

other systems. It can also use up more and more of the available storage space in the computer system, finally making the system unusable.

Extension

What is a Trojan horse?

Try to find out about different types of virus and what they are intended to do. Consider the fact that different measures are needed to counter different types of virus.

? SAQ

4 You have just discovered that a part of your hard disk is inaccessible, possibly corrupt, and you suspect a virus.

What can you do?

There are two main ways of combating a virus.

The first is not to get one in the first place! If you do not use the Internet on a computer or connect to a LAN, and do not allow things like USB sticks to be attached to it, then the virus cannot get in.

A stand-alone computer like this is sometimes used in high-security situations but is not very useful for most people. A firewall can protect a network-connected computer from unauthorised connections and can go a long way to protect us from virus attack.

However, a firewall can't protect a computer from external media connected to it, such as USB sticks and CDs, which may contain viruses. We can control how external media are connected to a computer so that any code on the media is not automatically run on connection. Some system administrators make sure of this; some even disable the use of all external media apart from on very secure, controlled PCs.

The second way is to use a **virus scanner** (also known as an anti-virus application) to find any viruses that do try to get in. A virus scanner is an application which looks for the patterns of data or commands that are typical in viruses. It then either deletes or quarantines the suspect code.

What properties of a file can be changed in order to make a hacker's job more difficult?

If a file is held on a stand-alone computer which is never connected to any others then it is not possible to hack into it. The part of the system which is vulnerable to attack is the medium used for communication and what the computer is connected to. By considering different methods of communication used with computers, try to rank different methods of communication in terms of their security against hackers.

Install anti-virus software on your computer. Why is it necessary to download updates regularly?

Questions

13 When would it be sensible to have a computer system which is not connected to other systems? Are there any ways that a hacker or a virus could still gain access to the system?

14 Most schools have two types of computer system, one that is used by students and teachers for things like project work and one that is used for school administration. As a group, quiz your teacher about the system that holds student projects and try to get answers to the following questions.

a What files are stored and how are they arranged?
b What measures are used to stop people looking at things they should not see?
c What sort of backups are done, how often and where are they kept?
d What protection does the system have from viruses?
e Has the problem of hacking been considered and what measures are taken to protect the system from hackers?

Ask the school administrator if they will come along and talk to the class about the school administration system. Ask the same questions that you asked your teacher, but this time about the school administration system. Discuss the differences between the two systems.

Extension

Many systems use firewalls to make it more difficult to access them maliciously. One type of firewall is a spam firewall that is placed between the main firewall and the email server. Organisations use this to check emails coming into the system for unexpected messages. Only valid emails are allowed through to the main email server.

Find out about different types of firewall and what they can protect a computer system from.

Our well-being

Health issues

Ahmed's son does not have to spend his working life close to molten metal but instead works in a nice air-conditioned control room. However, he is spending long periods using the computer and is therefore very susceptible to other health risks which can be prevented. Some of these health risks are shown in Table 6.1.

Table 6.1 Health risks of using ICT and their prevention.

Health risk	Prevention
Sitting at a desk all day means little exercise.	Take regular breaks to stand up and walk around.
Long periods sitting at a desk can cause back problems.	Make sure the chair has back support, the keyboard is at the correct height, and the screen is at eye level.
Staring at a computer screen for long periods, limits eye movemet. This can cause a lack of tears to lubricate to the eye and lead to sore eyes. The muscles of the eye are not being exercised enough, or, conversely, being forced to focus at one distance for long periods.	Look away from the screen regularly and have frequent eye tests at the opticians. Make the screen less stressful to look at by ensuring it is not reflecting bright light. Fitting anti-glare screens is useful.
Using a keyboard for long periods means muscles are repeating the same actions such as hovering hands over the keyboard or repeatedly clicking the mouse buttons. This can lead to Repetitive Strain Injury (RSI), which feels a bit like arthritis.	Regularly stretching the wrist and arm muscles in different ways can alleviate the problem. Simple devices like a wrist support help to keep the arm in the correct position without using the arm musles when typing.

Figure 6.8 A wrist support to help prevent the onset of RSI from repetitive mouse and keyboard use.

? **SAQ**

5 What simple thing can you do to avoid sore eyes? Racing drivers also have to remember to do this.

Safety issues

Computers and their peripherals are electrical devices which need to be cabled together and to the electricity supply. Add to that the possibility that a set of computers may be connected by cables in order to create a network and we suddenly have a lot of wires around. Simple precautions can be taken to overcome the safety problems that this can cause.

Ideally the installation of the computers will have been well planned and the cables will all be well hidden and out of the way. In most cases this does not happen. These cables can be very dangerous – someone could trip over them (Figure 6.9). If cables are trailing and causing a safety issue, cable-ties can be used to gather them tidily together and keep them away from people.

If a new printer comes out and we buy one, it will need to be connected up and we have the problem of where to put it. It will probably go on the shelf behind the computer. Was that shelf designed to carry that weight? Does the printer fit properly on the shelf or is it precariously balanced?

Devices must be placed in suitable positions. The position must be able to support the weight of the device and must be large enough to support the device under each corner. Devices need to be placed where users can get at them if needed.

Figure 6.9 An example of trailing and tangled cables that pose a safety risk.

Figure 6.10 An example of overloaded extension leads connecting computers and associated equipment.

Users who drink liquids near the devices are at risk because electrical devices and liquids do not mix well.

It is important to ensure that the electricity supply to the room and to individual sockets is not overloaded (Figure 6.10).

Some computer rooms have false floors which have removable tiles. These can be a source of danger if removed during installations or maintenance and should be clearly marked and screened off. They should be carefully replaced to avoid tripping.

15 Consider the computer systems in your school. Are all the safety points mentioned here followed? Do the users of the computer systems follow the health guidelines suggested?

What about your computer system at home, if you have one?

Investigate other hazards associated with modern technology in schools offices and factories.

Consider the toxicity of some of the things used, for instance toners in printers. Consider the value of low-voltage electronic devices and their limitations.

Summary

- ICT has had a marked effect on leisure pursuits and social interaction.
- ICT has led to great changes in patterns of employment – de-skilling, re-skilling, semi-skilled employment, different times of employment, different place of employment, different relationships between the people involved.
- ICT devices are extremely good at doing some things but we must remember that there are many things which they are simply unable to do.
- Web 2.0 is characterised by being more interactive than Web 1.0 and allows users to alter the content. It includes blogs, wikis, social networks and media sharing sites.
- We must take care when using the Internet because we are vulnerable to unreliable information, phishing and pharming.
- Copyright is the legal protection that authors and publishers have regarding the copying of their software.
- A hacker is someone who gains unauthorised access to a system in order to cause damage. Access can be controlled by the use of passwords and encryption, and by controlling access to the communication medium.
- A virus is a small piece of code which replicates itself. It is controlled using anti-virus software.
- Health issues that must be considered when using ICT devices for long periods include RSI, back and muscle problems, and eye problems.
- Safety issues that must be considered when using ICT devices include wiring and safe location of devices.

7.1 How ICT is used in everyday life

When you have finished this module, you will be able to:

- understand a range of ICT applications in everyday life
- appreciate the impact of ICT in:
  - communication applications
  - interactive communication applications
  - data-handling applications
  - measurement applications
  - control applications
  - modelling applications.

Overview

Fifty years ago, people did not use ICT in their everyday lives. Nobody had a computer at home and devices that were used in the home did not contain computers or microprocessors.

Nowadays, most people have a cell phone and live in houses that contain many devices which use ICT to make their lives easier. The workplace, whether it is your school or the organisation that you work for, will probably use many computer-controlled devices. When we consider that ICT has had such an effect on our lives it is essential that we study the various areas of life where we meet them.

In the first half of Module 7 we look at the ICT applications we meet in everyday life that have caused our lives to change so dramatically.

Communication applications

The use of ICT has caused major changes in the way we communicate with each other on a personal level, and also the way that organisations communicate with us. We will look at a number of different applications, including the hardware and software, the effects on the people concerned and how the organisation has been affected. We will also consider the way that the pre-ICT activities have developed to the present-day computer applications.

Newsletters

Organisations like schools and clubs have always produced newsletters for the parents or for their members. In the pre-ICT era, people used a typewriter to type out a page of news onto a waxed sheet and then used the sheet on an ink copier to print copies. The quality was poor, there was no provision for pictures or colour and only a limited number of copies could be made before the quality deteriorated.

The first improvements came when electronic devices could save the content of the typed page digitally. This meant that the original document could be printed out as many times as was needed without there being a decrease in the quality produced.

The quality was much better than with the waxed paper version of copying and simple diagrams could be included to make the page more interesting. Colour printing also made the newsletter more interesting.

Volume 11, Number 3
February 2011

NEWS LETTER

Trinity High School

Success in IGCSEs at Trinity High School

The purpose of a newsletter is to provide specialized information to a targeted audience. Newsletters can be a great way to market your product or service, and also create credibility and build your organization's identity among peers, members, employees, or vendors.

First, determine the audience of the newsletter. This could be anyone who might benefit from the information it contains, for example, employees or people interested in purchasing a product or requesting your service.

You can compile a mailing list from business reply cards, customer information sheets, business cards collected at trade shows, or membership lists. You might consider purchasing a mailing list from a company.

If you explore a Publisher catalog, you will find many publications that match the style of your newsletter. Next, establish how much time and money you can spend on your newsletter. These factors will help determine how frequently you publish the newsletter and its length. It's recommended that you publish your newsletter at least quarterly so that it's considered a consistent source of information. Your customers or employees will look forward to its arrival.

Try to include interesting facts and figures, like a colourful pie chart for example.

The opening article in the newsletter should be one of the greatest significance and interest, in order to immediately capture your audience's attention.

School dinners – no chips on menu?

This story can fit 75-125 words, so should be shorter and more snappy than the main article.

You should include catchy sub-headings for smaller articles. Though all headings should be interesting, the main heading at the top, the 'headline' is the most important, and should be considered carefully.

In a few words, it should accurately represent the contents of the story and draw readers into the story. Developing the headline will help you keep the story focused.

Include photos and illustrations where you can.

Inside this issue:

Exams	2
Holidays	3
School trips	4
After-school club	5
Choir	5
Teacher's corner	5
Coming soon	6

Special points of interest:

- *Exam results.*
- *What's happening to school dinners?*
- *Where do we go on our next trip?*
- *More computers for our school.*

Figure 7.1.1 Newsletter showing text in columns, headlines, text boxes, use of margins, and colour figures.

These advances probably increased the frequency with which a newsletter was released because it was so much easier to produce.

The introduction of word processing software enabled easy editing to correct errors and further advances brought spellcheckers and grammar checkers that improved the quality.

It became very easy (click a button) to format a document in very clever ways:

- using columns;
- altering the margins and the spacing;
- changing the character SIZE;
- using different typefaces – fonts – like Arial and Times New Roman;
- different effects – like *italic*, **bold** and ^{super}scripts;
- indenting of text;
- automated bullet points and numbering;
- full justification of text – as shown in the next paragraph.

The problem is that when you use too many effects, or you use effects for the sake of using them, it becomes difficult to read the document, which is rather counter-productive. There is a skill in producing a newsletter and part of the skill is to ensure that the document looks impressive while remaining readable.

Question

1 Look at the newsletter and the text above and try to spot as many uses of simple word processing techniques as you can.

Decide whether you think the newsletter is effective. How could it be improved?

The following piece of text about newsletters is produced without any of the different techniques that are available (apart from a keyword in bold). Either reproduce it and include any of the techniques available on a word processor to improve it, or describe how the text could have been improved.

Newsletters are often produced using an application which has been specifically designed for ease of producing such documents. It is called a **desktop**

publisher (DTP) and is very like a word processor. A DTP contains most of the features of a normal word processor but with added capabilities as well. DTPs are particularly good at moving text and images around. Generally, you will create text in a word processor and then copy it into the DTP.

DTPs require text to be in boxes called 'text boxes'. Selected text boxes and their contents can be considered as a single unit and can be manipulated as one. Text boxes are one example of a unit called a 'frame', whose contents can be of many types known as 'objects'. An object can be a picture, a diagram or a table. Objects can be placed on top of each other. If the top one is made transparent then it is possible to see the object in the top frame and also the one in the bottom frame, underneath it. Objects can be flipped or rotated, and colours and contrast adjusted. A frame can be cropped or the orientation changed (from portrait to landscape, for example).

DTP applications were designed to help with the production of documents like brochures, newsletters, business cards, flyers and posters. In order to help the user the application has a number of templates that users can adapt to the document that they want to produce (Figure 7.1.2).

? SAQ

1 You produce a newsletter that has five different typefaces with different font sizes. Why do you think your teacher will not think it suitable?
2 You want to put an image of your school logo over the top of text so that you can still read the text underneath. How can you do this with a DTP application?

The person who was normally in charge of producing the school newsletter was the school secretary. Nowadays, anyone who can use a word processor will have the basic skills to use a DTP and produce a newsletter. The skill is no longer in producing the work using limited resources; the skill is now one of being discriminating about which techniques are sensible to use.

Many people may now contribute to the production of a school newsletter. The people who receive the newsletter are now better served: the information is better presented;

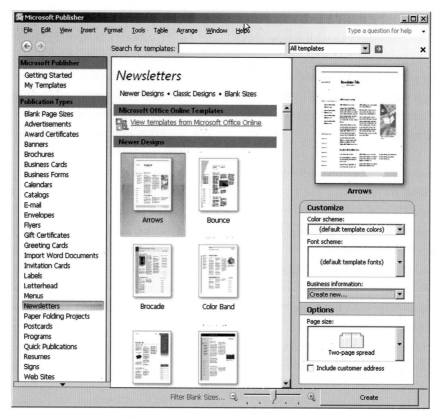

Figure 7.1.2 An example of different templates in a typical DTP (this example is from MS Publisher).

multiple pages are easy to do, probably double sided (duplex); and it can be produced more frequently than it used to be because the process is quicker. Duplex printing will require a duplex printer (unless the paper is manually turned over), which may be a colour one. A large print run would not be suitable for an inkjet printer because of the time taken to do the printing. Consequently, a colour laser printer will normally be used.

Question

2   Design the front page of a newspaper for your school, listing all the features of the software that you will use to help in the presentation of the page.

Flyers and posters

Although flyers and posters look very different to newsletters, the same sorts of considerations apply, so it is not the features of the DTP application that will tend to alter, or the methods of production. The difference is in the design of the finished product.

Figure 7.1.3 An example of a flyer. Its design contains more text than a poster but is eye-catching and more illustrative when compared to a text-heavy newsletter.

A poster needs to hold a minimum amount of information and must make that information accessible very quickly to people looking at it. A flyer can hold more information but not as much as a newsletter. The difference is that a newsletter is something which the recipient probably wants to receive. Parents are probably going to be interested in what is happening at their child's school. However, a flyer is something that is unsolicited and so if it does not make an immediate impact it will not be considered at all.

The production of posters used to be an exclusive trade before computer systems became common. Today, there are many high street businesses set up to produce simple posters cheaply and with relative ease using DTP applications and 'normal' printers. In theory, anyone with an ordinary PC, printer and a DTP application is able to make fairly decent posters or flyers. However, it is important to recognise that such posters cannot replace the work of highly skilled professionals who have the editorial, design and layout skills necessary to produce expert posters that are typically used in industry by large companies. Such posters also require specialised printers and printing houses. It is more typical for very small businesses, or an individual, to be those that make their own posters using DTP applications, or turn to the cheaper high street service.

To print posters it is necessary to use printers that can take paper sizes larger than A4, as posters need to be large to have a visual impact from a distance.

3 How do you think very large posters, such as for the side of a building, are printed?

Websites

A website is a collection of web pages, text, graphics, video and sound. A website is hosted on a web server on the Internet. The information in the website can be viewed by other Internet users using a web browser. Websites are used to raise the profile either of a person or an organisation and to communicate with others (Figure 7.1.4).

In order to produce a website you either have to write code or a use a web authoring application. The application's features are similar to those found in DTP software: the designer just needs to design the layout for the web pages on the website. Hyperlinks can be provided to jump to other web pages on the website or to other websites. More complicated, interactive websites require some programming knowledge to build them.

Figure 7.1.4 An example of a page in a generic website. This one is a template website for a business.

To input the various types of data to the site the designer will need:

- a digital camera linked to the computer by a USB connection;
- a scanner to scan in still pictures;
- a microphone to record sound files;
- the normal PC hardware to input text and to use the authoring software.

There are few requirements for the output – the website will be built and viewed on screen, so only a PC with a monitor and speakers is required. There will be a need to publish the website electronically. The usual way to do this is to hire space from a web hosting company or your Internet service provider. The website is built locally and uploaded to their servers.

A school website is used to raise the profile of the school in the community, which can help students when they apply for jobs. It is used to communicate with parents and other interested people to ensure that they feel fully involved with the school. The website is also used to advertise the school to people who currently have no connection with the school, potential new parents in particular, and it is also used to advertise events at the school.

This is a new technology which had no direct predecessor, so it has created new markets and new jobs.

There are companies that host thousands of websites; there are companies that will even build your school website for you. In your school, the website might be managed by a teacher, technician or group of senior students.

The Internet is used for advertising. Consequently, some old-style advertising is now no longer done and the advertising industry has suffered because of it. However, many advertisers have merely moved some of their business across to the Internet – it's just another medium for them to use.

Multimedia presentations

Multimedia presentations use a mixture of different media to present information effectively and maintain the interest of the viewer. The normal screen image containing text and graphics is supplemented by animations, video and sound. Sound can be synchronised with what is happening on the screen.

Changes from one screen to another can use complex transitions to make an effect. Transitions may involve one screen fading into another or one screen zooming into another. It can become a problem if complex transitions are used too much. The viewer may begin to look for the clever transitions rather than following the content closely.

Hyperlinks are included as a part of a single-user presentation to give the user the choice of path through it. Typical examples of multimedia presentations would be a presentation on a website or, in education, a computer assisted learning (CAL) package (Figure 7.1.5).

CAL presentations are interactive and give students the opportunity to manage their own learning by allowing them:

- to learn at their own pace;
- to repeat sections that were difficult;
- to omit sections with which they are happy.

This control over their own work encourages students and the different media assists in maintaining interest in the work and hence motivates the student.

A particular use in organisations is to aid the introduction of new computer systems into the

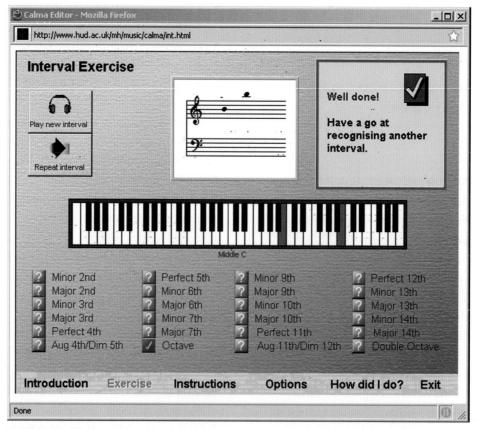

Figure 7.1.5 An example of a Computer Assisted Learning presentation for a music lesson. The screen is interactive, providing feedback as the student proceeds along at their own pace.

organisation by producing the training courses using multimedia presentations. They are placed on DVD so that the employees can then learn the new system in their own time.

? SAQ

4   If you wanted to give a user the option of repeating a CAL presentation, how could you do it?

A multimedia presentation can also be in the form of a slide show to be shown to an audience using a projector. The presentation is very similar in nature to that produced for a single user. The difference is that the use of links to move from one part of the presentation to another is not sensible because of the number of people in the audience.

Many chain stores use multimedia presentations on large screens. The presentations run in a loop while the store is open. They will typically use a lot of colour, fast cuts from one image to another and intricate transitions in order to keep the viewer's attention.

Question

3   Find some presentations that have used multimedia software. These could be software that you use in school for one of your subjects or presentations used by other departments in the school.

See if advertising presentations are being used in a local store. Look at some websites to determine whether they use multimedia presentations.

For each example that you find, identify the different features of multimedia presentations or explain why some are not being used.

Cartoons

Computers can be used to create cartoon animations. In the past, cartoons were created by producing thousands of drawings, each of which differed from the previous one very slightly. If each one was filmed for a fraction of a second and the pictures were then run together the effect was to create a moving picture. This process was highly skilled and very expensive as 25 pictures are required for 1 second of film, or approximately 100 000 hand-drawn pictures for a one-hour cartoon film. This could be reduced by cutting down the number of pictures per second, but any reduction also caused a reduction in the quality of the finished film.

Computers can be used to scan an image or the image can be created on screen with a graphic application. Then, if the user gives instructions as to how the image should move and where it should end up, the computer can calculate the intermediate stages and automatically produce copies of them. These copies can be displayed in sequence to produce the moving image. This is known as computer-generated imagery or CGI and is widely used in the film industry.

Music

Music is composed by a composer who creates a series of notes in their head or using an instrument and then writes them down if they are satisfactory. The music is written by inserting a series of symbols on a 'staff' or 'stave', which is a series of parallel horizontal lines. The position in which a symbol is placed determines the identity of the note.

Music composing software relies on the idea that if the instrument is connected up to a computer

Figure 7.1.6   A collage of typical screens from various MIDI interfaces. A MIDI interface translates incoming signals from the attached instrument into electronic data, which can then be stored and manipulated by a computer.

the software can read the notes as they are played. The standard way of connecting computers and electronic musical instruments is with **MIDI** (Musical Instrument Digital Interface – see Module 2 page 21). The music software can tell how long the note has been played for and how long the gap is between notes. It can even tell if some notes have been played together.

Sometimes music needs more than one instrument to play at the same time in order to produce the desired sounds. A piece of music can be played on one instrument and the score recorded by the software to a 'track'. This can be played back by the computer to the composer while the composer tries an accompanying part for another instrument. If the composer is satisfied, the new accompanying part can be saved as another track. The composer builds layer upon layer of tracks in the same manner.

If the computer is connected up to a printer then the software can print the score for all the parts (for the conductor) or individual parts (for an orchestra, for example).

Two of the most commonly used applications for this are *Sibelius* and *Cubase*. Sibelius will allow up to 48 instruments to be composed for at the same time. This technique of starting off with a basic tune and then enhancing it is called 'orchestration' and each instrument has its 'part'.

There are major benefits to composing in this way. The composer can hear immediate feedback of a new part of the composition and can also isolate particular instruments in the orchestration or even groups of instruments. You can edit the composition immediately or send it anywhere in the world electronically. Composers can collaborate with people all over the world on the same piece of music. Also, intermediate results can be sent to other places for inspection before carrying on with different parts of the composition. An example is a composer living in the UK who is writing the music for a film that is being made in the USA. As different bits of the music are produced the results are sent to the director in America for approval.

Notice that the process of writing the music is similar in principle to old-fashioned composition. The difference is that the software makes it possible to speed up the process, speed up the distribution and make remote collaboration possible.

Interactive communication applications

This section refers to the various interactive communication sites available for users on the Internet. Blogs, wikis and digital media uploading websites are specifically described in Module 6 and one of the questions asked you to discuss social networking websites. We look at social networking websites in more detail here.

Social networking websites

There has always been a need for friends, like-minded people, communities or groups with similar interests to be able to communicate easily with each other. Using the Internet as the communication medium has enabled many different social networking websites to achieve this.

Previously, email may have been used to put people on the same distribution list in touch with each other – an email sent to the distribution list would cause an email to be sent to everyone on the distribution list, whether they wanted it or not. This method is still in use but is inflexible – it is largely being overtaken by social networking websites. Whereas email was a one-size-fits-all way of doing things, each social networking website has a particular way of doing things that appeals to the users and makes their experience enjoyable.

They tend to operate by the user first getting a login account to the website and then putting in their **profile**. A profile lists the user's likes and maybe dislikes and gives some of their personal details. This is the information that the website's software needs to point the user at other users with similar details. For instance, the Friends Reunited website groups users according to the school they attended; on Facebook, once someone has accepted you as a friend, you are made aware of their friends. Other social networking sites allow you to select the groups that you want to join.

Privacy is an important feature of social networking sites. Generally, people are only connected with each other if they both agree (see Figure 7.1.7). Some sites limit access to other users' profiles or the less personal parts of their profiles. There have been instances where

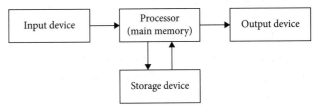

facebook

☐Remember Me Forgotten your password?

Email address   Password   Log in

Sign Up Facebook helps you connect and share with the people in your life.

This policy is effective as of 26 November 2008.

Facebook Principles

We built Facebook to make it easy to share information with your friends and people around you. We understand you may not want everyone in the world to have the information you share on Facebook; that is why we give you control of your information. Our default privacy settings limit the information displayed in your Profile to your networks and other reasonable community limitations that we tell you about.

Facebook follows two core principles:

1. You should have control over your personal information.
Facebook helps you share information with your friends and people around you. You choose what information you put in your Profile, including contact and personal information, pictures, interests and groups you join. And you control the users with whom you share that information through the privacy settings on the Privacy page.

2. You should have access to the information others want to share.
There is an increasing amount of information available out there, and you may want to know what relates to you, your friends and people around you. We want to help you easily get that information.

Sharing information should be easy. We want to provide you with the privacy tools necessary to control how and with whom you share that information. If you have questions or ideas, please take a look at our privacy help page.

Figure 7.1.7 Facebook Principles. This is an example of a privacy notice offered by the social networking website, Facebook.

spammers have used the information in profiles to gather lists of email addresses.

Social networking websites are a relatively new phenomenon. New ideas are being introduced by entrepreneurs all the time to try and capture a slice of the market. But how do they make money? Usually, social networking websites do not charge for membership and some have millions of members. What those members see is constant advertising. This pays for the development and administration and leaves enough left for the owners to make good profits. It is also used to pay for development of the next new idea.

 SAQ

5 Why isn't email popular anymore for social networking?

7.1c **Data-handling applications**

Many things that a computer is used for can be considered as **data handling** in one form or another. We have seen that the basic components of a computer and the flow of data around it can be illustrated as shown in Figure 7.1.8.

| Input device | → | Processor (main memory) | → | Output device |

Storage device

Figure 7.1.8 The main components of a computer. The arrows show the flow of data around the system.

The input to the system is data. In this respect all computer systems are to some extent data-handling applications but for this section our definition of data handling is slightly different. We are interested in applications which have a particular need for storing data for later use. For this section not only is the input data and the processing very important, but so is the storage, in particular the structure that the data takes when it is stored.

Surveys

The start point, whatever the data-handling application, is data collection. Sometimes this will be done automatically, and we shall see examples of that in this section, but another method is to use **surveys**. In computer terms we conduct surveys using **data capture forms**. Data capture forms can be used for many applications. The questions that are on the form and its structure will differ depending on its application. In general terms it is important to decide what data needs to be collected and then to decide what the questions should be to collect it. Data capture forms can be on paper or can be electronically based and filled in directly onto the computer.

Question

4 Search for some examples of data capture forms, both paper based and electronic. Look at the different questions on the forms and look for different types of questions which are asked.

Read the next section and then return here and answer the following questions for the forms that you have collected. Does the form look official? Is it obvious what the data that is being asked for will be used for? Are there instructions on the form to help the person to fill it in accurately? Is the data asked for confidential or sensitive? Are all the response boxes clear?

There are rules about creating forms. Sometimes it is necessary to break these rules but they should be stuck to most of the time:

- Make the form look official. It may be part of an official website. If it is on paper then the name of the organisation should be on the top together with a logo to give it credibility.
- Spaces should be supplied for the answers. People who fill in forms tend to follow what the designer of the form wants so the amount of space left for an answer is very important.
- Questions should have a small possible answer set. For example a question that asks what books you have read is meaningless. It does not limit the response and some people may want to write in a large number of titles. Even if it is restricted to a small number, what is the point of asking the question? It does not give valuable information because if you ask 100 people you may well get 100 different answers. The question should restrict the possible answers by asking, 'Which of these books

have you read?', and then giving a list of popular books. This now gives valuable information because it will be possible to determine which books are popular and which are not.
- Sometimes questions with open-ended answers need to be asked. If this is the care then a limited space can be given for the response to indicate the length of the required answer.
- A request for 'Name' needs to be carefully considered. Most people have more than one name. Which name do we want? Why do we want the person's name? Is it important? If the rest of the form is asking about sensitive things, shouldn't the form be anonymous?
- 'Date of birth' seems like a harmless request but there are two problems. First, it depends who you are asking – some people do not like to give away such information. Second, there are so many ways of writing the date down that the form must make it clear how the information should be given.
- Instructions about filling the form in need to be given, particularly if there are any unusual questions which may be difficult to understand.
- The method for collecting the data should be considered. We studied the use of OMR and OCR in Module 2. There are many types of form which use these two methods of input. The method of data input is important. A form that is completed by simply writing responses to the questions on it must have the data entered to the computer by an operator. This introduces a possibility of an error being made with the data.

The designer of the form must also have a clear idea of why data is needed and consequently which data must be collected in order to satisfy the needs of the application.

As an example, imagine that we have been asked to find out why people are not using the school library enough and make some suggestions for changes. The form that we have come up with is shown in Figure 7.1.9.

Once the data has been collected it needs to be stored prior to being used. The method of storage will differ depending on what the data is, how sensitive it is and how it is going to be used.

Library Survey

PLEASE COMPLETE THE FOLLOWING QUESTIONS

Name _____

Address _____

_____

_____

Form _____

Date of Birth [ ][ ][ ]

When was the last time that you were in the school library? _____

What did you go in for? _____

_____

Which books do you like? _____

_____

What would you like to see in the library apart from books? _____

_____

Do you ever go into the library to use the computers? _____

Are the staff helpful? _____

Any other comments? _____

_____

Thank you for filling in this form.

Figure 7.1.9 An example of a data capture form for a school library. The purpose is to discover why the library is not being used enough.

Address lists

When you fill in a form, an interesting question to ask is, 'What happens to all the information which you supply on the form?'

One of the pieces of information which we are often asked to supply is our address. Address lists are very valuable. Organisations which deal through mail order need to be able to send brochures to potential customers so a list of names and addresses is something which they can use for their business.

As an example, imagine a business which specialises in publishing science fiction novels and selling them by mail. The first and most valuable list of addresses is that of all the people who have bought books from the company in the past. This list is particularly valuable because everyone on the list has already proved that they are interested in the type of books that are being sold by the company because they have bought them in the past.

The business wants to expand their list of names and addresses. If they just use a set of addresses at random, like the names and addresses in the phone book, then most people will not be interested in their books and the costs of the brochures and the mailing will have been wasted. However, if they were to use the results from a survey similar to the one for the school library and only mail those people who said that they liked science fiction books, then they could expect a higher proportion of people to respond. The list is now a more specialised one because it is a list of people who share a particular quality.

Lists like these are very important to organisations.

Question

5 Consider the library form. Comment on the layout of the form and the way the questions have been asked. Are all the questions sensible questions? Would you feel confident filling in this form? Could you fill in the form properly? Do you understand what all the questions are actually asking you?

Redesign the form so that it could be used in your school. Would the design change if you decided to put it on the school website instead of handing out paper sheets? Would the design of your form change if it was for a specific age group of students?

Question

6 The next time you, or one of your family, is asked for their name and address on a survey, try giving all the correct information except for the initial of your name. Make up a fake initial. It is then interesting to wait and see if you get some junk mail addressed to the name with the fake initial. If you do, then it means that your name and address has been passed on to another organisation. Is this fair? Is this legal? If organisations were not able to do this, where could they get their lists from?

Extension

Targeting with lists is used to great effect in electioneering. Political parties have lists of voters along with a profile of each voter showing what they like and do not like. Individual letters can be sent to each voter which are tailored to that voter, telling them what they want to hear. This was first done in USA as part of the 1984 Presidential election, but has now become common practice. In the 2008 US Presidential election the same techniques were used with email addresses and cell phone numbers.

Investigate how the techniques can be used with electronic communications and consider how communication using lists of one sort or another may be used in the future.

Question

7 Consider the example spreadsheet in Table 7.1.1 that could be used for the running of a tuck shop. What improvements could be made to the layout? How would you improve the contents of the cells to make it more understandable? Does the spreadsheet carry enough detail to make it very useful? What problems could be caused by the inclusion of 'Apples' as a record in the sheet which will not be true of the other records? Three different formulae were used to make the spreadsheet. What are the formulae and which cells would they be in?

Tuck shop records

If your school has a tuck shop it is probably run on a simple basis of buying some snack foods and selling them for slightly more than they cost. However, if the tuck shop is a bit more complex than that or if it is decided that it is necessary to make the tuck shop run on a more formal basis, then it will be necessary to keep accurate records. This may involve keeping the records using a computer system. The records will be used for numerical purposes and hence a spreadsheet would be the most sensible form of record keeping to use (Table 7.1.1).

Figure 7.1.10 An example of things on sale at a school tuck shop.

Should a school tuck shop keep a record of suppliers? Probably not because it is on such a small scale. However, if it did it would store the records in a database so that information about a supplier could be linked to the products. Staff records could also be kept if it was thought to be necessary, but this would be for a larger tuck shop than is common in most schools.

Clubs and societies

Clubs and societies need to keep data on their members. This data can be searched for specific members of the club so that they can be contacted. It can also be searched for specific data – for instance all the members who are in a particular age group so that a team can be chosen to represent the school.

Table 7.1.1 Example spreadsheet for school tuck shop.

Name of snack	No. in box	Cost per box	Price	No. of boxes	Profit per box	Profit
Tweeks	48	6.78	0.19	3	7	21
Star	60	4.76	0.1	5	1.24	6.2
Big drinks	24	3.88	0.25	7	2.12	14.84
Apples	50	7.24	0.22	4	3.76	15.04
			Total Profit			57.08

ID	First name	Family name	Form	Position in league	Phone number
5	signa	ahmed	6dy	14	0785123345
6	james	aimes	2fr	25	0798543321
7	afroz	akin	5de	16	0784653452
8	betran	awdren	6jt	14	0756324565
9	ravi	boparra	3we	1	0715624354

8 Consider the extract from a database which shows some of the members of a school chess club. The records have been ordered. Which field has been used to order the data? How else could the data have been ordered? Criticise the data that is being stored. What other data might be useful in the running of the club? How could the best team of sixth-form students be chosen? Is this a sensible use of a computer or would the data be better kept in some other way?

If this were a club outside school then a lot more data would be necessary. One set of data would be about membership fees, which is numerical data. Does this mean that the information would need to be kept in a spreadsheet? Decide what numerical data would need to be kept and investigate the effectiveness of using a database or a spreadsheet to store all the data.

School reports

To understand the use of ICT in producing school reports we need to consider what information is on the reports (the 'files' referred to here are those discussed in Module 5):

- **Data which is individual to that student.** This would include the student's name and form. This information is already on the computer system. It is stored in the 'student file'. If the template for the reports is stored on the computer then the system can be told to produce a set of reports for every student in the school or just for a year group or even for all the girls in the hockey team. Any subset is possible. These reports will be stored electronically and await further information being imported to them.

- **Student progress.** The form teacher will probably have to write a report on the student's progress and hence their name will need to be on the report. This can be found by using the form name as the foreign key and looking up the name of the form teacher in the 'teacher file'. This can then be added to the report.

- **The number of absences that the student has had and the number of times they have been late.** This data will be stored on the attendance register, which is often computerised. If it is, the computer can quickly calculate how often a student has been absent or late to classes and insert the figures on the report.

- **Teacher comments.** The teachers will have to write a comment for each of the students that they teach. These comments tend to be repeated many times for different students as there is a limit to the number of appropriate comments that can be made. A set of responses can be stored on the computer system and the teacher then simply chooses the comments that apply to that student and they are added to the report by the computer. This set of comments is called a comment bank.

- **Date of the report.** This can be in the form of the actual date that it was completed. This is easy for the computer to do as it knows the date anyway. Alternatively it may just say which term the report is for, in which case the same information will be on every report.

When the reports are completed they can be printed out for distribution to parents. Note that the most suitable printer needed for this will be a laser printer. It is fast enough to print the large number of reports quickly and also can print to the necessary quality. A colour laser printer may be used if the school uses a colour logo and wants to give a good impression.

XAVERIAN COLLEGE

Advanced Progress Report – Spring 2005

Student: James G.

Tutor Group: 04-U6-TU-TH-09-C PN

Subject: Art A2

Subject Teacher: Mr Gornall

% Attendance: 82.72

Late for class 1 times

Ex - Excellent	**G** - Good
S - Satisfactory, **minimum standard**	**P** - Poor, **cause for concern**

Commitment

	Ex	G	S	P
Effort / Motivation	✓			
Attendance				✓
Punctuality			✓	
Attitude	✓			

Subject Knowledge

	Ex	G	S	P
Background knowledge	✓			
Understanding	✓			
Factual recall	✓			

Communication Skills

	Ex	G	S	P
Oral	✓			
Written	✓			
Contribution to group work	✓			
Presentation of work	✓			

Target Grade Range	C/A

Achievement

Internal Assessment Grade reflecting current standard of student's work	C
External Assessment Grade the most recent module/unit grade	C
Estimated Grade based on current progress and effort being maintained	C

Study Skills

	Ex	G	S	P
Ability to meet deadlines	✓			
Ability to work independently	✓			
Ability to organise learning	✓			

Analysis / Evaluation

	Ex	G	S	P
Application of knowledge	✓			
Ability to discuss / evaluate ideas	✓			
Ability to analyse problems logically	✓			

Comment and/or action to be taken:

James has impressed me greatly this year. He is an intelligent, articulate student whose enthusiasm has been a fine example to his classmates. James has the potential to achieve a very good grade in the summer, despite his disappointing AS result last year. All round, an excellent student and a very personable, charming young man.

Subject Teacher .... **Date** 10/04/05

Figure 7.1.11 An example of a school student report. This example has been filled in by hand, which is much more time-consuming for the teacher and less efficient. The teacher will have to keep rewriting generic sentences that apply to all children, and might even include spelling errors by mistake.

Questions

9 The system will also attach the names of the individual teachers to the subject areas for each of the individual reports. Refer back to Module 5 and describe how the system can find out which teachers teach particular subjects to individual students and then access the information that should be put on the report.

10 Look at the school reports that are produced at your school. Are they hand written or produced on a computer? Try to identify the parts of the report that can be filled in automatically by the computer system. Identify parts of the report that the computer system can help the teachers to fill in. Are there any parts of the report that the computer cannot assist with?

Extension

How could the system be extended to ensure that teachers fill in the correct reports and keep track of which have been completed by the teachers and which have not?

School libraries

Some libraries in schools are too small to require computerisation. The geography department library for sixth-form geography students which has about 20 books and perhaps 10 students is really not appropriate for a computerised application. However, it is a good example to show how a system would work for a larger library.

We will use this as an example, except we will only have five books and six students. It will be enough for us to understand how a larger library system might work in our school library.

The two files (7.1.2 and 7.1.3) can be used to identify the books that are held in the library and the students who are allowed to borrow the books. However, the files here are very restricted in the way that they can be used. Apart from looking to see whether or not a title is owned by the library and checking to see whether a particular student is allowed to take a book from the library, there is little else that they can be used for.

Table 7.1.2 Student file.

Name	Form	Geography group
Boparra	6dy	Mr. Khan
Broad	6ft	Ms. Anderson
Flintoff	6dy	Mr. Khan
Harmison	6ft	Mr. Khan
Shah	6ft	Ms. Anderson
Strauss	6dy	Mr. Khan

Table 7.1.3 Books file.

ISBN	Book title	Author
978 2 489 768734 1	Economic Geography	Daniel Vettori
978 1 453 62456 1	Geography for A level	MS Wicksamaringhe
978 1 123 49876 4	Glacial valleys	Sachin Tendulkar
978 9 123 45678 5	Meteorology	Wasim Akram
978 0 234 56789 5	Volcanoes	Jacques Kallis

The main thing that computers need to be used for in libraries is to keep a check on which books are out on loan and who has them. In order to do this we need to include another file in our library database. At the moment there is nothing that links a particular book to a student because there are no foreign keys. To allow us to keep track of books we need another file called the Loans file (Table 7.1.4). This will contain the student names and also the ISBN of the books. This means that the three files are now linked together using the Name field and the ISBN field as foreign keys.

If the teacher wants to know where a particular book is and how to get it back if it is still on loan, they

Table 7.1.4 Loans file.

ISBN	Name	Returned?	Date due back
978 2 489 768734 1	Flintoff	yes	16/05
978 1 453 62456 1	Shah	yes	23/05
978 1 123 49876 4	Boparra	no	29/05
978 9 123 45678 5	Flintoff	no	29/05
978 0 234 56789 5	Strauss	yes	30/05

only need to know the title of the book. For example, a teacher wants to know where *Meteorology* by W. Akram is. The Books file is searched for the title and author. The ISBN is then taken from the Books file. The ISBN is then used in the Loans file to find out firstly whether or not the book is in the library or out on loan. In this case it is out on loan; Flintoff has it. Using this name the teacher can then ask the computer to search the student file to discover that Flintoff is in 6dy. The teacher can then go to the correct form room to speak to the student.

Notice that in order to be useful it is necessary to have three files with two sets of foreign keys.

Questions

11 Why is it necessary to have the third table of Loans? Can the problem of keeping a track of the books and the loans be solved in another way? (Can the loan be added to either the Books table or the Student table? Try both methods with the data given in the Loan table here and see what happens.)

12 Find out what system is used in your school library. Is it a manual, paper-based system? Is it a computerised system? Whichever it is, try to decide how it works and think about the way that the three tables of information that are in this solution are used in your library.

What are the special items of hardware that would be needed in a library system? Would it be reasonable to type in the ISBN of a book every time it was taken out on loan? How about the identity of the student taking the book out on loan?

 Measurement applications

Let us start by considering what a measuring application is. Clearly it has something to do with measuring a value or a set of values. Then a computer is used to display the values to the user in a meaningful way, which represents the magnitude of the thing being measured.

The values that are being measured are physical values that occur around us in the world. In order to measure something in the outside world the computer needs to be given some data to describe the measurement that needs to be taken. These measurements will be taken by devices that can automatically take measurements and return the values to the computer.

We studied a number of these devices, called **sensors**, in Module 2. Most of the data that is measured will be analogue data. Throughout this work we should remember that any analogue data that is measured will need to be changed into digital data so that it can be used by a computer system.

ICT can provide great precision in taking measurements; far greater than a human being is capable of. However, some things benefit from computerised measurement and others do not. Take for example a school groundskeeper who needs to know the size of the sports field in order to work out how much fertiliser is needed. Would the precision offered by ICT be important in measuring the field? No, because the groundskeeper only needs an estimate, since a very accurate measurement of the field wouldn't have any noticeable effect on the quality of the grass after fertiliser application.

Compare this with the requirements of an automatic weather station (Figure 7.1.12). Precision in the measurements taken is very important because they are used in making weather forecasts, which many people, such as farmers or sailors, depend on. Similarly, the temperature within a reactor vessel during a chemical reaction may need to be accurately measured. If the temperature gets too low the reaction will stop but if it gets too high the pressure could make the whole vessel dangerous. These temperature points may be very precise.

Figure 7.1.12 An automatic weather station. Typically these consist of a rechargable battery, a data logger and various sensors.

6 If you want to measure barometric pressure and use this data on computer, what would you use?

Where would you use it?

Precision and safety are not the only reasons for using ICT in measurement. If measurements need to be taken over a long period of time, a human being may forget to take them or may not be available at the right time. So ICT systems have a number of advantages over humans when taking measurements:

- **Precision.** ICT can provide more accurate measurements than a human.
- **Reliability.** ICT can be relied upon to take the measurements every time.
- **Accuracy.** ICT will ensure that the measurements are taken at exactly the right time.
- **Non-interference.** Measurements can be taken without disturbing the thing that is being measured. A human being might need to put a thermometer into the reaction vessel to measure the temperature, or the heater may need to be turned off to allow the human to get close enough to take the measurement.

13 Make a list of the things that happen in your life – in school, at home, around the town that you live in – that require measurements to be made. For each one consider:
- what is being measured;
- how accurate the measurement needs to be;
- how often the measurements need to be taken;
- for how long the measurements need to be taken;
- how easy it would be for a human to be able to take the measurements.

For each one, decide whether it is sensible to take the measurements by computer (expensive) or by a person. Try to justify your choices by referring to the points in the list above.

Using ICT to measure values does not have to be on a small scale or on something that we can see around us.

Gravity is different at different points on the Earth's surface. This difference means that we are lighter at the poles than we are at the equator. This difference in gravity is so small that it does not affect us directly but it does affect the tides in the oceans. A space craft has been sent into space which will accurately map Earth's gravitational field.

Another space mission is mapping the sea bed.

Try to find out about these and other measurements that are taken from space. How can measurements about the Earth be taken from space? What types of measuring instruments are used?

Scientific experiments

There are many different scientific experiments that need to be controlled by processors which can take measurements and then make decisions based on the measurements that have been taken.

Why is the use of sensors to take measurements during scientific experiments so important?
- Often the experiment being done will be dangerous to human beings. Sensors can be used where human beings cannot.
- The findings from scientific experiments are based on the accuracy of the measurements that are taken.
- There is a need for the measurements not to be missed or the results of the experiment will begin to be questioned.
- It is important to ensure that nothing interferes with the experiment which may change the results.

Compare this set of requirements against the set of generic requirements that were listed in the opening section. They are very similar.

Scientific experiments that use ICT to collect the data will need to use sensors. The three types of sensor which were studied in Module 2 were temperature, pressure and light sensors.

Temperature sensors can be used to measure the temperature of the chemicals that are reacting in a vessel or the temperature of the chemicals that are being prepared to enter the reaction vessel. They may be used to measure the temperature of an engine part in an engineering workshop to ensure that the friction in the engine is not excessive. They may be used to measure the surrounding temperature in order to allow a comparison of the temperatures in an experiment and in the surroundings. Each experiment will be different but many experiments will need a temperature sensor.

Figure 7.1.13 Temperature sensors are also used in engine rooms. Here, you can see the circular dials (gauges) that display the temperature as it is being constantly measured.

Experiments may also need a **pressure sensor**. Pressure sensors are very important in chemical experiments. Some reactions will only work if they are done at particular pressures and the computer must ensure that the correct pressure is used. Also, chemical reactions often involve the chemicals changing their state and creating large volumes of gas. If kept in the same reactor vessel, there will be large pressure build-ups, which can be very dangerous if the pressure becomes too great.

Figure 7.1.14 An example of a pressure gauge for an industrial chemical reaction. The sensors would be in the vessel inself and attached to the gauge for read out.

The use of **light sensors** is less obvious. They may be used, for example, in a biological experiment about plant growth (Figure 7.1.15). The computer can be used over long periods of time to take measurements at regular intervals of the levels of light. The data can then be used as part of an experiment to determine growth rates of different plant types in different growing conditions.

Figure 7.1.15 A biologist positioning a light sensor in the rainforest, for an experiment about plant growth.

When the data has been collected it needs to be sent to the computer. This will be via an **analogue-to-digital converter** so that the signals that arrive at the computer can be understood. The data can be processed by the computer in one of two ways. Either the computer has been programmed to play some active part in the experiment or it is simply collecting the data for later use.

If the computer is playing an active part in the experiment then the data that is sent to it will be processed and decisions will be made. Output devices (Module 2) carry out the actions resulting from the decisions. This is a good example of real-time processing (see later in Module 7.2 page 127).

? SAQ

7 You want to control a light to come on at dusk when it is freezing. What two sensors do you need?

Alternatively, the data can be collected for analysis. The data is likely to be numerical so it will probably be collated in a spreadsheet which will allow graphs to be drawn in order to allow the results to be easily interpreted. A spreadsheet will also allow the user to ask 'what if...' type questions of the data (see later in this module).

Question

14 Make a list of the various experiments that you have done in science lessons in your school. Which ones used computer-controlled measurement to carry out the experiment? In which did you take the necessary measurements? In these experiments, was it essential that you took the measurements or would it have been better to have used sensors linked to a computer?

Electronic timing

Electronic timing can be very accurate. But the critical thing about timing is not so much the measurement of time itself but the starting and stopping of the timer.

Figure 7.1.16 A typical stopwatch used for school athletics. It measures time to the accuracy of one-hundredth of a second but it is manually operated so some accuracy is lost.

Using a stopwatch at the school athletics day is a good way of timing a race. The person using the watch might be a bit late in pressing the button at the start and they might be a bit late again at the end, but overall they won't be much more than a quarter of a second out. The watch itself might be a few seconds out over the course of 24 hours, but not enough to make any difference to the times awarded at the school sports.

However, at an international athletics meeting the timings are measured to the nearest one-hundredth of a second more precisely by using a computer. The need for a greater degree of accuracy is now more important and electronic timing is essential. A computerised timer will be used as well as computerised start and stop actions.

Figure 7.1.17 An example of an electronically operated timer at the Berlin Marathon. It also measures to the accuracy of one-hundredth of a second but a computerised start and stop means the measurement is much more accurate than a stopwatch.

The start and stop actions are supplied by sensors. The start of the race is signalled when the starter fires the starting pistol. You may have noticed that there is always a cable attached to the pistol. This carries the signal from the sensor in the pistol to the computerised timer, which now starts.

At the finish line a simple light beam across the track will be broken by the runner who crosses the line first. The light sensor senses the break in the signal and sends a signal to the computer to indicate the timer should be stopped.

8 When is manual timing better than computerised timing? When is computerised timing better than manual timing?

Question

15 How can sensors be used to determine whether there has been a false start in a sprint race? How can a false start in a long-distance race be determined?

The text says that breaking a light beam will be used to stop the clock at the end of the race. This could be used but there is a problem. What would happen if a bird flew across the beam before the athletes reached the end? Try to find out what method is really used for ending the timing of the race.

Extension

Consider electronic timing and the starting and stopping of the clock in swimming races. What about Formula 1 Grand Prix racing? How are pit stops timed?

The global positioning system (GPS) relies on the time taken for a signal to get to the GPS device from the satellites which are orbiting the Earth (Figure 7.1.18). Timing in this example is not to the nearest hundredth of a second but needs to be very much more accurate.

The distance to the Moon can be very accurately measured because a mirror pointing back to Earth was left on the surface of the Moon by one of the lunar landing missions. When a laser is fired at that mirror from Earth, the laser light is reflected back. If the length of time that it takes the light to get back to Earth is measured then, because we know the speed of light, we can work out a very precise distance to the Moon.

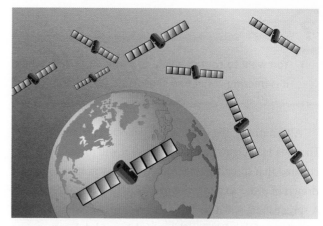

Figure 7.1.18 GPS satellites orbiting the Earth. (Please note that this is an artistic representation and does not reflect the true number or relative location of GPS satellites).

Some experiments need to measure time in very small divisions indeed: this can only be done by electronic timing.

Extension

The Large Hadron Collider (LHC) is used by the scientific community to study the composition of the smallest atomic particles. It fires particles around a large circle in order to increase their speed to very close to the speed of light. It then forces them to collide in order to split them into their component parts. The scientists who use the LHC use units of time called nanoseconds to control the electronic equipment. They regularly use units called picoseconds when measuring the effects of the collisions. One nanosecond is 1/1000 000 000 of a second. One picosecond is an even shorter time period: 1/1000 000 000 000 of a second. They also use even smaller time periods for some of their experiments. Timings like this are not going to be possible for a human being to conduct so electronic timing is essential.

Research the LHC and the small time periods discussed.

Environmental monitoring

Environmental monitoring is concerned with monitoring the quality of the environment. Frequently, it is about measuring the levels of pollution in the environment and reporting the levels over long time periods. Computers are often used for this purpose.

Figure 7.1.19   Exhaust fumes being released from a vehicle.

Particularly important are levels of gases like carbon monoxide and nitrogen dioxide which are produced by vehicle exhausts (Figure 7.1.19). These can be monitored by installing specialised sensors that will detect the levels of the particular gas and report back to the computer via an analogue-to-digital converter. The computer can be used to:

- draw graphs to show the recent levels in an understandable form;
- store the data over a long period and report the findings when the user asks for the results;
- store the results in a spreadsheet which will allow the user to predict future levels;
- produce information in table or graph form for importing into a report which can then be published.

If the data is going to be recorded for future use then it is important to decide when to take the readings.

As an extreme example, consider the setting up of a carbon monoxide sensor at a busy intersection in a city centre. The expectation would be that the sensor would show high levels of carbon monoxide because of the high levels of traffic. However, after collecting information for a year, the sensor shows that levels of carbon monoxide were actually very low. How can this happen? In this case the sensor was set to take a reading every 24 hours and the readings were taken at 3.00 am every morning. The readings will be low because there are not many vehicles on the road at that time in the morning! If the readings had been taken at 9.00 am they would have been completely different because at that time the roads are full with people trying to get to work.

There are two timings to be set in any experiment. The first is the time interval between the readings being taken. It is important to ensure that this is not on a regular cycle otherwise the readings will be unrepresentative. The other timing to consider is the length of time that the experiment will go on for. The example above was for a year. Is this sensible? Why couldn't we take a reading every hour for a week, or even every five minutes for one day? (If the day was at a weekend would the figures taken be representative?) This decision is partly decided by the urgency of the results and partly by the reasons for collecting the information. If the information is collected to determine whether there is a problem then it needs to be collected as quickly as possible so that any necessary action can be taken. However, if this is intended as a monitoring exercise then the sensors could be set up to monitor conditions on a permanent basis.

The atmosphere near busy road junctions is one type of environmental monitoring; there are many others. Any part of the environment in which we live can be monitored.

 SAQ

9   In environmental monitoring, what are the two critical timings that need to be decided?

16 Consider a river. It is necessary to ensure that the river's water quality is maintained to make sure that the water can sustain the fish and other creatures that live in it. A problem has arisen because a factory has been built on the bank of the river. The factory takes water in from the river in order to use it in its production process. It then discharges the water that it has used back into the river further downstream.

The important environmental question is: has this affected the quality of water in the river? Decide what sensors are necessary to answer the question. Decide where these sensors should be placed. Explain how and at what time periods the data will be collected from the sensors. Describe how the data will be used when it has been collected.

Notice that this section has been about monitoring. At no point have we suggested that the computer system can do anything about the conditions that it finds. There is no suggestion that the computer finds too much carbon monoxide in the atmosphere and so decides to remove some of it. The system is there to monitor conditions, not to control them. The next section discusses the use of computer systems which can control the environment rather than just monitoring it.

Control applications

In the last section we were studying the use of computers to take measurements in the outside world and present the results. When we talk about 'computer control' we are talking about applications where the computer is not only taking measurements from the world around it, but has been given command over some devices which will allow decisions to be made and actions to be taken that will have a direct bearing on the results that are taken next time.

The devices that are used to take action – motors, buzzers, heaters and lights – were explained in Module 2 and in this section we are interested in how they can be used rather than how they work. The example applications here are the ones that are mentioned specifically in the syllabus but readers should be aware that there are many others that may be asked about in the examination.

Turtle graphics

LOGO is a simple computer programming language which was developed in order to encourage children to think in a logical way (hence the name). Part of the language is completely graphical and was developed to be used to control the movements of a small robot device which looked a bit like a turtle. Hence, the language that made it move was called turtle graphics. The original turtle contained a pen so that it could draw a line as it moved. Nowadays we don't need the physical turtle, but the concept is the same even if we draw directly to a screen. There are many commands that are available in turtle graphics but the ones that students are likely to need in examinations are listed here with advice as to how they are used.

In each of the diagrams the turtle is represented by a triangle shape. The shape that is used to show the position of the turtle does not really matter except that it needs to show the direction that it is pointing in. The turtle is normally considered to be at the position where the triangle is pointing.

Most turtle graphic commands are made up of two parts: the first is the name and the second gives a value which tells the computer how much needs to be done. For example FORWARD 5 would tell the turtle that it must move forwards and that it needs to move 5 units. This is not always true, as we shall see later, but it is a good place to start. The actual command word is FORWARD but it can become very annoying to have to write it in full every time it is used, so each of the command words have shortened forms. The short form will be put in brackets after each of the commands given.

1. Moving forwards
FORWARD 5   (FD 5)

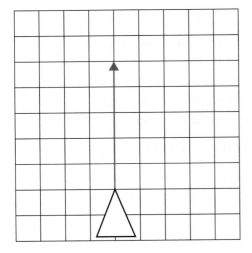

2. Moving backwards
BACK 5   (BK 5)
This makes the turtle go backwards. This is very rarely used in exam questions because it is always possible to turn completely around and then go forwards.

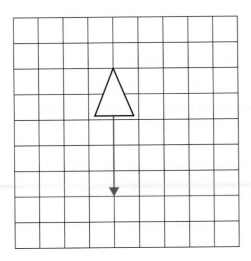

3. Turning sideways
There are two commands that make the turtle turn to face another direction. The command must tell the turtle which way to turn and then tell it how much to turn. The number is the number of degrees in the angle that has to be turned. Almost always this will be 90 or some multiple of 90 in an exam question. The reason for this is that any other angle is very difficult to represent on an exam paper, although 60 and 45 are sometimes used. You can ask the turtle to turn left or right.

LEFT 90   (LT 90)

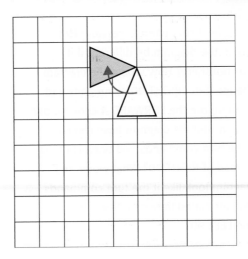

Notice that it looks as though the turtle has moved to the right, but if you imagine the line that will be drawn by the turtle if it goes forward now, you will see that it has moved to the left. Be careful with turns – it is easy to get mixed up.

RIGHT 90   (RT 90)

4. Moving the pen

Sometimes you want the turtle to move without leaving a line behind it. If this is the case then before you move the turtle it is necessary to tell it to lift the pen off the paper. The command is PENUP. This does not need a number after it. The turtle will now move around without drawing anything until it is told to put the pen back onto the paper. The command for this is PENDOWN.

Imagine you want to draw a square of side 4 units. The commands would be:

FORWARD 4	(FD 4)
RIGHT 90	(RT 90)
FORWARD 4	(FD 4)
RIGHT 90	(RT 90)
FORWARD 4	(FD 4)
RIGHT 90	(RT 90)
FORWARD 4	(FD 4)
RIGHT 90	(RT 90)

The result would be:

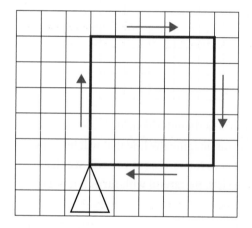

Question

17 Is the final command necessary? How would the diagram be different if it was not there? How would the diagram change if the RIGHT 90 commands had been before the FORWARD 4 commands? How would the diagram have changed if the turn commands had been LEFT 90 instead of RIGHT 90? What would the diagram look like if the turn commands had alternated between RIGHT 90 and LEFT 90?

An important hint for doing questions that are based on turtle graphics: it is very easy to become confused between RIGHT and LEFT as the turtle moves around the page. Always make sure that the turtle is pointing away from you before you try to do the next command. You can do this by moving the paper, book or exam paper around as the diagram is drawn. Another hint is that exam questions more usually ask for the candidate to produce a set of commands rather than drawing a diagram from a set of commands. If a question does ask for a diagram to be drawn, make sure that the line that you have drawn on the paper stands out well because the examiner must be able to see it properly.

5. Repeating

The set of commands that drew the square were a bit tedious because they are the same commands done over and over again. This can be shortened to make it easier to write down. Also, if the number of commands is reduced there is less chance of a typing error being made.

Consider the commands – there were four pairs of:

FORWARD 4   RIGHT 90

If these are going to be put on the same line we need to make sure that they are kept separate so a comma is put in between them:

FORWARD 4, RIGHT 90

Now, this pair of commands needs to be done more than once:

REPEAT   FORWARD 4, RIGHT 90

We don't need the gap, but we do need to make it clear what commands we want to be repeated, so these commands are put in brackets:

REPEAT (FORWARD 4, RIGHT 90)

This will certainly draw the square, the problem is that it will go round and round the square for ever because there is nothing to stop it. We need to tell the computer the number of times that it should do the commands in the bracket. The answer in this case is 4 because a square has 4 sides:

REPEAT 4(FORWARD 4, RIGHT 90)

The REPEAT command is the last of the commands that are needed for the exam work.

Question

18 A student has been asked to write a command for drawing an equilateral triangle. The command produced is REPEAT 3(FORWARD 5, LEFT 60). Draw the diagram which this command will produce and explain why it does not work. What should the correct command be? Try to produce a command which will draw a regular hexagon.

What would be the result of running the following command:

REPEAT 4(REPEAT 4(FORWARD 4, LEFT 90), RIGHT 90)

Try to produce some simple drawings and the commands that will produce them.

Extension

LOGO is a very powerful programming language. Investigate how it can be used. If your school has a copy of it, investigate the commands that are available for producing sounds.

Control of lights and lamps

Lamps can be controlled in two ways depending on the effects that need to be controlled. If the application turns lamps on and off according to the time of day then a mechanical timer is needed which controls a switch between the electricity supply and the lamp. The effect will be that when the timer switch goes from the off position to the on position, the lamp is connected to the electricity supply which will turn it on. This is not a control application because no decision is being made; this is a simple switch. We can only change the timing periods by mechanically adjusting the pins on the timer face (Figure 7.1.20).

If the lamp is controlled by a system which measures the available light and then switches the lamp on when it starts to get dark, this is becoming more like a control system. It will need a light sensor and a decision will be made about turning the lamp on depending on the amount of light. Many street lights use this system.

Figure 7.1.20 An example of a timer switch. The timing periods are set by manually adjusting the pins on the timer face.

Question

19 What can stop the light being turned on if a bird sits on the light sensor in the middle of the day?

How can the lights be stopped from turning themselves on if there is an eclipse?

Imagine a more sophisticated system in a house. The light level could be measured and found to be low. This starts a random sequence of lights to be switched on and off through the night so that it looks from outside the house as if there is someone at home. Now, we have something more like a control system:

- light sensors are needed to tell the system when it should be working;
- decisions are needed in order to make the sequence of lights believable;
- a timer may be incorporated.

Some specialist lighting systems require the use of more sophisticated control systems. Consider the control of

How ICT is used in everyday life **113**

traffic lights at a busy junction. The lights will be controlled by a sequence of commands, not unlike the commands that are used in LOGO programming. This will be a simple sequence of commands unless sensors are used to tell the computer controlling the lights something about the traffic conditions. If this is done and the computer now knows that one road has more traffic than any of the others, it can make a decision to keep the lights for that road on green for longer than for any of the other roads.

This is now a true control system because the computer is controlling the output dependent on information from sensors about what is happening. The computer may wait for a few minutes and then take more information from its sensors. If the queue of traffic has not reduced then the computer knows that it has not given enough extra time on green, so it might make the decision to allow even longer on green to see if this will help. However, the extra time on green may have made a queue build up on another road. The computer may decide to allow that other road some more time as well. The computer is no longer just making a decision based on what was reported about the outside world by sensors. The computer is now able to decide whether it made a good decision and what to do if its previous decision has not worked. This is extra information. This information which allows the computer to decide how well the previous decision worked is called **feedback**.

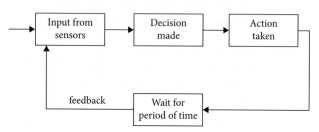

Figure 7.1.21   A visual representation of a typical feedback loop in a control system.

Question

20   Why is there a box on the diagram labelled 'Wait for a period of time'? What would happen if that box was not there?

What will happen if there has been an accident close to the traffic lights which is causing the long queues of traffic on that particular road?

When considering a control application there are six factors that should be considered:

1   **What are the inputs?** What are the important things that the computer should know in order to be able to make sensible decisions? In the traffic lights example, inputs might be the roads where there is a vehicle waiting and the current timings on red and green. An additional input might be an indication of the lengths of the queues of traffic for each of the roads.

2   **What is the desired outcome?** In other words what do we want the result of the decision making process to be? In this example the desired outcomes might be firstly to ensure that the light sequence is safe and secondly to keep the queues of traffic to a minimum.

3   **What outputs are needed to produce the desired outcome?** The outputs will be the sequence of traffic lights and the amount of time each road will have a green light.

4   **The processing done by the computer.** How is the computer going to arrive at the decisions which need to be made? How does the software turn the inputs from the sensors into the outputs which will achieve the correct outcome? In this example the lengths of the queues at the lights are turned into decisions about the amount of time the lights should be on green for each road.

5   **The time before taking the next inputs and adjusting the decision.** In this case a wait of perhaps two cycles of the traffic lights may be right. The wait needs to be long enough to ensure that there has been enough time for any decision made to have had some effect but not too long otherwise if something has gone wrong it will not be spotted quickly enough.

6   **Dealing with unmanageable situations.** What is going to happen if the control application cannot cope with a situation that arises? There must be some way that an alarm can be raised. This could be a message sent to the headquarters of the traffic police to say that there is a problem at this particular set of lights which seems not to be solvable and that it should be investigated.

? SAQ

10   a   Why wait before adjusting the decision?

b   What can happen if the system waits too long?

Control of washing machines

All new washing machines have a microprocessor embedded into them (see Module 6). This microprocessor will have the software which controls the washing machine permanently stored on it. This software will require inputs and the means to produce outputs which will affect the washing machine.

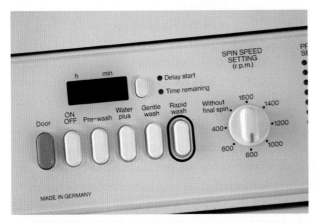

Figure 7.1.22 A washing machine control panel allows you to select what cycle you want. The details of the cycle are stored in the microprocessor to which it is linked.

We need to apply the six factors for control applications to the example of the washing machine:

1. The machine will need to know whether or not the door is shut, so there will need to be a pressure sensor or microswitch on the door. It will need to know that the water has been put into the wash drum and it will also need to have a temperature sensor so that the temperature of the water can be reported to the microprocessor.

2. The desired outcome from the wash cycle run by the machine is that clothes will have been washed.

3. In order that the outcome can be achieved the microprocessor will need to have control of a number of output devices:
   - a heater to make the water hot enough;
   - a motor to spin the drum to agitate the clothes;
   - lights on the front of the machine to show the user the stage in the wash cycle that has been reached;
   - actuators to turn the inlet valves on to allow hot and cold water into the machine;
   - an actuator to turn the outlet valve on to let the water out of the machine when the wash has been completed;
   - an actuator to control the pump.

4. Software will be necessary to make the decisions which will allow the clothes to be washed. This part of the system is described in further detail below.

5. The machine will have a timer as part of the software. This is used to time the different wash cycles, such as when to use the soap that is in the soap dispenser and when to put the fabric conditioner in if there is any being used. Another form of timer will be used to time the delay in measuring the temperature of the water if the heater is on. If the water is not hot enough the microprocessor will decide to turn on the heater in order to heat it up. If the microprocessor immediately takes another measurement of the temperature it will not have changed because the heater has not been given enough time to have an effect. There needs to be a delay before the next reading is taken from the temperature sensor, so a timer is necessary.

6. If the door is not shut then the microprocessor probably cannot shut the door because it does not have an output device that can do this (but note that the door can be locked by the microprocessor if it is closed and the wash cycle starts – a safety feature). It needs to be able to draw the user's attention to the problem, usually with a buzzer and a particular light illuminated on the control panel.

Question

21 Decide how the microprocessor will be able to tell if the machine is overloaded with clothes. How does the microprocessor know how much water there is in the machine so that it knows when to turn the valve actuators on and off? Would it be something as simple as a humidity sensor?

We need to consider how the microprocessor makes its decisions.

The first decision is whether or not the door is shut and then what action to take. This can be considered in the form of a diagram (Figure 7.1.23).

Notice the shape of the box which asks the question. It is usual to put a question in a diamond to make it stand out from the rest. Also note that the question has two possible answers which are usually 'Yes' or 'No'. If a question has more than two answers it is necessary to change the question into a series of questions with only two possible answers for each one.

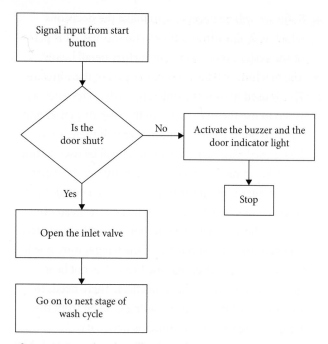

Figure 7.1.23 Flowchart illustrating how a washing machine microprocessor decides if the door is shut, and then what action to take next.

When the diagram has been drawn it is possible to go on to the next stage, which is to decide how the microprocessor can make the decisions.

The program for the diagram above would need a way of getting the input from the sensor.

The command used could be:

> INPUT door

Notice the way that the command is in capitals, just as it was for the turtle graphics work. The term 'door' just stands for a signal from the pressure sensor on the door.

There will need to be a way of asking the question. The command used could be:

> IF door is open THEN sound buzzer, END
> 　　ELSE open inlet valve

It is usual to put another command ENDIF when the IF has finished. The ENDIF just makes things neat and tidy and tells the reader where that statement finishes.

The whole routine would be:

> INPUT door
>
> IF door is open THEN sound buzzer, END
> 　　　　ELSE open inlet valve
> ENDIF
> ……
> ……

Try to understand this piece of program, which will decide the temperature of the water:

> INPUT the desired temperature, DT
> INPUT the temperature from the temperature sensor, ST
> IF ST < DT THEN OUTPUT turn on heater
> 　　REPEAT
> 　　　　wait for 1 minute
> 　　　　UNTIL ST >= DT
> OUTPUT turn off heater
> OUTPUT turn on wash motor
> ……
> ……

Notice the pair of commands REPEAT and UNTIL. This pair of commands can be used to make the computer do the commands that come in between them over and over again. It stops the processing when the condition in the UNTIL line is met. This is very like the REPEAT command in turtle graphics. The < symbol means 'less than' and the >= symbols together mean 'greater than or equal to'.

Questions

22 This stage should have included a check to make sure that the water was actually being heated up otherwise an alarm should be sounded. Try to adapt the instructions above so that this is carried out. (This is very difficult, but can be done using only the commands that we have used up to now.)

23 After the door is safely closed and the water is the right temperature, the next stage is to keep the wash motor running for the right amount of time. Write a series of instructions that will do this. Don't forget to use the soap in the soap dispenser tray.

Notice that controlling an automatic washing machine is quite a difficult and complicated process, but that if it is split up into its different parts each part becomes much simpler and then you just need to join them together.

Control of automatic cookers

An automatic cooker has two inputs made by the user: the desired temperature and the length of cooking time.

A sensor measures the temperature in the cooker and the microprocessor controls a heating element to keep the temperature constant. The microprocessor controls a light or a buzzer to inform the user when the time is up. The diagram to control the cooker will look like the flowchart shown below (Figure 7.1.24)

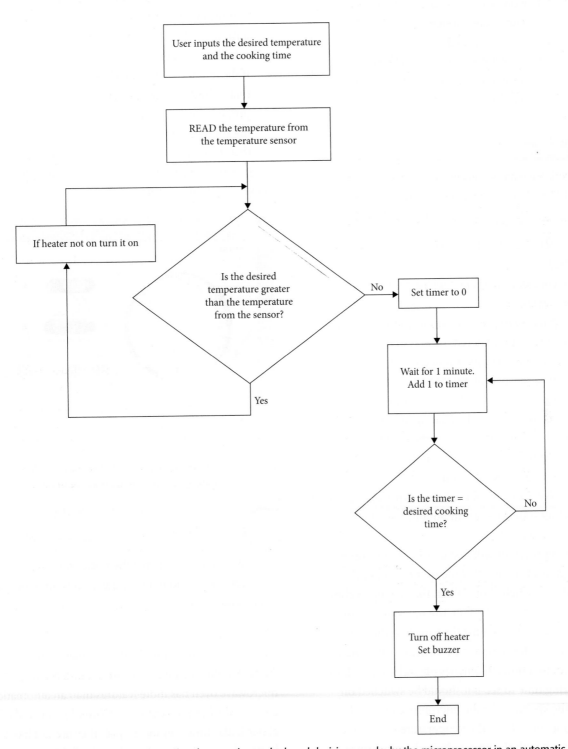

Figure 7.1.24 Flowchart illustrating the questions asked, and decisions made, by the microprocessor in an automatic cooker.

24 Figure 7.1.24 looks very complicated but only because the whole process has been presented in one go rather than splitting it up into small steps like the last example. The box which is labelled 'If heater not on turn it on' is too much of a simplification. Try to devise a series of steps which would be better here. It should include an alarm signal if the heater does not seem to be heating the cooker up. How long will the buzzer sound for? What turns it off?

Extension

Try to work out what the instruction 'Add 1 to timer' will look like when it is written down as an instruction.

Central heating controllers (air conditioning controllers)

We need to consider the six factors for control applications again:

1 What inputs are needed? Inputs from the user: room temperature required; time system turns on; time system turns off. Inputs from the system: temperature sensor will input the actual room temperature; clock gives the time of day.

2 The desired outcome is the heating or cooling of the room to the temperature which the user has input. This should only be carried out at the times when the system should be switched on.

3 The microprocessor will need to control a boiler (for the heating system) or an air conditioner (for the cooling system).

4 The microprocessor will first check the time on its clock against the time that the user has input that it should be switched on. When the system reaches that time and is switched on, the microprocessor compares the time against the time that the user has input for the system to be switched off. When it reaches that time, it switches off and goes back to comparing time to see if it should be switched on. When the system is on the microprocessor reads the temperature from the temperature sensor and compares it with the preset, desired temperature. If

the temperature is too low (heating system) it will turn the boiler on until it is warm enough. If the temperature is too high (cooling system) it will turn the air conditioner on until the room is cool enough.

5 The microprocessor will need to monitor the temperature sensor on a continual basis while the system is switched on, but a boiler or an air conditioner takes time to alter the temperature of a room so the time delay will need to be about five minutes between taking measurements.

6 If the temperature is not changing then it may mean that a window is open or that the boiler is not lighting properly or that the air conditioner is broken. The microprocessor needs a method of informing the user that the system is unable to control the temperature.

Most of the devices that are computer controlled follow these rules in much the same way.

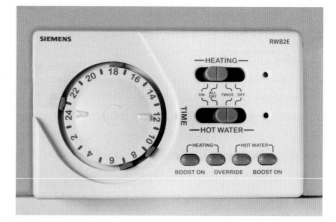

Figure 7.1.25 A typical controller for a central heating system. The user sets the required temperature as well as the on and off times of the system. The microprocessor makes decisions based on the user inputs and the readings from the sensors.

 SAQ

11 What might happen if the microprocessor only senses the room temperature every 15 minutes?

Microwave ovens

These are very similar to the devices that we have already studied in this section. There are a few differences. A microwave oven has more features than an automatic cooker. Most can be set to turn themselves on and off at particular times (in this respect they are just like the heating/cooling systems just described). They can also be set to different power settings; like setting the temperature in the last example. Otherwise the control system is going to be very similar to the one for the automatic cooker.

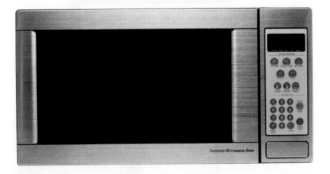

Figure 7.1.26 A typical modern microwave oven with a control panel to the right.

Video recorders

Video recorders used to record to tape, but now record to either optical disk (DVD or Blu-Ray) or to hard disk. The recording media will change with advancing technology but the control applications will have common characteristics.

They share a need for timing to be used in the control process: when to come on and when to turn off. The channels that need to be recorded need to be chosen by the user and some of these devices also allow the user to time the recording of a whole series. To do this the recorder needs to be able to access information from the broadcasters so that detailed information about programme availability is available to the microprocessor.

This is becoming too complex for this course in terms of the control programs that are necessary. The control instructions themselves are just as simple as the ones that we have already seen. However, the microprocessor has to do many more things than the control applications we have seen so far.

One important difference between this and the systems that we have studied so far is that the recorder can be programmed and the microprocessor can control part of the system while at the same time the user can be in manual control of part of the system. This adds a new complication to the system.

Computer-controlled greenhouses

The temperature in a greenhouse will be controlled as we have seen for the central heating controller.

The humidity in the greenhouse must also be controlled. A humidity sensor tells the computer how humid it is and the computer can then make a decision to turn on the water supply to the sprayers.

The windows will also be operated by the computer. It will be important to have the windows open as much as possible in order to allow insects in to pollinate the plants and to keep the air moving in the greenhouse so that there is no build up of disease. However, opening the windows will let the warm air escape so there is a balance that has to be made between the benefits and the drawbacks of opening the windows.

Greenhouses may also have blinds on the glass that can be computer controlled. A light sensor measures the light intensity. When the sun is at its strongest the computer actuates electric motors which draw the blinds down so that the plants are shaded.

Computer control can be used on a single greenhouse in a garden but it is more likely to be used in

Figure 7.1.27 **a** The inside of a large commercial greenhouse. The pipes seen here disperse water and will be tightly controlled by programmed computers. **b** Such large greenhouse complexes need to be computer-controlled and monitored.

commercial areas and large greenhouse complexes. Here it is simply not feasible for human beings to carry out the large number of necessary adjustments to maintain optimal growing conditions.

Burglar alarms

A simple burglar alarm detects when a door or window is open using a simple magnet and contact switch. A signal is sent to the control application which sets off the alarm.

This can be made more sophisticated by increasing the number of sensors and by using different types.

One sensor that we have not mentioned yet is a movement sensor. These use infra-red light to detect when there is movement within the range of the sensor. The reflection of the infra-red light back to the sensor should be constant. If there is something moving in range then the pattern of the reflected infra-red light changes and the sensor detects this change. These sensors are called passive infra-red sensors (PIRs).

Figure 7.1.28 A typical control panel for a modern burglar alarm. The user inputs a code to set the alarm when they leave the house, and a code to stop the alarm being triggered when they re-enter the house.

 SAQ

12 How do movement sensors ignore small animals?

Sensors can also be used together to make them more effective, as we described in Module 2.

The computer at the centre of the system can get its information from a sensor in two ways. The first is that the sensor sits there doing nothing (hopefully) until something is sensed. When it senses something, a signal is sent to the computer which can immediately decide what to do. This means that the computer will only be monitoring the burglar alarm system when it gets a signal from a sensor. For the rest of the time the computer can be used for something else. This is called an **interrupt system**: the sensor interrupts whatever the computer is doing if it is triggered.

The alternative is for the computer to send a message to each sensor in turn asking if there is a change to its condition. If the answer comes back that there is no change then there is no burglar; if the signal comes back that something has been detected the computer has a decision to make. This is called a **polling system** because the computer is continually asking (polling) all the sensors in turn to report their condition.

Questions

 25 Find out about movement sensors. There are many different types of sensor – many very specialised ones as we saw when studying environmental monitoring earlier in this module. Try to find some more sensors and give some examples of how they may be used.

 26 Discuss whether polling or interrupt systems should be used on burglar alarm systems. Will the type of premises that is being protected make a difference to the choice?

Consider the computer room at your school. The room has a lot of valuable equipment in it. This equipment needs to be protected and so a new burglar alarm system needs to be installed. Decide which types of sensor are going to be used and where they are going to be placed. Work through the six necessary factors of computer control which we have used in this section and see if you can plan the introduction of this burglar alarm system.

Modelling applications

Computer modelling uses mathematical formulae to describe something. The formulae are used to analyse or predict how something will behave in different conditions. For example, a computer model of a building could test how it will react to an earthquake or to hurricane force winds. A computer model of a new aircraft could see how tightly and how fast it can make a turn before the wings are damaged or it is forced into a stall.

Modelling using computers does not mean building a physical scale model.

From these examples it is evident that there are two obvious reasons for modelling a situation: to test situations without endangering anybody; to test their feasibility without spending large sums of money (building a prototype to find it doesn't work is expensive).

If a computer model is produced of a new design of car, the individual parts of the car can be studied in great detail in specific conditions. One big advantage of computer modelling is that the particular component under test can be isolated away from the rest of the vehicle and can be tested under very specific conditions. A rear suspension system can be modelled (as a set of inter-dependent mathematical formulae) and its performance tested under different conditions. The design can be modified, as a result of the testing, by changing the formulae used to model it.

This is a difficult concept. It has been made easier for users by the use of graphic outputs from the computer model. Animations can be used which reflect what is happening in the formulae. Some will be realistic; some will use other ways of visualising the thing being modelled.

The 'thing' being modelled can be anything from an atom, to a rear suspension system, to a reservoir, to a planet!

A good example is the use of computers by meteorologists to model the weather. The better the model that can be produced, the better will be the resulting weather forecasts. **Weather forecasting** models are created by thinking of the atmosphere as a number of cubes of air. There are lots of cubes needed to cover a land mass and the cubes can be one on top of the other in order to represent different layers of the atmosphere. In this way a 3-D model is created of our atmosphere.

There are rules that have been developed over many years of studying the weather. These rules state how the weather in one area will affect the weather in an adjacent area. This means that if we can tell the computer model what the weather is like in a particular cube the model should be able to work out what it will be like in adjacent ones by using mathematical formulae based on the rules. A simple rule may be that if the wind is blowing from the west and it is raining in the cube on the west then we can predict that it will start raining here in the future. If we know what the wind speed is then we can use another formula to predict how long the rain will take to get here.

If the cubes are very big then it becomes very difficult to give a general statement about the weather within that cube. If it is raining in only a small part of the cube does that mean it will still be likely to be raining here in the future? The smaller we can make these cubes, the better the forecasts will be because the effect of chance has been reduced. However, there is a disadvantage to having cubes that are too small. Each cube will react with six other cubes around it and they in turn are interconnected, which means that the amount of calculation is enormous to produce a forecast for a large area. So, the smaller the cubes are the more of them there are and the more calculations need to be done. Computers can work very quickly but there is a limit to what even a super-computer can do in a short period of time and the work must be done quickly otherwise it is of no use. There is no point in taking three days to forecast tomorrow's weather.

The quality of weather forecasting continues to improve. As computer processing power increases

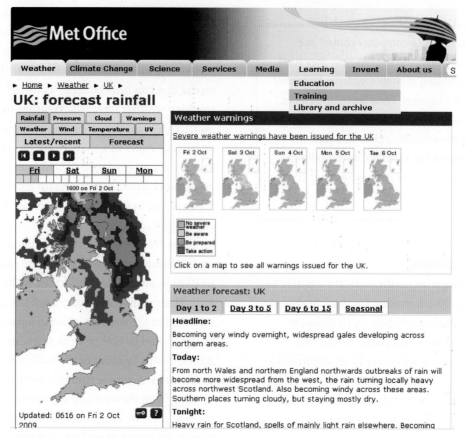

Figure 7.1.29 The Met Office website. The Met Office is a worldwide climate and weather forecaster. They use a complex weather forecasting model to make their predictions.

the number of cubes can be increased. Also, when a weather forecast is inaccurate, meteorologists will study what was forecast and come to conclusions as to what went wrong. They then alter the formulae in the computer model that was used in order to more accurately represent what happened and so improve the forecast when the same thing happens in the future.

Simulation

Once we have modelled a system, we can **simulate** how that system responds to other systems that interact with it. If we consider a car suspension system, then a simulation of this would include the speed of the wheels, the tyre pressures, different turning angles, the road conditions and so on. We can vary all these things and see the results graphically. The simulation lets us learn a lot about a system and also lets us predict what can happen under certain circumstances.

Flight simulators are used to train pilots. Trainee pilots can be placed in realistic situations which will let them learn techniques for coping with the different situations they may face. All the displays and sounds are controlled by the computer-based simulator; all the

Figure 7.1.30 The inside of a flight simulator used to train pilots. The inside mimics that of a real plane and the simulator creates scenarios for the pilot to respond to.

movements of the controls are fed into the simulator. The flight simulator also gives a simulation of the outside of the aircraft – the airspace, runways and other planes.

The training can be done safely because the 'plane' is not going to crash. Specific uncommon situations can be set up which a pilot might never meet in their training if it were done any other way. The one disadvantage is that however good the simulation is, it is not a plane and the pilot will always know that there is no danger. This may change the decisions that the pilot makes, for instance they might be quite happy to take a risk that they would never take if it were a real aircraft.

The same comments about training of pilots apply to the training of drivers via **driving simulators**.

Architectural simulations are often used by architects who want to test a part of the design that they have produced. Take as an example an architect who has designed a new shopping mall. Before the mall is built it is important that the procedures for evacuating the mall are tested in case there is a fire. To wait until the mall is built could lead to disaster. Even if the mall was built so that it could be tested, it could still not be set fire to.

The architect will build a computer model of the mall and use it to test the procedures. The computer will be given a mathematical model of what the mall will look like. The walkways will be featured as will the width of the walkways and the number of people who can walk through them at a time. The exits and entrances will be highlighted and the estimates of the number of people who will be in the mall at a particular time and how they will be distributed around the mall will be included. The model can be instructed that a fire is discovered at a particular point and the computer will be able to show how the people evacuate the mall.

Special features could be included on the model for things like customers who are disabled and hence will need assistance or a school party of young children being taken to the cinema which is on the top floor of the mall.

When the model is run with all these values put into it, it is called a simulation. The simulation will produce a set of results. The architect will then adjust some architectural things on the model: perhaps the width of the walkways; perhaps the cinema is moved to be on

the ground floor. The architect may run the simulation using different scenarios, such as changing the location of the fires, or blocking one of the exits because of building work.

Once the computer model has been set up the architect can alter whatever they want to on the model and come to the best solution for a design as far as evacuating the mall is concerned. Most buildings are designed like this nowadays and it would be difficult for a builder to get approval to start construction of a major public building unless the architect could show that these simulations had been run.

 SAQ

13 What are the advantages of simulations?

Spreadsheets

Spreadsheets are very valuable for simple computer modelling because they allow '**what if…**' questions to be asked.

A family can store their family finances on a spreadsheet. A school tuck shop can store the records of the shop on a spreadsheet. It allows questions to be asked like: 'Star chocolate bars are preferred to other bars but students do not buy them because of the price we are charging. What would be the effect of cutting the profit we make on every bar?'

If our assumptions about the preference of the bar are valid then we should be able to reduce the cost of a bar on the spreadsheet model and increase the number sold. We would need to factor into our spreadsheet the likes and dislikes of students. The spreadsheet should then be able to **predict** the increase or the decrease in the profits.

If we are deciding to buy a new family car to replace our old one, then we could use a spreadsheet to find out how much the cost would be. The sorts of data that would be input to the sheet would be: the cost of the new car; the amount that we would be given for our old car; the number of payments that we would make to pay back the cost; and the amount of each payment. We could also take into account the cost of the new tyres that we would have to buy for the old car and the fact that it is due to have a major service. These would both count as savings because we would not have to pay for them if we buy the new car.

The new car will also be worth a lot more than the old one would be in four years' time when we will need to think about changing the car again. Also the new car has a much better fuel consumption figure and so will be a lot cheaper to run.

All of these figures could be input to a spreadsheet and the true cost of changing the family car will be produced.

Figure 7.1.31   A family test driving a new car.

Question

27 Create a spreadsheet model of your family finances. You should include all the things that are paid out on a regular basis and the outgoings that are a bit less reliable, like the amount that is spent on food each week which will tend to vary. Then it is necessary to include all the income to the family. Try to set up the areas of the spreadsheet to represent all the incomes and expenses and then use formulae to link them to find out what the difference is over a year. This will then allow the values to be changed so that the effects of changing some spending habits are immediately shown on the sheet.

WARNING: This is an interesting exercise to do and it can be genuinely useful, but be careful: your family's finances are private and other people should not know them. The structure of the spreadsheet can be designed at school and dummy numbers can be put into it to practise and to see if the formulae are linked up properly. Do not put your family's personal information into the spreadsheet while it is on the school computer. Only use real data if the spreadsheet is on your home computer so that it can be seen by your family and nobody else.

Summary

- Understand and appreciate the impact of ICT applications in everyday life.
- Communications applications are used to create:
  - newsletters – word processors and desktop publishing applications have made their production very easy;
  - flyers and posters – similarly easy to produce nowadays;
  - websites – uses web authoring tools on a PC;
  - multimedia presentations – these can be used for learning, training and advertising;
  - cartoons – CGI has largely replaced the traditional, laborious, hand-drawn process;
  - music – for performance, composing and production of music scores.
- Interactive communication applications are used for social networking websites with lots of new ideas being introduced all the time.
- Data-handling applications can be used in:
  - surveys – data capture forms have to be carefully thought out;
  - address lists – more specialised lists are useful in targeting a particular audience;
  - tuck shop records – keeping numerical records of stock is a simple but expandable use;
  - clubs and societies – searching on specific data is possible if the structure is well thought out;
  - school reports – these are highly structured to enable flexible use;
  - school libraries – several data tables with foreign keys will be required.
- Measurement applications have advantages over humans in terms of precision, reliability, accuracy and non-interference and are used in:
  - scientific experiments – different types of sensors and analogue-to-digital converters combine with the computers;
  - electronic timing – from timing races to measuring the distance to the Moon;
  - environmental monitoring – particularly measuring levels of pollutants over long periods.
- Control applications go one step beyond measuring or monitoring and have the capability to make decisions based on inputs:
  - turtle graphics – helping children to learn simple programming techniques to control an object;
  - control of lights and lamps – used with sensors and computers to make decisions using feedback;
  - control of washing machines – the microprocessor needs to consider the six factors for control applications;
  - control of automatic cookers – timing and temperature are controlled;
  - central heating (and air conditioning) controllers – timing and temperature are controlled;
  - microwave ovens – timing and power are controlled;
  - video recorders – the recorder can be programmed, adding a new complication;
  - computer-controlled greenhouses – need humidity sensors to control sprayers and windows;
  - burglar alarms – used with many different kinds of sensor to detect movement and signal alerts.
- Modelling applications are particularly suited to computers as large amounts of data need to be handled. Once produced, they can be used in:
  - simulations – to see how the model reacts with other systems as in flight simulators or architectural simulations;
  - spreadsheets – allow 'what if…' questions to be asked to predict events.

7.2 Work-related ICT applications and their effects

When you have finished this module, you will be able to:

- understand the differences between batch processing, online processing and real-time processing
- have an understanding of the following applications and how they can be used:
  - communication applications
  - publicity and corporate image publications
  - robotics and production line control
  - billing systems, stock control and payroll applications
  - school management systems
  - booking systems
  - banking applications
  - medical applications.

Processing types

This module is based on the study of a number of ICT systems in the workplace. To understand the individual systems it is necessary to understand first that the systems that we are going to study are one of four different processing types.

Let's consider a factory in which each of the workers has to input an ID number when they come to work and then enter it again when they leave. The computer system will be able to work out their pay because it knows how long they have been at work and their hourly rate of pay. It would be inefficient to process the individual workers' pay every time somebody came into work or left at the end of their shift. Instead, all these pieces of data are stored up in one large **batch** for input to the computer.

The computer system may be used during the day to respond to prompts and activity from all the input devices both locally and over the network. Computer time is scheduled so that when the batch data is entered, there will be little input activity and the computer is lightly loaded.

When data is collected together in a batch before it is used in the system, this is known as **batch processing** (see Figure 7.2.1). Usually, batch processes run unattended.

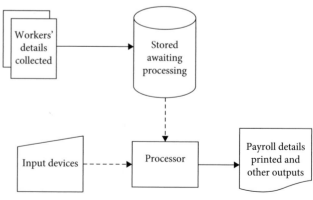

Figure 7.2.1 Batch processing.

Now consider a bank that conducts most of its business with its customers either over the telephone or over the Internet. When a customer calls the call centre or accesses their Internet account, they will want instant information about their account. The databases that hold the customer accounts must be ready to receive queries and provide answers instantly.

When the input to an application needs to be dealt with immediately the type of processing is called **real-time processing**.

To react so quickly, the call-centre operators or the users themselves have securely connected through a private or public (the Internet) network and been routed to the bank's computer, which has accessed the database and retrieved their information.

When the input goes directly to the computer like this, the system is said to be **online**. (Note that this is not the same as using the Internet. It is common to say that online work means using the Internet but that is not an accurate enough definition of working online.) When the input data is saved and sent to the computer later it is called **offline**. Online and offline working are illustrated in Figure 7.2.2.

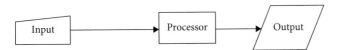

Figure 7.2.2a Online processing: input from the user is sent directly to the processor for immediate action. The input is dealt with quickly enough so that the output produced will affect the next input.

Figure 7.2.2b Offline processing: input made by the user is sent to a storage device and is only sent to the processor after all the input is collected.

Real-time applications are said to be online applications, while batch processing is said to be offline because the input is collected before being processed.

? **SAQ**

1 a When would be a good time to run a batch process?

   b You connect from home through the Internet to your school's intranet. What are you online to?

Communication applications

We have already looked at several communication applications in Modules 6 and 7.1 related to social use. The applications that we shall look at here are more work related.

The Internet

The **Internet** is the largest network of computers in the world. The information stored within it is not controlled and neither is access to it, although it is necessary to have an access point through an Internet Service Provider (ISP).

The Internet is huge and grows larger every day. To find anything, you need the help of a program called a search engine. Search engines find Internet websites containing information about what you have asked for (search terms). Sometimes there seems to be too much information. For instance, a research on 'William Shakespeare' results in a list of 43 600 000 sites from one search engine.

Unfortunately the sites are not all about the playwright William Shakespeare. Many are about Shakespeare societies all over the world. Some just happen to have the name 'Shakespeare' in them, like the William Shakespeare public house in Bristol or the Shakespeare Marine Engine Company. The problem here is not that I cannot find information, but that I find too much. I have to guess which are the best sites for me to go to in order to get the information that I want, probably by just looking at the ones on the first page. Alternatively, I can refine my search by adding more search terms. Some search engines help you by offering search terms. They also offer you advanced search options. Search engines can order the 'hits' by websites that most accurately meet the search terms.

2 You want to find information about one of the characters in a particular Shakespeare play. What search terms would you use?

How would you ensure that the search engine only searches on 'William Shakespeare' and not 'William' or 'Shakespeare'?

Another problem with the Internet is that nobody controls the information. Anyone can create a website saying anything at all. So, it is possible that someone has set up a website stating that Shakespeare was Chinese, that he did not write any plays and that he was a famous aircraft builder. All of this is nonsense but if someone who knows nothing about Shakespeare visits that website they may end up believing it. Always be very careful not to believe everything you read on the Internet because much of it is either inaccurate or simply untrue. There are also fake websites to contend with (see Module 6).

The Internet can also be used for personal and group communication. **Electronic mail, fax and electronic conferencing** have been covered in Module 4. These applications allow quick communication which can be made private by the use of passwords and encryption techniques (Module 4). Referring to speed of email communication can be a little misleading because this depends on the recipient and how quickly they decide to open their email, but the email becomes available to them immediately it arrives. If you are online to your email provider, you will get a notification (a sound or a message flashed on the screen) when an email arrives for you.

An advantage of email communication is that communications are addressed to the person rather than a physical place. A letter will be delivered to a place, whether or not the person is actually there, whereas, an email is delivered to the person. They can then collect it using any computer wherever in the world they happen to be. This ability to stay in touch is important to anyone who travels a lot, especially to business people who need to be mobile.

Much of the information contained in company communications will be sensitive and needs to be protected from unauthorised eyes. Many companies and organisations set up their own versions of the Internet which look very similar but have a strictly controlled membership. These are called **intranets** (Module 4). The fact that access to them is password controlled means that confidential information can be considered to be safer.

Sometimes an organisation will want to extend access to the intranet to others who are not employees. For example a company might allow access to some parts of their intranet to customers so that they can make orders electronically. When other people are allowed access to parts of the intranet it is called an **extranet**.

Extranets are very important in business. A company may want to use the Internet to advertise and communicate with other organisations. Some of the communication and information should only be seen by people within the company and for this they create an intranet. Access to their intranet will be password controlled. The company then decide that it will be good for their customers, and hence for the company, if customers are allowed access to some parts of the intranet via the Internet. This extended access creates an extranet. Still password controlled (but probably limited to certain areas), access to the extranet makes customers feel important and builds a loyalty to the company. It also makes communication between the company and these customers easier.

In business, it is important to build customer loyalty and a good way to do this is to make them feel special. Giving them access to the extranet can do this very easily.

Mobile telephones

Mobile telephones are often called cell phones. They work by maintaining communication with a ground station which is a radio communication mast. The power of the transmitter on the phone is limited and it needs to be within about 10 km of a mast to work (Figure 7.2.3). The area that is covered by a single mast is called a **cell** – hence the name 'cell phone'.

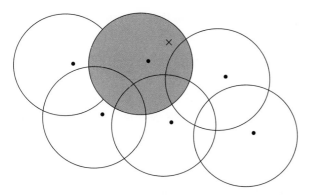

Figure 7.2.3 The dots represent the masts at the centre of each cell and the X is a phone. The cell which the phone uses is the one with the strongest signal.

To make a call, the signal from the calling phone is received by the mast and is then converted to the correct format for being sent over the PSTN (Public Switched Telephone Network). The signal is then sent to the mast whose cell is the one in which the receiving phone happens to be and a signal is sent to the phone from that particular mast (Figure 7.2.4).

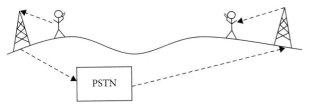

Figure 7.2.4 Making a call using a mobile (cell) phone.

Mobile phones can be very useful in business as people who are away from the office can be contacted almost anywhere. They do not need to keep their office informed of where they are. Usually, a company that requires its workforce to be mobile will issue mobile phones to them and pay all the bills.

Internet telephony

Internet telephony uses an Internet connection to make phone calls. The basic hardware is used as for connecting to the Internet, but the router will need a socket to plug the telephone in or there may be an adaptor or a special phone. Software is required which can make the Internet behave like a telephone service. Voice over Internet protocol (**VOIP**) is the software which allows the Internet to be used like this.

The big advantage is the reduction in cost for most calls. In fact, if the recipient of the call uses the same ISP as the sender then the call is usually free. This is a major advantage if the calls are international. However, calls that need to pass from one ISP to another, or that need to be passed to the landline system, can be expensive.

VOIP services are used particularly by businesses who wish to employ people to work from home on call-centre jobs. The calls come from clients to a central server which then sends them via the Internet to the workers at home. The business does not need to pay for a building to house the workers or for heat or light (but this home cost would be reflected in the workers' pay). It does not even pay for the phone calls because the client who rings in will pay the expensive part; the passed-on segment from server to worker will be free.

A common type of VOIP software is Skype, but there are many other providers. It also allows for instant messaging and file transfer; messages and files are transferred in real time from person to person.

7.2b Applications for publicity and corporate image publications

Businesses need to make potential customers aware that they exist and to ensure that present customers do not forget about them. Traditional forms of advertising like newspaper advertising, billboards and television are not targeted at the single audience that the business may want to attract. The business hopes that some of the people who see the adverts are going to be interested in the content of the advert.

ICT applications have allowed businesses and others to focus their advertising where it is likely to be most effective. We have seen the impact that websites and paper forms of advertising can have (Module 7.1).

Some forms of advertising are intended for even smaller audiences.

Business cards are produced in order to identify the person who hands them out. The cards are about the same size as a credit card and will contain:

- some means of identifying the person giving the card out – normally their name and position in the firm;
- identification of the firm that the person represents – normally the firm's name;
- some way of showing that the card is official – the firm's logo is often used;
- a way of contacting the person – their telephone number, their email address or their postal address, or some combination of all three.

Figure 7.2.5 Someone passing their business card to another individual.

The amount of information that is on the card is important. The card is small and to put too much on it will make it difficult to read. It needs to stand out among all the cards that a person may be given.

Choice of fonts will be important. They must be easy to read, so anything like Algerian or Old English text can be counter-productive. Size of text is also very important because people with poor eyesight will not be able to read very small font sizes.

Colour is very important for two reasons: not only in order to make an impact but also to create a **corporate image**. A company will use the same colour schemes and fonts throughout the various materials that they produce. In this way the combination of colours or the use of a specific font becomes identified with the company.

Business cards are very easy to produce using either word-processing or DTP applications.

 SAQ

4 How would you produce credit-card-sized business cards? Can you get card that small?

Question

2 Collect some examples of colour schemes and fonts that are easily recognisable. Try to work out what it is about them that make them recognisable.

Letterheads serve much the same purpose as business cards. All the relevant information about the company is placed at the top (and sometimes the bottom) of a sheet of letter paper. Letter heads are used to promote the business by encouraging instant recognition of which business is represented and reinforcing their corporate image. If individuals were left to produce the letterhead whenever they needed to write a letter, everyone would produce a different set of information in the letterhead: the information would be placed in different positions and the fonts and colours would differ. It is important to ensure that the information being given is acceptable to the business.

It is usual for a business to outsource the production of letterheads to a good quality printer who will use letter-quality paper. When you come to write a business letter, the laser printer will be loaded with the letter-headed paper and you print to that.

Of course not all letterheads are paper-based. You may wish to email a business letter which contains your letterhead to another company. In this case you need to have a **template** containing your letterhead already composed. In your word-processing application, you would create a new document by first selecting the letterhead template, write your letter in the space provided, attach the document to an email with a covering note and then send the email. The recipient can open the attachment and read it on screen or print it, or both.

Question

3 Produce a letterhead for a letter that you are going to send out from your school to a supplier of paper. Compare the contents, colours and fonts used with the letters that have been designed by other people in your class. Discuss the differences and decide on a common letterhead which has been agreed by all. You should be able to justify all the choices you made as a group. Compare the group effort with a piece of genuine headed notepaper from your school. Explain why yours is better in some respects than the genuine school notepaper and equally explain what features are better on the school notepaper than on yours.

Applications in manufacturing industries

Robotics

Robots are machines that are controlled by computers and can be used for a variety of tasks. If a machine simply carries out the same mechanical tasks every time and a change in the design of the item being produced by the machine would mean the machine being redesigned, then it is not a robot. A robot can carry out the same task over and over again, and it can be reprogrammed to change the task. Because it is computer controlled, a robot can also make decisions.

Robots can be categorised into two different types: fixed and mobile.

Some are fixed to a single point in the factory and the work that needs to be done is brought to them. This type of robot is usually called a **robot arm** because, like our arm, it is fixed at one end and yet has a large degree of movement available. A robot arm consists of rigid sections of different lengths connected together by joints which allow the attached sections to move.

The length of each of the sections will depend on the distances that the robot arm is expected to reach and the number of joints will dictate the flexibility of the arm and also the complexity of the control program that the processor will need to run in order to operate the arm effectively.

Robots are used in production lines because they:
- produce more consistent results than human workers;
- are more precise than a human being;
- can work continuously without a break;
- do not require heat or light;
- do not need to be paid, although they do cost a lot to buy in the first place;
- can work in areas or with materials which would be dangerous for a human being.

Figure 7.2.6 Robot arm operating in a factory production line.

A robot can be programmed by having a program written directly for it. Alternatively, a technician can move the arm to each of the positions that it needs to be and make it carry out all the actions that it needs to carry out. The computer which controls the robot records all the positions that it was moved to and all the actions that it was made to do as numerical sequences. It may be necessary to do this several times. The computer can then command the robot to repeat the actions by replaying the sequences.

The robot may rely on the other components (maybe another robot) positioning the item to be worked on correctly. However, a robot with a more sophisticated program can reposition itself according to the position of the item.

Some robots are mobile and can move to position automatically. Robots like these can be used on production lines to move items from one place to another. A car's bodyshell on a robotic platform may first move to the station where robot arms fit the wheels. It then moves the bodyshell to another station where more robotic arms fit the seats, and so on until the car is built. The robotic platform may be programmed to move to particular stations where different things are added according to the model of car being produced. So the first may need cloth seats and the second is a GLX version which has leather seats and so goes to another station to be dealt with by a different robotic arm.

Production lines

A **production line** is used to create an end product from raw materials or other components. Computers can be used to control the flow of materials along the whole production line. Factory production lines are often controlled by sensors, sending data to a processor which then uses actuators to change a parameter or start an activity on the production line if that is necessary.

Consider a system which starts with bars of very hot metal. By passing it through a series of rollers it flattens the metal into sheets – a bit like rolling out pastry into sheets when baking a pie. One of the problems with the metal sheets is that the accuracy needs to be precise, but the metal is so hot that people cannot go close enough to measure it until it cools down.

A simple system uses sensors that are set at specific thicknesses so that when the metal is passed between them the thickness of the metal is measured and the

Figure 7.2.7 Car shells being carried on robotic platforms to different robot arms in a car factory.

Figure 7.2.8 Hot metal sheets passing along a production line.

data sent to a processor. The processor can then make decisions and send messages to actuators to bring the presses closer together to make the sheet thinner, or move them apart if the sheet is becoming too thin.

Question

4   A bar of metal is presented to a robot. When the bar leaves the robot it should have a hole drilled in the middle and it should be turned through 90 degrees.

Instructions given to robots must be very precise otherwise they can be misinterpreted. What is wrong with the instructions here? Are they unambiguous?

Try to write a set of instructions that will tell the robot how to carry out the task. (You do not need to use robot language but try to be precise.)

Extension

Imagine that the metal bar needs a series of holes drilled in one face. The holes need to be in a line with each hole 2 cm from the previous one. Rewrite the instructions for drilling a single hole in the bar. Comment on the way that the methods that were learned in Module 7.1 about turtle graphics can be used here.

7.2d Applications for finance departments

Manufacturing businesses rely on buying goods or raw materials and then doing something to the material that is bought. This may be simply a matter of repackaging it or marketing it (using some of the techniques we have already studied). It may be that the raw material is processed in some way to create a product for sale. The business will then sell the finished product. In this process there are a number of applications for the business's finance department:

- The raw materials coming into the business must be paid for.
- The finished product will be sold and the customer needs to be billed for the goods.

- New stock of raw material must be ordered when the stock level gets too low and the production department must be told to produce more of some items when stock of that finished product becomes too low.
- The people working for the business need to be paid.

Billing systems

The business will have agreements with suppliers as to the price that will be charged for the goods that the business buys. Agreements will have been made to cover discounts for bulk buying and for customer loyalty. Details like these, along with details of the suppliers, will be stored on the supplier file on the computer system. When the business buys some materials an invoice will be sent from the supplying firm listing the goods bought and asking for payment. For example, Cottonwoods Ltd might need to buy certain goods that a company Rea Industries produces. Cottonwoods would order and receive these and then get an invoice (see Figure 7.2.9).

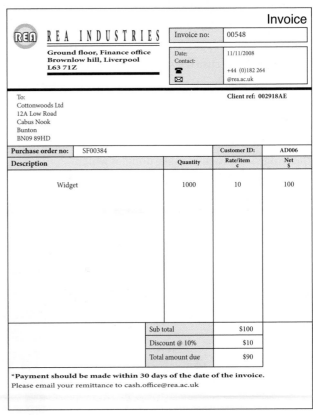

Figure 7.2.9 Invoice from Rea Industries to Cottonwoods Ltd. Here, 'widgets' is used to represent a manufactured device. In a real invoice, the actual item(s)/product would be listed.

When the finance department (often called the accounts department) receives the invoice the first thing that will be done is to check with the data sent by the warehousing department (see later on in this section) to make sure that 1000 'widgets' were actually received. The supplier file will then be checked to ensure that the correct discount was offered. The same record on the supplier file will then supply details of how payment should be made. This payment will normally be done by transferring money from the Cottonwoods bank account to the account of Rea Industries. This is a simple process that can be dealt with online to the bank that handles the Cottonwoods account. The information needed to transfer the payment is:

- proof of identity that the person handling the transaction is actually an employee of Cottonwoods and that they have the authority;
- the amount to be transferred;
- the account number of the Rea Industries account so that the money can be credited to them.

The money is then debited from the Cottonwoods account and credited to the Rea account. This form of payment is immediate. There are no problems with cheques going astray in the post and the money can stay in the Cottonwoods account until just before the date on which it is expected to be paid. This is an obvious advantage for Cottonwoods because they can keep the money longer, but it is also an advantage to Rea Industries because they are certain of payment arriving with no delays.

Stock control

The widgets are used to make dongles which Cottonwoods Ltd sell for $2 each. This order is dispatched to them by the warehousing department. When widgets are taken from the warehouse to the production line to make dongles, the bar code on the side of the box of widgets is read by a bar code reader and the worker types in at a terminal the number that have been taken out of the warehouse.

The file of raw materials will have that many widgets deducted from the number that were in stock. For example, if there were 1000 and 500 have been taken, then the file will show that 500 are still in stock. The reorder level has been set to 350 so there are still plenty of widgets left, consequently no order is produced to Rea Industries.

One of Cottonwoods' main customers is Carnforth Retail who sell dongles in their shops. Carnforth Retail have placed an order for 200 dongles. The warehouse had 150 dongles and made another 100 with the widgets, so that there was a total of 250 dongles in the warehouse. When Carnforth Retail's order is processed and 200 dongles leave the warehouse, their bar code is read and the file of finished products is searched for the record of dongles. Subtracting 200 from the 250, this leaves 50 in the stock file.

An automatic order is placed on behalf of the sales department to the manufacturing department for more dongles.

In order to make them the manufacturing department needs to take more widgets from the warehouse. This will probably mean the number of widgets going below the reorder level and this, in turn, will produce an automatic order which is sent to Rea Industries for more widgets. A copy of this

Figure 7.2.10 Movement of stock is recorded by reading the bar code.

order will be sent to the finance department so that when Rea Industries send in their invoice the finance department will be able to check that more widgets were ordered.

The whole process has now gone full circle. It relies on the accurate counting of goods into and out of the warehouse so that the system knows how many of each item is left and can predict when reordering is necessary. This process is known as **stock control** and applies just as much to the warehouse of a manufacturing company as it does to the stock in a supermarket.

The two essential benefits are still the same though. The processes should mean that the company will not run out of stock because it is able to anticipate a need arising and they do not have to store a lot of stock in case they forget to produce enough. This type of stock control has a special name – it is called **just-in-time** stock control (or JIT). The reason for this is that the orders are placed just in time to stop the warehouse running out of stock and yet not so early that the warehouse ends up with too many of an item.

Notice that the processing described here is an example of real-time processing, as the data is processed immediately to produce a useful output.

Payroll

The workers will be paid weekly. Their pay will depend on their rate of pay (taken from the staff file) and the amount of work that they have done during the week. The method of processing the pay was described at the start of this module. When the processing is done the output will probably be a transfer of money, electronically, to the workers' bank accounts and an output of the pay for individual workers called a payslip (see Figure 7.2.11).

Cottonwoods Ltd	
Record of pay for week ending 04/05/11	
R. Thornton	Manufacturing Department
	Grade C employee
	Employee number 123456B
Bank Details	LancsBanks
Sort Code	07-13-29
Account No.	6543 543 2345
Tax No.	AD379684-25
Number of hours at standard rate	33
Standard rate:	$7
Number of hours at overtime rate	6
Overtime rate	$12
Gross pay	$303.00
Tax paid at source (Rate of 30%)	$ 90.90
Net pay	**$212.10**

Payment will be made to your bank account on the first working day following the date shown above.

Figure 7.2.11 A simplified example of a worker's payslip.

Question

5 Write down the processes involving widgets and dongles that Cottonwoods Ltd's systems are designed to go through. You should make sure that the processes demonstrate the order properly and that it is clear where decisions are being taken. Make a list of the pieces of information that the finance department would expect to receive during the process and the data that it needs in order to carry out the necessary financial tasks.

This is difficult work to which there is not a 'right answer'. Many answers will work. When you have finished your version compare it with some versions produced by other members of your class and discuss where your versions are the same and how they differ.

Question

6 The payslip shown is a simplified version of a real payslip but it shows the three different types of data that are used. They are:
  • data that is common to all workers;
  • data that is specific to the particular worker whose payslip it is;
  • data that is calculated.
Identify the three different types of data on the payslip shown. What will a blank payslip look like before it is printed out for a particular worker?

School management systems

7.2e

The use of computers in many parts of school life have already been considered in Module 7.1. Data handling of the stock records in a school tuck shop was studied, as were the processes involved in keeping track of books and borrowers in a school library. The storage and use of records on school students and their use for compiling school reports was described in the same section. There is one part of a school computer administration system which has not yet been described – the school registration system.

Registration systems

School registration systems are based on OMR system technologies. This type of input was described in Module 2. Sheets are printed with ink that is readable by human beings but not by the scanning process. These inks tend to be blue or pink pastel shades. Instructions are given to the user using these inks on the paper and areas are assigned in which the user can make marks. The positions of the marks rather than the marks themselves are the important thing. When the page is scanned the only thing input to the computer will be the coordinates of the marks and the computer can then tell which areas have been shaded in and hence what the user intended to be input. School

Name	Week commencing: 4 April 2011									
	M		T		W		T		F	
	P	A	P	A	P	A	P	A	P	A
1. JOE										
2. ANDREW										
3. SAM										
4. MICHELLE										
5. RONALD										
6. JASMINE										
7. MERRY										
8. CHRISTIE										
9. LOREY										
10. MARISAH										

Figure 7.2.12 Part of school registration form for a class. The form has been designed for use with an OMR system. The teacher marks the appropriate box for a given student; P = Present, A = absent.

registers are an ideal use of OMR technology. Each student, each day, has two areas that could be filled in and one must be chosen. The areas simply stand for present and absent.

The sheets are sent to the school office and fed into the computer system. There is an element of batch processing about this system as all the sheets from all the classes will be collected as a batch and scanned into the computer as one job. However, there is also an element of real-time processing because the processing will be done quickly enough to put lists of absent students on the notice board in the staff room so that staff can check on students who are missing from their classes. This is a reasonable assumption to make, but in reality this is a batch processing system because the processing is not done until all the data has been collected for input to the system.

Booking systems

7.2f

Consider a concert being held in a theatre. It is necessary to sell the 1000 tickets that are available to people who want to buy a ticket in advance. The promoter of the concert decides that instead of just selling the tickets at the theatre they will be on sale at a number of different shops in the area. Each shop needs to be allocated blocks of seats to sell otherwise the same seat may get sold twice. The promoter decides to let each of the ten shops have 100 tickets to sell. The problem of the same ticket being sold twice will not happen now because each of the tickets is unique. However, there is now another problem. Some of the shops might sell out and have to send people away without a ticket, while other shops do not sell all their allocations and this will mean empty seats on the night of the concert. This would not happen if there was a way of allowing the popular shops to sell the unwanted tickets from the other shops. This could be done by physically moving the tickets from one shop to another or it could be done by leaving the tickets in one place and allowing the individual shops to have access to them via computer communications.

Theatre booking systems

Theatre booking systems allow booking agents in different locations to be in communication with a central computer system which stores details of the available seats for shows.

When a customer rings or goes into the agency or shop they:

- State their requirements which will include the name of the show or concert, the date for which tickets are required and the number and type of tickets that are wanted.
- The agent will then go online to the computer system and search for suitable tickets. While this is being done no other customers can be serviced because of the danger of selling the same ticket twice. This is called locking the file so that no one else can change anything. More sophisticated systems just lock individual seats to avoid jamming the system up.

When the tickets are agreed:

- The customer pays by card (or cash if the shop has that facility agreed with the theatre).
- The seats that have been bought are changed to show 'sold' on the computer system.
- The file of seats is unlocked so that other customers can make bookings.
- The ticket is printed out at the shop or a receipt (an eticket) is printed out which will be exchanged for the full ticket at the theatre.

This system allows for the sale of all the tickets because there is never a risk of the same ticket being sold twice. This is an example of a real-time computing application.

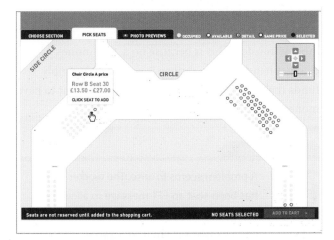

Figure 7.2.13 Online booking for a theatre. The customer can click on the seats (circles) on the seating plan to find the price, availability of seats and to book.

This system can be extended to allow the same sort of booking on the Internet. The advantage is that the customer can order tickets over the Internet without having to go to a shop to do the booking. Money is saved because the purchaser does not have to pay a fee to the shop. The customer simply sees the same screen that the shop worker sees when they book a seat for you.

A problem can arise because the payment must be made over the Internet which can be subject to interception. However, great strides have been made by the financial industry to ensure that payments over the Internet are secure and all personal details are encrypted.

Cinema booking

Cinema bookings can be done in much the same way. Customers can book over the Internet; they can even book using the keypad on a mobile phone. The payment may be done immediately or the seats may be reserved and the customer given a reference number. When the customer gets to the cinema they go to a ticket machine and type in their reference number and feed in their credit or debit card. The machine debits the card and prints out the ticket.

Figure 7.2.14 Father and daughter collecting pre-booked tickets from a cinema ticket machine.

This allows the owners of the cinema to reduce their costs by employing fewer people than they would otherwise have to without the automated system. If it is a cinema complex with a number of screens, then the screen that is showing a particular film can be changed if the bookings show that it is very popular. Screenings do not have to be finalised until the complex opens on any particular day.

There are many applications used here that have to work together seamlessly.

Travel applications

The **travel industry** allows bookings to be made by individual customers using the Internet or by travel agents. It is just as easy for customers to do their own bookings as it is to use a travel agent, but many customers continue to use travel agents to book holidays. The reasons are:

- Some customers do not have Internet access.
- Travel agents give insurance against the travel company going out of business. If the customer books the holiday themselves they may find it difficult to get their money refunded or may have difficulty if they are actually on the holiday when it happens.
- The process is rather harder than booking a cinema ticket and it may prove too daunting for some people to contemplate.
- Travel agents have access to some holiday packages that are not available over the Internet.

The basic principle of booking a holiday, or a seat on a plane or on a train or any other travel-related service, is the same as booking a seat in a theatre. If there is a central file or database holding all the details of the holiday or the travel service, then there cannot be a double booking made. Also the number of people involved in providing the service is reduced which will mean that the wage bills will be reduced and the cost of the services can be reduced.

Airlines commonly encourage passengers to book over the Internet. Internet booking allows the costs of tickets to be reduced. Actually, 'tickets' is the wrong term to use because an old-style airline ticket is rarely used nowadays. Instead the passenger is issued with a reference number, which is emailed to them after a successful booking has been made. At the airport, the customer can enter their reference at a machine, check in their baggage and be issued with a boarding card without the need of troubling a human being. Again, this saves a lot of money that would otherwise be spent on wages

and reduces check-in time. There are some airlines that will not allow customers to book in any other way than through the Internet; also passengers may not be allowed to check in at a check-in desk in the old way.

? SAQ

5 If you pay over the Internet for tickets, how can you be sure that the transaction is secure?

Banking applications

Electronic funds transfer

Earlier we studied the use of computers in producing the payroll for a company. Part of that process was that after calculating the amount that a worker had earned during the week, the computer arranged for the money to be paid into the worker's bank account. This does not involve cash being taken to the bank and paid in over the counter. This movement of funds is called **electronic funds transfer (EFT)**. An EFT message is sent to the company's bank asking that the money be taken out of the company account. A EFT message is then sent to the worker's bank stating that the correct amount of money should be added to the worker's account. The flow of the data is shown in Figure 7.2.15.

Notice that this process is not called 'electronic money transfer'. This is because no actual money changes hands and no money is moved. It is simply funds that are moved – in other words, the right to have money in your account.

Questions

7 A problem seems to arise. The worker's bank has been sent an EFT message to allow the worker to have their pay, but no money has been transferred into their account. How is this solved? Is this a real-time process or a batch process?

8 Is this process popular with the workers? Do they appreciate having their money paid into a bank account rather than being given cash in hand?

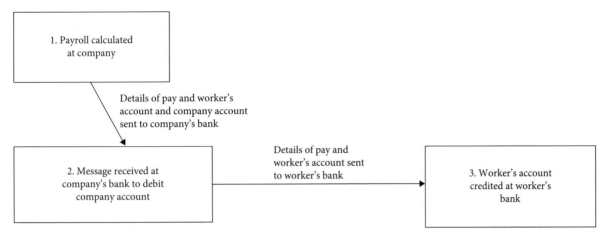

Figure 7.2.15 Using EFT to pay workers.

EFT is used at checkouts in supermarkets. It is still possible to pay at a supermarket checkout using cash, although bank cheques are rarely acceptable nowadays. However, the preferred payment method is now either a debit or credit card. The card is inserted into the card reader at the point-of-sale (POS) terminal (see later in this module). The funds are then transferred electronically from the card holder's account to the supermarket's account in the same way as the worker's pay is transferred (Figure 7.2.16).

Individual customers can also use EFT while carrying out their banking requirements using **Internet banking**. The customer is asked for their

identification checks and is then allowed to state specific accounts to which they want to transfer money from their own accounts. The only other details which are needed are the bank code and the account number that the funds should be sent to. The transfers are then carried out immediately. The problems are going to arise from keeping the accounts safe from being hacked, but it does mean that banking is far more accessible because there are now fewer reasons to have to travel to the bank.

Customers can also arrange to carry out **telephone banking transactions**. The method for doing this is very like banking over the Internet. In truth, it is the

Figure 7.2.16 Chip-and-PIN machines allow customers to use a suitable card (normally debit or credit) and a PIN number to pay by EFT.

Figure 7.2.17 Bank employees talking to customers during telephone banking.

same because all that is happening is that the customer is talking to a bank employee in a call centre who is carrying out the Internet tasks on a computer at the direction of the customer.

ATMs

Another piece of technology makes it even less likely that a customer will have to visit the bank personally. An **automated teller machine (ATM)** is the machine outside banks (sometimes in other locations) which allows the customer to carry out transactions without actually going in to the bank.

Figure 7.2.18 ATM being used by a man in the street. He is able to carry out transactions with his card and PIN number, without having to enter the bank.

The customer needs to provide identification and also proof that they are who they say they are. This is normally done by using a plastic card provided by the bank and a PIN (personal identification number). This method was explained in Module 2. The customer can then request a number of services. Typically this will be the withdrawal of cash. The machine will have to check that the PIN is correct and then check the account to ensure that the funds are available. There will also be a check made to ensure that the customer has not withdrawn more than an agreed amount in the last 24 hours. This is to stop someone stealing the card, finding out the PIN and then taking all the money from the account.

These processes are all real-time processes because the account needs to be checked and updated without delay.

Question

9 Another service that the customer can ask for at an ATM is a statement of their account. Is this process a real-time process or a batch process?

Credit/debit cards

When a card is used, the same sort of funds transfer is carried out as described in the EFT example at the start of this section. There are slight differences about where the funds come from.

If the card used is a **credit card** the message is sent to the credit card company. The credit card company then arranges for funds to be sent to the account of the organisation which has accepted payment using the card. The credit card company then stores the information that the card has been used, where it was used and how much was spent in the transaction. This information is collected together once a month and a statement is sent to the card holder showing them how much they owe. Notice that the use of a credit card requires both real-time processing for payments and batch processing for the production of statements.

Debit cards are used in the same way but the customer is dealing with their bank when they use their debit card rather than a credit card company. The bank will debit the customer account immediately (a real-time process) rather than waiting to produce a statement at the end of the month. The transaction will simply be shown as a payment on the normal bank statement.

Applications in medicine

The study and practice of medicine is an enormous subject and continually growing. Computer technology is important in helping health professionals provide as reliable and efficient a service as possible and also in keeping them aware of medical advances.

Diagnosis systems

When a patient goes to see a doctor they may have symptoms of an ailment. They go to see a doctor because of the doctor's expertise and experience, but no doctor can be expected to be an expert in every part of medicine.

The problem is that there is so much information about diseases and symptoms that doctors need help to make sure they have not missed anything. They used to get this extra information from books but nowadays this has been superseded by information held on computer systems.

Computer systems can hold more information, can be updated regularly and can use computing techniques to aid searches for information. In order to produce a system which will be useful for doctors, the accepted knowledge about diseases and conditions and their symptoms are collected together. This means interviewing expert doctors to collect their knowledge and using information from books. This knowledge is all collected together and stored in the computer. There needs to be some way for the doctor to interrogate the data that is stored and also for the computer to output answers to the doctor's questions. There needs to be a set of rules which tell the computer how different parts of the data fit together and interact with each other. Finally, there needs to be a program which is able to apply the rules to the data to come up with sensible results. When all these parts are put together a system is created which in some respects is more expert than the doctor. It is called an **expert system**.

There are many types of expert system. We consider here an expert system for **medical diagnosis.** On its own, used by a non-expert, it is not reliable for diagnosis. Diagnosis needs experience and the human ability to relate to individual patients. However, it is a powerful tool for the doctor.

The four parts of a medical expert system are:
- the facts about illnesses and conditions – the **knowledge base**;
- the means of asking questions and getting responses from the system – the **user interface** or human–computer interface (HCI);
- the set of rules which the data has to abide by – the **rule base**;
- the program that can apply the rules to the data in order to get sensible results – the **inference engine**.

All expert systems have these four parts (although some textbooks will say there are only three parts because they say the data and the rules are stored together). Figure 7.2.19 shows how the parts of an expert system are related.

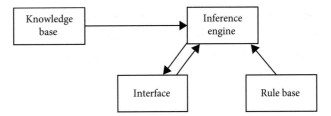

Figure 7.2.19 Flowchart representing an expert system.

 SAQ

6 What advantages does a doctor who uses a medical expert system have over a doctor who doesn't use one?

Information systems

When a doctor has diagnosed a patient's problem they may prescribe medicine. There are thousands of medicines available, each of which has possible side effects and lists of other medicines that they should not be mixed with. All this information can be found in large reference books which doctors use. However, things change so often that the books are always out of date.

What the doctor needs is all this information stored on the computer. Information stored like this is an **information system**. The doctor can search the system for possible medicines to prescribe and can see the information that is available on each one. This sounds very like an expert system. The difference is that the emphasis in the diagnosis system is on the expert system making decisions. When considering the medicines information system the emphasis is on providing information.

Hospital records

The storing of records on computer systems has already been discussed more than once in this book. The question that arises here is: what is different about hospital (or patient) records? Apart from the need to keep the information secure, the main difference is how long they will be stored. If you belong to a library it is unlikely that the library will store your loan records longer than a few months. Your school records may be kept for a few years after you leave school in case you ask for a reference in the future, but they will be destroyed eventually.

Your medical records are stored for life because a doctor could want to see your medical history at any time. It is possible that something that happened to you as a baby may affect you at any point of your life. Another difference is that there will be a need to store X-ray photographs, ultrasound or MRI scans and so on. This may be done physically but it is better done electronically because the records are then available via the Internet wherever you are in the world.

Question

10 How long will it be before we all have a computer chip implanted under the skin which contains our medical history? What would be the advantages and disadvantages of this?

What else could it be used for? For each use that you think about consider the advantages and disadvantages.

Extension

Investigate the use of computers and robots in carrying out surgical operations. What are the advantages and disadvantages for the patient and for the hospital? Investigate the use of the Internet and particularly video conferencing when conducting complex surgical operations.

7.2i Applications in libraries

The use of computers in school libraries was covered in detail Module 7.1. The same points that were made then will apply to the uses made of computer systems in larger libraries.

In a larger library there will be a different form of input. This will almost certainly be by bar code readers. The readers will use the bar code from the book that is being borrowed and will read the member ID from the member's library card.

Figure 7.2.20 Bar codes and bar code readers can also be used in libaries. They are used to identify the customer account, as well as books.

Question

11 Why will the ISBN of the books in the books file be replaced by a book ID?

Discuss the other differences between the school library system and a larger, public library system before reading any further. Note that there are no 'right answers' here because all libraries tend to use similar but different systems.

Extension

What is the Dewey system of classification? What part will that play in a computerised library system?

Note that there will be a need for a member ID to identify the member rather than using the name as was done in the school library example. The reason for this is that there are far more members of a public library than there are of a school library. Also, if there were clashes of name in the school library example then each student also belongs to a class and a combination of the name and the class can be used to uniquely identify the student. However, this is more difficult in a larger library. The unique identifier is especially important in the loans file which keeps track of the loans that have been made and are still outstanding. The difference between the school example and the public library is that the public library will have an extra field in the member file called the member ID, which will be the key field. This key field will then appear in the loans file instead of the name of the borrower.

One area of use that will be very different from the school library system is the method of dealing with overdue books. The loans file will be searched each day for books that are overdue. Any records that represent loans that have not been returned will have the member ID and the book ID read. The member ID can be used to search the member file for the details of the member who has not brought the book back. The book ID can be used to search the book file for details about the book. These details can then be used to produce a letter (see Figure 7.2.21 on the next page) or an email which can be sent to the member telling them that the book is overdue and asking for it to be returned.

The use of expert systems
Expert systems were explained above where an expert system to aid medical diagnosis was described. The same principles of collecting knowledge from experts in the field and then making it available through a computer system can be applied to many other fields.

Mineral prospecting
Mineral prospecting differs from medical diagnosis because of the types of data that the expert system works with. There is still the knowledge base which is created by using the combined knowledge of as many experts as possible. However, there are other forms of data that can be used:

- Satellite data can be input. This can be in the form of pictures of the Earth's surface, which may show outlines of the ground that are not otherwise visible.
- Sensors can be positioned on the ground to capture tiny movements, which may show that there is seismic activity in the area.
- Data from geological surveys can be input. For example, an explosion is set off on the surface some kilometres away from sensors that are placed on the surface. According to the length of time that it takes the shockwave to reach the sensors and the strength of those shockwaves, it is possible to create maps of what is beneath the surface.

Using all this data, the expert system can then make **predictions** as to the likelihood of finding particular minerals in that area. Note that what is produced is a prediction – certainty of an outcome is not possible. This type of expert system will predict whether a particular mineral is present by giving a **probability** of its presence as a percentage. 'Iron ore 20%' would mean that it was unlikely (20/100 or 1 in 5) that iron would be found there, whereas 'Iron ore 80%' would mean that it was highly likely (80/100 or 4 in 5) that iron would be found.

Question

12 Consider the letter shown in the illustration. Which parts of the letter are standard contents which will appear on every letter about an outstanding loan? Which parts of the letter are found in the different tables and which tables do each of the pieces of information come from? Which parts of the letter are calculated by the system?

How can the tables be slightly altered so that a similar letter is not sent again tomorrow? How will the system know about members who still do not return books despite having been sent a letter?

SAQ

7 In what other ways can iron ore be detected? How could this be used as data in an expert system?

AnyTown Library

Mr. T. Johnson
15 OurStreet
Anytown

20 April 2011

Dear Mr. Johnson

You borrowed the book *Council Wars* by Sarah Fishwick on 4th April 2011.

This book is now overdue. The current fine payable is 56 cents. Please return the book as soon as possible.

Yours faithfully,

L. Kreicbergs

(Chief Librarian)

AnyTown Library

Address: Any House, 23 Any Road, Anytown, ANY 12345   Phone: 01234 567890   Fax: 01234 567890
Email: libname@anytownlib.hotmail.com   Website: http://www.anytownlib.com

Figure 7.2.21   A letter from a public library to a member regarding an overdue book. The book and the member will have been identified using the member ID and the book ID and the system of files on which this information is stored.

Car engine fault diagnosis

Information about things that can go wrong with cars is collected from experienced mechanics and stored in the knowledge base of the system. When the car is brought into the garage a mechanic working on the car can input details of the faults by answering a series of questions through the HCI. The system will then interrogate the knowledge base using the rules in the rule base and produce a result for the mechanic on the interface screen. This is the standard way to use an expert system but this application can be set up to be rather more automatic than this.

Many cars have processors which monitor the working of the engine continually and warn the driver of problems that are occurring. If this is the reason why the driver brought the car into the garage then the mechanic would connect the car's processor to the expert system and the details of the fault can be downloaded automatically.

Figure 7.2.22 A mechanic is using an expert system to help determine what is wrong. The car is connected to the diagnostic and through a series of questions and a bank of information and rules, a diagnosis can be determind.

The expert system can also be connected to the exhaust system of the car. The exhaust gases can be analysed automatically and the details entered into the expert system to give further data which can be used to diagnose any faults that the car may have.

Extension

Try to find out what types of sensor are used to provide evidence for a car engine diagnosis expert system.

Chess computers

Chess-playing computers are expert systems. Originally they were given lots of good moves for particular circumstances that might be met in a game. These moves were the result of asking many expert players. The problem with this is that chess is a very complex game with an infinite number of possible situations; it is simply not possible to predict all the moves that may happen in a game.

Better chess computers are programmed with strategies. They are able to quantify how good their position and the opponent's position is. At each turn they work through possible moves trying to analyse what the outcome will be and hence find the strongest move.

The best machines have a degree of intelligence in that they can learn when they do something wrong. When these computers are beaten they will analyse the moves so that if the same situation arises in a future game they will not make the same mistake again.

Expert systems that 'learn' in the way that the best chess-playing systems do have gone one stage beyond a normal expert system and are said to use **artificial intelligence**.

7.2k Applications in the retail industry

Stock control

Stock control has been covered in Module 7.1 and earlier in this module. In the data-handling application example, a school tuck shop could keep levels of stock automatically. However, the reason for doing so would probably be to enable it to keep a check of whether any stock is going missing rather than to use automatic reordering facilities.

Then we saw a financial application where the levels of stock were automatically monitored and decisions were made which would lead to automatic ordering if the levels of stock were too low.

Many retail organisations use a third method for ordering stock. The same monitoring system is used as in the Cottonwoods Ltd example except that orders for new raw material or products are not made automatically. Instead the system will flag items that have fallen below the accepted minimum level and will then rely on a human being to decide whether or not an order for the product should be made.

Consider a supermarket where the levels of sales of ice cream have been relatively low through the winter months. The weather is improving and the minimum stock level has been reached. If the system automatically orders the ice cream from the supplier then it will probably not order enough because demand is likely to be higher than it has been over the winter. Conversely, at the end of the summer, where sales have been very high, an automatic system is likely to order far too much and the supermarket will not be able to sell it all because the weather is no longer very good.

Figure 7.2.23 Ice cream cartons on freezer shelves in a supermarket.

Another example could be that sales of a particular type of tinned ham are not very strong so when it comes to reordering an automatic system would be set to order relatively little of the product. However, the manager of the store has been informed that the company are to start a major television advertising campaign. The system would only order a few tins whereas the manager will probably decide that the campaign means that a much bigger order is necessary.

 SAQ

8 Can you think of products where the minimum stock level will be allowed to fall to zero? Can you think of times when the system would automatically set the minimum stock level to zero?

The same basic stock ordering is the same in a retail system as it is in the Cottonwoods Ltd system. The difference is that the retail system will not automatically send the order but will send a list of products that have hit the minimum reorder level together with the suggested order that should be made and allow the manager to adjust the order before it is sent.

Notice that this has become a batch system rather than a real-time system. The original system sent orders as soon as the minimum reorder level was met – this is real-time. However, the system is now collecting all the necessary orders for the manager to consider together. This collection of the information is what turns the system into a batch process.

POS/EFTPOS

Point-of-sale (POS) terminals are terminals that are set up at the exits to supermarkets which allow shoppers to pay for their goods in the following way:

- The shopper presents their purchases.
- The items are scanned using a bar code reader.
- The stock file is searched for the bar code.
- When it is found:
  - the number in the stock file has one taken from it;
  - the number in the stock file is checked against the minimum stock level and a need to order more of this stock is added to the list to be sent to the manager at the end of the day;
  - the description and price of the article is sent to the terminal.
- The price and description are displayed on screen.
- The price and description are printed on a till receipt.
- The price is added to the total so far.

This means that the shoppers have a printed record of their purchases and are able to check for errors. The system proves to be very popular with shoppers which pleases the management of the supermarket because more people come to shop in the store.

If there is a chip-and-PIN reader added to the POS it becomes an **electronic funds transfer at the point-of-sale (EFTPOS)** terminal. Not only does the system control stock levels and produced itemised receipts, but it also controls the way that payment is made. Customers are encouraged to pay by card because this will reduce the amount of cash being handled at the tills.

SAQ

9 Why don't supermarkets like being paid in cash?

Question

13 Refer back to the discussion work in Module 6 (Question 5). This was about two shops which both used old-fashioned methods of serving customers. One shop decides to introduce new computerised systems and the questions were about the effects that this would have on the customers of the shops, the workers in the shops and the shops themselves. Here are some more questions for discussion (there are no precise answers, but try to justify your decisions):

a What would you expect to be the effects on the stock in the two shops?

b Why does the store with the new system have fewer specially discounted items on the shelves which are out of date?

c Why does the store with the new system have more special offers available?

The store with the new system decides to offer a new service whereby customers who are too busy to get their own shopping or who are disabled can use Internet shopping. They can email an order to the store over the Internet. The store will then arrange to have the order delivered.

d How can the store ensure that the goods are paid for?

e What are the disadvantages to the store and to the customer of using this form of shopping?

f What are the advantages to the store and to the customer of using this form of shopping?

g Is this very different from the old system that allowed customers to telephone in their orders?

h Is the system coming round full circle?

Summary

- There are four different processing types that we need to recognise – batch, real-time, online and offline.
- Communications applications:
  - The Internet can overload us with information.
  - Email has advantages over traditional mail.
  - Intranets can be extended to extranets.
  - Mobile (cell) phones use radio masts and the PSTN for communication.
  - You can phone over the Internet using VOIP.
- Business cards and letterheads market your company's corporate image.
- Robots are controlled by computers and have advantages over human beings. Some are fixed as on production lines. Some are mobile and can be used to transport materials around.
- Production lines use sensors and control applications to control the flow and production of materials, and end products.
- Financial applications:
  - Billing systems need to bill customers and pay suppliers.
  - Stock control systems need to hold records of raw materials and end products so that when they run down, they are replenished.
  - Payroll systems calculate workers' pay and initiate transfers of money.
- School registration systems use OMR.
- ICT enables booking systems to be used over the Internet.
- Banking applications:
  - Funds can be easily transferred over the Internet using EFT.
  - ATMs can carry out transactions without the user going into a bank. There are many security checks in their use.
  - Credit cards use EFT. Credit card systems use real-time and batch processing for payments and statement production, respectively.
- Applications in medicine are used for diagnosis systems, information systems and hospital records.
- Large library systems will use databases and automate some processes, like overdue letters.
- Expert systems are all broadly similar with a knowledge base, HCI, rule base and inference engine. Medical diagnosis systems have moved towards expert systems. Expert systems are also used in mineral prospecting, car engine fault diagnosis and chess-playing computers.
- Retail systems use stock control, point-of-sale terminals and chip-and-PIN readers in combination to manage stock, sales and payments.

8

Systems analysis and design

When you have finished this module, you will be able to:

- name the stages of the waterfall model of the systems life cycle
- describe the process of improvement by iteration
- understand the individual stages of systems analysis and design:
  - the analysis stage consists of problem definition, a feasibility study, information collection and a requirements specification
  - the design stage starts with output design, then input, storage and processing
  - the development and testing stage consists of dividing the coding work into modules which are subsequently tested before testing as a whole
  - there are four types of implementation
  - documentation is important to the maintenance of the system and consists of technical and user guides, which have recommended formats
  - the evaluation stage looks at how well the solution meets the requirement specification and then defines how the system needs changing
  - maintenance goes on throughout the system's operational life.

Overview

When an organisation (often referred to as the client) considers that one of its systems has problems or is in need of improvement, a **systems analyst** studies the system to determine where the problems are and how the system can be improved. The analyst then plans the implementation of the solution and hands the plans on to a software team to produce the solution and test it. The analyst then plans how the system is going to be imported into the organisation and arranges for continuing maintenance of the system. This whole process is known as the **systems life cycle** and can be summarised as:

- analysis
- design
- development and testing
- implementation

- documentation
- evaluation/maintenance.

Don't worry too much about the names of these stages or the fact that when you look in another text book they may differ from this one. Most software system life cycles are similar to each other; the stages named here are those in the IGCSE ICT syllabus.

It is important to note that when a problem is solved in this way, we should not think of the stages of the solution as being in a straight line. The analyst does not start at the beginning and work straight through to the end. They may reach one stage and realise that they have to go back and find out something else or plan things a little differently. They may find that something does not work properly, so they have to go back and change the design. This process is called the **waterfall model**

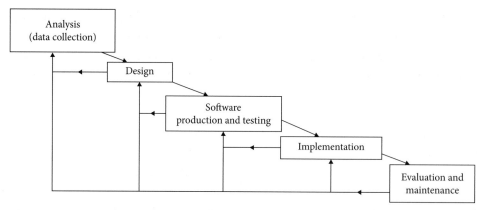

Figure 8.1 Waterfall model of the systems life cycle.

(see Figure 8.1) or cascade model of the systems life cycle. At each level it is possible to go back to any of the previous stages to refine the end product – this is known as **iteration**.

8.1 Analysis

The analysis stage starts with problem definition and a feasibility study. It is necessary to understand the problem in terms of the client's requirements and needs, otherwise the solution that is proposed may be solving the wrong problem.

Figure 8.2 A systems analyst and client working together at a laptop.

Problem definition always involves a compromise between people in the organisation and the systems analyst. The people in the organisation know how their business works, what the nature of the problem is and how much they can spend. The analyst knows about computer systems and what is possible. In response to the problem definition the analyst produces a report which states what is possible – the **feasibility study**. At this

stage the proposals are still very sketchy. If the feasibility study is accepted then the analyst needs to find out as much as possible about the organisation and the problem to be solved. The collection of information begins.

Information collection

The information can be collected in a number of ways:

- **Observation** – The systems analyst can learn a lot from simply watching what is going on in the area of the organisation that has the problem. The intention is to understand how things are done and the relationships between people. It is very useful because no detailed planning is necessary and it does not involve working with other people. The disadvantage is that people tend not to work in a normal way if they know they are being watched. Point a camera at someone and see what happens!

- **Interviews** – The systems analyst will want to find out how things work and, particularly, what is not working properly in an organisation. The obvious thing to do is to ask the people who operate the system at the moment. Questions do not have to be fixed in advance, but it is helpful if the analyst has a logical, enquiring mind and knows how to probe for information. In a simple example a question is asked about the information that needs to be stored. If the person being interviewed says that it is necessary to store information about their customers, the next question will need to be something about security and privacy of this information: 'Does that mean that we will need to protect the information by placing a password on the file?' On the other hand if the reply was that the only data stored was going to be the details of the stock, the follow-up question might be: 'How often do the details of the stock change?' A disadvantage of interviewing is that it is very time-consuming.

- **Questionnaires** – Many people's views can be obtained in a short period of time. Questionnaires are much less time-consuming for the analyst and they give everyone the feeling that their views matter. Each person also has the chance to consider their answers before filling it in. The disadvantages are that some of the people may not take it seriously and the questions cannot be changed halfway through the process as in an interview.

- **Document collection** – Documents reveal a lot about an organisation. Processes and procedures tend to be captured in documents. But input and output documents should also be examined. The analyst will be looking for answers to questions like: How is the data collected? What data is collected? What happens to this data after it has been collected? A disadvantage is that documentation is often difficult to understand for someone who is outside the organisation, so it may be necessary to interview someone to explain it. A more serious problem can arise because the documents may give the wrong impression of the process which is carried out. The documents may say one thing but everyone does something else.

The information collection methods outlined above will provide a large amount of data about the present system. This raw data needs to be collated and studied, so that it can be turned into useful information and recorded. Sometimes this will bring to light areas where there are gaps in the data collected. For example, the analyst may realise that important questions were not asked in the interview because some of the documents that were collected after the interview seem to suggest that there are other files that were not mentioned. This would mean that a further interview was needed in order to clear up the confusion.

The best way to deal with information like this is to record it in a diagram that shows the passage of data through the system and the different files that are used. It should identify all the system's inputs and outputs and how data is processed. It would also show details of storage of the files and how the files are related. Other diagrams could be used to show the hardware involved in the system. All the features of the existing system should be identified.

Requirements specification

As the analyst collects data about the existing system and the problems, a list will be forming of things that will be necessary in the solution. This list is the **requirements specification** and will include what the organisation wants the system to do, details about the storage requirements, and information about the desired hardware and software. Think of this as being a contract between the systems analyst and the organisation.

The requirements specification lists the things that, after consultation, the organisation has decided must be successfully done in order to satisfy them and the analyst has agreed that this is what can be delivered. This agreement is extremely important to both parties and must be clear in what is expected. It is going to provide the 'rules' around which the final evaluation will be carried out.

An agreed requirement specification leads to the next stage.

 SAQ

1 What two documents need to be agreed during the analysis stage? What do you think would happen if the client doesn't agree with them?

1   In the three applications given below, each of the owners wants a new stock control system installing. Discuss how the analyst would collect information in each case and why the methods might differ. Also discuss ways in which the information collected can be represented.

   a   A small general purpose shop wants to install a computerised stock control system. All stock control has been done manually until now. The owner is the only person who works in the shop.

   b   A dress shop has used a computerised system for some time for selling items and giving receipts to customers. However, the stock is still controlled manually. The owner looks after all the ordering of stock and record keeping but does not work in the shop. The owner has decided that she wants some help in dealing with suppliers and stock control in the shop. There are six shop workers.

   c   A large supermarket uses a fully computerised stock system together with POS terminals. The owner has decided that the present system needs updating, mainly because a rival supermarket has installed a more modern system. There are in excess of 100 workers who work in different departments in the supermarket. The supermarket stocks in excess of 30 000 items. Some workers work as shop assistants, others as supervisors; some work in the accounts department and others in site management because it is a very big store.

2   Companies communicate using documents. Some of the documents that are produced and received by Cottonwoods Ltd have been assembled by the analyst during the 'document collection' stage. You can see these documents on the next page.

   a   Discuss what these documents show the analyst about the way this company communicates with others about orders.

   b   If the system is to be computerised, what information is there on the documents that would help the analyst decide what data input, storage and output will be necessary when planning the supplier and customer files?

   c   Which documents do you think that the analyst has failed to find? Will this be important or is there enough information here to satisfy what the analyst needs to know?

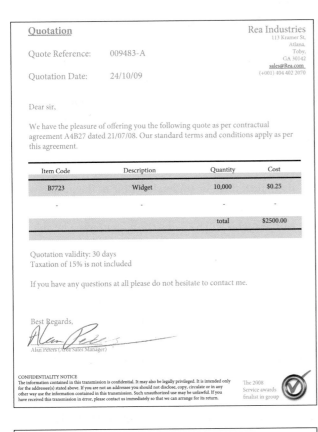

Quotation

Rea Industries
113 Kramer St,
Atlana,
Toby,
GA 30142
sales@Rea.com
(+001) 404 402 2070

Quote Reference: 009483-A

Quotation Date: 24/10/09

Dear sir,

We have the pleasure of offering you the following quote as per contractual agreement A4B27 dated 21/07/08. Our standard terms and conditions apply as per this agreement.

Item Code	Description	Quantity	Cost
B7723	Widget	10,000	$0.25
-			
		total	$2500.00

Quotation validity: 30 days
Taxation of 15% is not included

If you have any questions at all please do not hesitate to contact me.

Best Regards,

Alan Peters (Area Sales Manager)

CONFIDENTIALITY NOTICE
The information contained in this transmission is confidential. It may also be legally privileged. It is intended only for the addressee(s) stated above. If you are not an addressee you should not disclose, copy, circulate or in any other way use the information contained in this transmission. Such unauthorized use may be unlawful. If you have received this transmission in error, please contact us immediately so that we can arrange for its return.

The 2008
Service awards
finalist in group

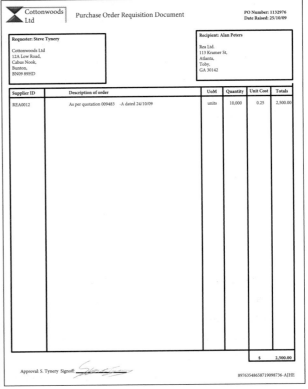

Cottonwoods Ltd
Purchase Order Requisition Document

PO Number: 1132976
Date Raised: 25/10/09

Requester: Steve Tynery
Cottonwoods Ltd
12A Low Road,
Cabus Nook,
Bunton,
BN09 89HD

Recipient: Alan Peters
Rea Ltd.
113 Kramer St,
Atlanta,
Toby,
GA 30142

Supplier ID	Description of order	UoM	Quantity	Unit Cost	Totals
REA0012	As per quotation 009483 -A dated 24/10/09	units	10,000	0.25	2,500.00
				$	2,500.00

Approval: S. Tynery Signoff:

8976354865871909873 6-AJHE

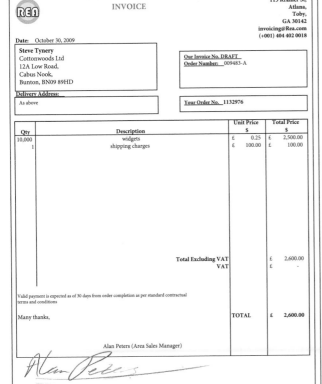

REA

INVOICE

113 Kramer St,
Atlana,
Toby,
GA 30142
invoicing@Rea.com
(+001) 404 402 0018

Date: October 30, 2009

Steve Tynery
Cottonwoods Ltd
12A Low Road,
Cabus Nook,
Bunton, BN09 89HD

Our Invoice No. DRAFT
Order Number: 009483-A

Delivery Address:
As above

Your Order No.   1132976

Qty	Description	Unit Price $	Total Price $
10,000	widgets	£ 0.25	£ 2,500.00
1	shipping charges	£ 100.00	£ 100.00
	Total Excluding VAT		£ 2,600.00
	VAT		£ -
	TOTAL		£ 2,600.00

Valid payment is expected as of 30 days from order completion as per standard contractual terms and conditions

Many thanks,

Alan Peters (Area Sales Manager)

CARNFORTH Retail

7 Carnforth Road,
Carnforth,
Lanarks,
LN38 7BC

Tel: 01524 584003
Fax: 01524 584096
Email: enquiries@CRLTD.net

Date: 2nd November 2009

Steve,

Following our verbal conversation, I would like to request a quotation from yourselves for the supply of:

(500 off) dongles

Please advise cost, inclusive of shipping and handling and a lead time so we can inform our clients

Best regards,

(Dominic Rostell) Partner

This document is intended solely for the stated person(s) above. If it has been received in error, please contact CarnforthRetail Ltd and we shall arrange its return or otherwise.

Design

All computer systems consist of:

- input
- processing
- output
- storage.

Output designs

The purpose of the design stage is to decide what the output will look like. It may seem odd to start from what appears to be the wrong end, but the analyst's job is to produce a system that will do a particular thing. In other words, the really important part is to decide what the organisation wants to happen in the end. If the client likes the output, they are likely to accept the whole solution.

Imagine that the client is a mail order company and that the analyst has been asked to produce a system that will allow the telephone receptionists to take orders over the phone. The client is only concerned that the receptionists can search to see if stock is available and then place an order. They are not really interested in how the system does it. The analyst will design what the output screens must look like and then produce what is known as a **prototype**. It won't work yet because no processing has been designed and there is no data yet! However, this prototype is realistic

enough to allow the client and workers to tell whether it will be suitable for the tasks that they want it to do.

Care must be taken when designing the screens that the layout is produced properly. The entire area of the screen needs to be used and care must be taken not to place too much detail on a single screen. Text can be made to flash to draw attention to it or the characters might be in a different colour. Choices of colours to be used should take account of the contrast between the colour of the writing and the colour of the background otherwise it won't be easy to read. The content of what is output on the screen must be understandable to the people who are going to be using it. At all stages the client and the workers who will be using the system must be able to have an input into the acceptability of the screen designs.

The client may decide that the company logo must appear on every screen and that the corporate colour scheme should be used for the backgrounds. One of the workers may be colour blind and consequently some colour schemes should not be used. This sort of detail should have been found out in the analysis stage, but it is the sort of thing that can be missed. These are examples of the sort of things that can happen which force the analyst to go back to a previous stage and change the requirements specification, and hence the design.

Figure 8.3 Example output design for the ordering system of a mail order company.

? SAQ

2 In these examples, what term is used to describe going back to a previous stage which results in an improvement to the end product?

Input designs

Once the output has been designed it is clear what the inputs should be and it is then possible to design the input screens. These input screens go through the same prototyping process as the output screens. Not all input data will come from input screens, however. The analyst has to decide how that data will be collected and design a method of inputting it. For example:

- Will automatic data collection be used? For example, a sensor tells the system when someone enters a building or what the temperature of a process is.
- Are questionnaires (**data capture forms**) going to be used? If they are, should they be designed so that the answer sheets can be read by a special OMR or OCR machine?
- Is the data going to be input by someone using a keyboard and a screen?

When data is input to the system it will have to be checked for accuracy because any computer system can only be as good as the data that is used in it. Special routines called **validation** routines are set up to do this. The method that is going to be used to **verify** the data input also needs to be decided. The method used will either be a visual check on the data entered or double entry of the data and then comparing the two sets of data. (Validation and verification were covered in Module 5.)

Many people design on paper with a pencil and ruler. While there is nothing wrong with doing this, there are a number of different design aids and wizards that are available on the computer to help in this work. So designing straight onto the screen is an option.

Data storage

Now that the analyst knows what the input and output will be, it is possible to design the data storage. Among the questions that need to be considered are:

- How much data needs to be stored about each item?
- What is the volume of data that needs to be stored and will the volume of data change in the future?
- How often are the different data items going to be accessed? How quickly does the required data need to be accessed?
- Who should have access to the data? How will that access be controlled?
- What sort of hardware is going to be needed for the storage?

Processing

Finally, the analyst can design how the input data is processed to produce the outputs required. At this point there should be a good understanding of the system design and of how the different parts work together to achieve the required results. The system design specification is produced and this is used as the input to the next stage.

Question

3 Refer to Question 1 in this module where three example applications were outlined.

For each of these applications decide what the important points about the input and output to and from the system are. What validation and verification of the data input will be necessary? What form will the output take? What data needs to be stored? What are the important features of the data and how will these affect the hardware and the structure of the data files? What will be the form of the access to the data?

8.3 Development and testing

Development

The system design comprises a number of different sections – at the least there will be an input section, an output section, a storage section and a processing section. There may be many more or the analyst may have divided a section into several sub-sections. These different sections are called modules and the development of most software is done in modules. Each module can be coded by different programmers to speed up the process. When the modules are completed they can be linked together to form the complete software solution.

Figure 8.4 An example of the kind of coding programmers would use.

Test strategy

Before the software is produced, it is important to consider how the system will be tested to ensure that it meets the requirement specification.

The danger of leaving how the software will be tested until after the software has been produced is that there is a tendency to make the testing fit the software rather than the other way around.

To do this a **test strategy** is needed. This involves:
- deciding which parts of the software functions need to be tested;
- drawing up a **test plan** that includes:
  - the tests to be performed
  - the data to be used in the tests
  - the expected outcome
  - the purpose of each particular test.

The test strategy will include testing all the different parts of the solution and making sure that the results are as expected. This will include testing the input, the output and the storage as well as the different functions that the software is meant to be able to carry out. File structures

should be tested. Validation routines should be tested to ensure that as much inaccurate data is spotted as is possible.

Testing

The functionality of the individual modules will be tested as stand-alone units. This is referred to as **unit testing**. Any errors found will be reported back to the module's programmer and it is their responsibility to correct the error. The particular failing test will be re-run to check the error has been fixed.

When unit testing is complete, the modules are linked together for **integration testing**. At this point the full functionality and performance of the design can be tested, checking that all the modules coordinate with each other correctly.

Both test data and real data should be used in the testing. Test data is specially prepared to test that a particular part of the processing is working. A good example would be a system which allowed examination marks out of 100 to be entered. A validation check will ensure that marks greater than 100 will be rejected. A test to show that the validation check is working might be to input a mark of 105 and see what happens. Test data includes some data that could be part of the solution, some that would be right on the edge of being acceptable and some, like 105, which should produce error messages. These sorts of test data are called normal, extreme and abnormal data, respectively. Real data will be used to ensure that things like the volume of data will not inhibit system performance.

? SAQ

3 What are two advantages of developing solutions in modules?

One thing to remember is that you cannot exhaustively test whether a piece of software will always work. Imagine a simple program that will add two numbers together. A sensible test to see if it works would be to input the numbers 3 and 4. If the software gives the answer 7 it has passed the test. What about 5 and 9?

What about 7 and 3.5? An infinite number of tests need to be carried out to show that the software always works, but that is impossible. A better approach is to try to think of tests that will prove that the software does not work. If the tests cannot cause a failure, then the assumption is that the software works.

If the testing shows that part of the solution does not work properly then consider the waterfall model that we introduced at the start of this module. When something does not work properly the analyst needs to go back in the work to find the area of design or analysis which caused the problem and have another look at that part of the work in the light of the test results. Changes may be needed to the specification or the design or both.

The client should always be a party to the test plan. They have to be convinced that the software works as agreed. If the testing follows the test plan and the results are satisfactory, then they will accept the product and the next stage can be entered.

Question

4 Refer to Question 1 in this module where three example applications were outlined.

For each of these applications, consider what test data would be sensible to include in the test plan. What would be the important parts of the test strategy? What areas of the proposed solution will need to be tested? What validation testing will need to be done?

Will the testing of the third application be any more important than the testing done on the first application?

8.4 Implementation

When the system has been produced and thoroughly tested, it then has to be implemented into the organisation for which it has been designed. How this is done will be decided beforehand because there are some choices to be made and a lot of work to be done.

If a completely new system has to be designed, doing something that was not done before, then there is no choice – the system has to be put in place and switched on. However, most systems are designed to take over a task from an older system, so a changeover plan is necessary to manage the change from one system to the other:

- **Hardware** – The first thing to be done is to buy and install any new hardware which will be necessary for the new system. It is possible that all the old hardware will be good enough but this is unlikely. If only some of the equipment needs replacing then staff may be able to carry on working. However, it is quite likely that the business will need to shut down, although it may be possible to install the new hardware while the business is normally shut (overnight or at the weekend), ready for operation when it opens as normal.

- **Data files** – After the hardware has been installed, the files of data have to be loaded onto the new system. They should be in electronic form so that they can be loaded up quickly from a storage device. However, the records might be held on paper files or they may be in a form that is not suitable for the new system which will mean considerable work preparing them for being entered. It may be necessary to employ data-entry staff temporarily in order to ensure that the data is entered properly. Note that it is important that these data files are as accurate as possible when the new system starts to work. Decisions will have to be made about how the data entry should be checked for accuracy.

- **Training** – The staff who are going to be using the new system will need to be trained how to use it. If they are familiar with a computerised system already then the training may not need to be very extensive. However, if they are not used to a computerised system the training has to be very carefully planned. An important question to be answered is 'What form will the training take?' Typically the staff can be trained by having training days where a tutor is brought to the firm and the staff are trained in various aspects of the use of the system. This has big advantages: there is someone who can answer specific questions which the staff may have; the management can be sure that everyone has actually done the training. A disadvantage is that the staff have time off while the training sessions are held. Another method is to put all the lessons onto a DVD and each member of staff is given a copy so that they can do the training when it suits them. Advantages of this are: the firm can run normally while the staff are learning; staff can learn at their own speed; staff can skip sections they already know or can redo sections that they find difficult. A disadvantage is that the staff have to use their own time to do the training.

Question

5 Discuss the advantages and disadvantages of the two types of training for the staff and for the firm. What other forms of training could be used?

Figure 8.5 Adult users being trained in an IT classroom.

Even with training, some of the workers may not be able to learn how to use the new system. This can cause a major social problem because these workers may be made redundant or moved to other, less skilled jobs.

System implementation

The implementation of a new system can be carried out in four different ways.

As an example we will consider an examinations board that needs to change the system that it uses to store candidate results; collate the results for each candidate from all the subjects; produce all the results for each candidate; and send the results to the centres around the world. The old system is proving to be very slow and unreliable because there has been a large increase in the number of candidates taking the examinations recently.

Direct changeover

The old system is shut down and the new system is started up. The old system is no longer available so if something goes wrong it is not possible or very difficult to go back to the old system. Although this sounds a simple method of implementation, it requires careful planning. All the files must be loaded up and ready to use, all the workers must have been properly trained and the system must have been fully tested.

In the example, the information stored is too important to be lost during the changeover and if the part of the system that produces the results does not work properly the results will not be produced in time. This is an example of a time-sensitive process which is very important to the organisation and hence a direct changeover is not appropriate.

This was how the UK stock market was computerised in the 1980s. The old market closed on a Friday night and when it reopened on Monday morning the new computerised systems were ready for operation. Unfortunately there was an error in the software: when a share fell in value by a certain amount, the software was programmed to sell all of those shares that they had in order not to make any more losses. By the time human beings intervened, massive amounts of money had been wiped off the value of some companies and some people who had shares in the companies were ruined. It doesn't often happen, but when a system implemented using direct changeover goes wrong it can be disastrous.

The advantage of a direct changeover is that it is simple and cheap to do but the disadvantage is that if it is not properly planned and tested the organisation might have to shut down.

Phased implementation

In a phased implementation, one part of the system is changed but the rest of the system continues to use the old methods.

In our example the input of the marks might be done using new input methods from the new computer system while the processing and the production of the results is still done with the old system. It allows the new input system to be thoroughly tested before going on to replace the processing part of the old system with the new processing software from the new system.

A disadvantage is that there are two systems running at the same time and that the staff will need to use two different systems to process one set of data, but in important applications it is often worth the extra work. Notice that all the different results for all candidates in all subjects are treated in the same way. The system has been split up according to the processing rather than the data used.

At the next phase, another part of the system is changed over, and so on until the whole system has been implemented.

Pilot implementation

This type of implementation is very like a phased implementation except that the division of the tasks is done according to the data rather than the processes.

In the examination results example the decision might be taken to change all the IGCSE results to the new system while the rest of the results were still produced on the old system. Note that there are now some results that will be using the whole of the new system while some will be using the old system. In this way the scale of the problem is reduced if the new system is faulty. Again, the workers will need to use both systems until the full changeover is done but the organisation gets the experience of a live system before introducing it throughout the company.

The example here is based around the data being divided by the different levels of exams. It could just as easily have been divided according to country – all the Indian results done by the new system and the rest of the world remaining with the old methods. Or it could have been by subject with all the maths results produced by the new method and the rest of the subjects using the old system.

Once the pilot is seen to be operating correctly and there are no outstanding problems, the implementation can be extended to full coverage.

Parallel running

This method of implementation involves both systems running at the same time. They will continue to run

side by side, producing two sets of results, until the client is satisfied that there are no faults with the new system.

In the example it would mean that the data will be input twice, the results will be stored in two systems, the processing will be done twice and the results will be produced twice. Obviously this is an expensive method of changeover, but it is worth it if the system and its results are very important to an organisation. It provides an excellent way of testing the system using real data, because it is possible to compare the results produced by the two systems and if there is a difference then there is a fault in the new system.

SAQ

4 a Which of the four implementation types do you think is also known as 'big bang'?

   b Which is the most disaster-prone implementation type?

Question

6 Refer to Question 1 in this module where three example applications were outlined. For each of these applications, consider:

   • the need for training of staff and how it will be carried out;

   • the data files that will be needed and decide how they will be produced and what measures should be taken to try to ensure accuracy of the data held in the files;

   • the different methods of implementation.

   For each of the examples explain why some implementation methods are not sensible and justify a choice of which one should be used.

8.5 Documentation

To maintain an information system the organisation cannot rely on the knowledge held in people's memories. This knowledge has to be recorded in a structured way. Likewise, the users have to be guided in the use of the information system. Guides to the systems are usually produced as two separate sets of documents known as **technical documentation** and **user documentation**, respectively.

Figure 8.6 An office worker overwhelmed by paper records. Information needs to be ordered in a structured and easily accessible way.

Documentation is not just tacked on to the end of a solution: it should be produced while the system is being developed. This is especially important for the technical documentation because there will almost certainly be more than one person producing the solution and each person involved needs to know what everyone else is doing.

Technical documentation

The technical documentation is the information about the solution that a technician needs in order to understand how the system works. It is required when updating or fixing problems with the system. It will include:

- **Purpose of the system** – This is the definition of the problem that the system solves, as agreed with the client. This definition supplies a means of measuring the scope of the solution and leads directly to the next item.

- **Limitations of the system** – There will have been some limitations put on the system in the initial discussions between the client and the analyst. For example in the examination board example in the previous section, the client might have intended to have included an electronic method of distribution of the results to centres. But once the analyst had done the feasibility study, it was decided that this would add too much to the final cost, or it would mean that the project would not be ready on time. This is a limitation to the system. It may be reported towards the end of this documentation despite being part of the initial discussions. The reason for this is that other unforeseen limitations may arise when the system is tested. There may also be an issue with some of the original requirements not being met because they were not possible within the time limits set for the system's completion.

- **System flowcharts** – System flowcharts show the complete information system, sometimes referred to as the **system architecture**. The flow of the data is described diagrammatically along with the different data-handling and storage hardware and the individual programs needed to achieve the requirements of the system. The programs, or processing requirements, will only be in outline form because the full details of the programs are covered in the program flowcharts. There are a number of different sets of acceptable symbols that can be used in a system flowchart. The important thing in any of these representations is that the logical flow of the data through the system is correct. The basic symbols are:

Terminator (start or end)	Input or output	Storage

Process	Decision

Question

7. Produce a systems flowchart for an application that inputs changes to be made to a membership system in a library. Include procedures that will check on the accuracy of the inputs and the uses of different files and the production of outputs from the system which will include membership lists and regular users.

- **Program coding** – Details of any programming done will need to be included. This will include the original designs for the program, possibly in the form of **program flowcharts**. Flowcharts will range from those which show the basic ideas behind the code and how it joins together, to detailed flowcharts that describe the coding. These detailed flowcharts should match the program code so that it is easy to see how the decisions in the code were arrived at.

  The code itself must be fully annotated. **Annotations** explain what the code does and is contained within the code itself. Each of the lines or sections of the code needs to have a simple explanation attached to it explaining what it does. Fully annotated code is code that has enough annotation in it to allow another programmer to produce the same code when they can only see the annotation.

- **List of variables used** – Details of any variables that have been used in the program are listed here. This will include the name of the variable, the reason it is being used and the data type. The reasons for this list are twofold: to help the technician follow the program if some maintenance needs to be done; and to ensure variables are not duplicated.

Question

8. An entry in a list of variable names looks like this:

   X This stores the total of all the items bought so far 'Number'

   Criticise this entry in the list and say how it could be improved.

- **File structures** – This defines the data types of all the fields in the files used by the system (see Module 5). It also shows the linkages between the files. If the system uses databases, then the database management system will have a view that shows the relationship between the files, which can be included here (See figure 8.7). This information is needed in case the file structures need to be modified in the future.

- **Hardware and software requirements** – The hardware needed to run the system is listed, including estimated file sizes so that storage choices can be justified. There may be diagrams to show how the servers, peripherals, storage devices, network and user terminals are interconnected. Software requirements should also be listed, including details of software that has been bought in, that has been modified or that has been specially written. Minimum system requirements for running the software will also be included.

- **Validation routines** – Reasons for using validation were given in Module 5, as were the different validation routines that can be used. Details of the different validation routines that are used to check the input data are given in this section of the technical documentation.

User documentation

The other part of the documentation is provided for the people who are going to use the system. Users do not need the technical details of how the system works, but they do need to know its features and functionality. The user documentation tells them how to use the information system. It includes:

- **Purpose of the system**
- **Limitations of the system**
- **Hardware and software requirements**

This seems to be the start of the list for technical documentation! It is, but this time the emphasis is different. The purpose of the system will not list the agreement between the client and analyst: it will be in terms that the user can understand and will simply state what they can use the system for. Similarly with the limitations and the hardware and software requirements. In the technical section the hardware requirements

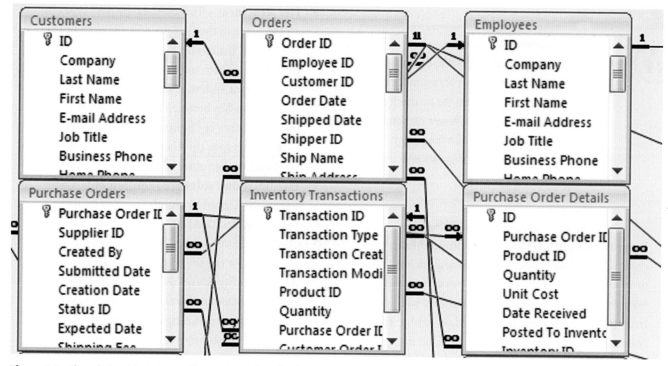

Figure 8.7 The relationship between files as shown in a database management system.

were dictated by the power of the hardware necessary to allow the system to run. In this section it is more about what to use it for and how to use it.

- **How to use the system** – This will include details about how to input data, what sort of data needs to be input and in what **format the input** should be made. If a price is to be input for instance, is it always necessary to have two digits input after the point? What sort of **output** is required? How is it to be produced and what should it look like?

- **Sample runs** – The outputs from some successful runs of the software so that the user has a reference how the system should look if it is used properly. These may be screenshots of input and output screens, for example.

- **Error messages** – Things will go wrong with any system and when they do it is important that the system has been designed to output error messages (see Figure 8.8). Users can look these up to find out what has caused the error and what can be done about it. Error messages can vary from simple messages that inform the user that there is no paper

left in the printer, for example, to error messages informing the user that something serious has happened and that some of the saved data in the system has been corrupted. One particular set of error messages tells the user when there has been a validation error caused by an input to the system which was in the wrong format or was outside the range set for the data. The message should advise the user what was expected. These error messages need to be in non-technical language.

- **Trouble-shooting guide** – There should be some assistance given for minor problems that can arise with the system, otherwise every time things go wrong it will be necessary to call a technician. The trouble-shooting guide tells the user how to identify that certain things have gone wrong and what can be done about them when they have.

- **Frequently asked questions (FAQs)** – There are some things which experience has shown are problems or questions that many users have. These problems are drawn together with the answers that go with them.

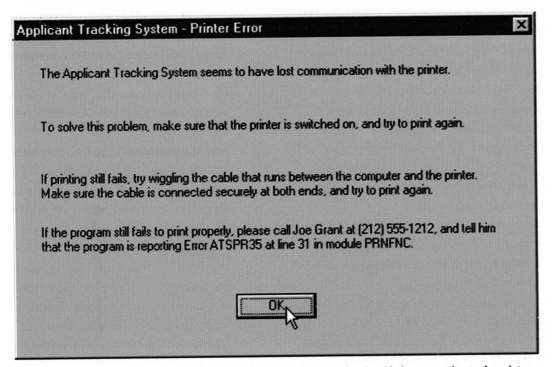

Applicant Tracking System - Printer Error

The Applicant Tracking System seems to have lost communication with the printer.

To solve this problem, make sure that the printer is switched on, and try to print again.

If printing still fails, try wiggling the cable that runs between the computer and the printer. Make sure the cable is connected securely at both ends, and try to print again.

If the program still fails to print properly, please call Joe Grant at (212) 555-1212, and tell him that the program is reporting Error ATSPR35 at line 31 in module PRNFNC.

OK

Figure 8.8 An example of an error message. In this example, the problem is with the connection to the printer.

 SAQ

5 As a result of testing the system it is found that a module of code does not pass data to the next module as intended. It is rewritten and causes the user interface to change. Where would these changes be recorded and why?

Question

9 Refer to Question 1 in this module where three example applications were outlined.

For each of these applications decide who the audience is going to be and then decide what content would be necessary in each of the user and technical guides.

8.6 Evaluation

At some point after the new information system has been operating as a normal business application it is time to review the project.

Evaluation against the requirements specification

Before the solution was produced, the systems analyst and the client organisation agreed a set of things that the finished solution should do. This was the requirements specification. It was the list of requirements that needed to be met for the system to be a success. If the system does not satisfy these requirements the problem may not have been solved. The solution will be considered a success if all the requirements are met. It may even be considered a success if most of the requirements are met. The test plan was set up to provide the evidence that the requirements have been met and that the software does everything that is required of it. Also, the users must be asked for their view of how the implementation has gone and how well the system works for them. Is it easy to use? Can it be used efficiently? Users tend to discover problems that computer-literate testers do not think of.

Limitations and improvements

As a result of the evaluation, we build up a list of required changes.

Some of the changes are needed to address the limitations – a shortfall between the requirements specification and what has been delivered. That is, what is delivered is not what was agreed initially. This shortfall can be identified because there is not enough evidence that all the requirements in the specification have been met. Evidence here means test results, and these test results are what supports the systems analyst's assertion they should be paid. This type of testing is known as functional testing. Functional testing does not prove that the solution is perfect or even that it is carried out in the best way, but it does provide evidence that the solution satisfies all the requirements made of it.

Other changes will address improvements identified during operation of the system, perhaps in response to the client's changing needs or to accommodate changes in the external environment.

The production of the finished solution is not the end of the process. Continual evaluations and improvements to the system can be made. Refer back to the waterfall model (Figure 8.1) – we can go back to any other stage either to address problems or to make improvements. Reference to the technical documentation is critically important in making the changes. It is also necessary to update the documentation to record any changes made.

Maintenance

This continual process of changes to the system is known as **maintenance** and will take place throughout the system's operational life cycle. There are three forms of maintenance:

- **Error correction (corrective maintenance)** – All complex software goes wrong sometimes. We call the errors that cause this 'bugs' in the software. The system support staff have to be able to find these bugs and fix them.
- **Added functionality (adaptive maintenance)** – Things change in the organisation. The original problem that the system was built for may have altered. We may need the system to do something else. For example, suppose the examination board in the example used earlier in this module has expanded into a different country. The authorities in the country want the results to be presented in order of the marks that were awarded rather than according to the centres that the candidate was in. This will require a different program to accomplish it and will also mean different output techniques.
- **Performance improvement (perfective maintenance)** – Organisations are always looking to speed up processes or make them more efficient. Or it may be that the system has simply grown beyond its original capacity – such as a larger user base or increased number of products being handled. The systems analyst has to consider how to solve these issues. It may be a change to the hardware – higher performance servers,

Figure 8.9 A computer engineer carrying out maintenance on a server.

for example – or changes to the software – using a relational database instead of flat files, for example. Any changes will require careful planning and implementation.

SAQ

6 The system has been operating satisfactorily for three months since implementation. A user tries to do something differently that causes an error to be reported by the software. They submit a bug report to the system support staff who investigate the error and conclude that the user is trying to do something that the system wasn't designed for.

a How will the support staff have reached this conclusion?

b What can they do about the error?

Question

10 Look back to Question 1 in this module where three example applications were outlined.

For each application decide what sort of evidence the analyst should provide to the management of the organisation so that the performance of the solution can be evaluated. Give examples of the types of event that would mean that the three different types of maintenance would be needed.

Summary

- There are six stages in the waterfall model of the systems life cycle – analysis, design, development and testing, implementation, documentation and evaluation/maintenance.
- System analysis and design is a continual iterative process that refines the solution.
- The analysis stage consists of problem definition and a feasibility study that, on agreement, is followed by information collection, resulting in a requirements specification.
- Designing the output is the first part of the design stage, followed by input, storage and processing design.
- The development and testing stage consists of dividing the coding work into modules which are subsequently tested individually before integrating them together and testing as a whole.
- Implementation starts with installing new hardware and data and training the staff. The changeover to the new solution can be carried out in four different ways – direct changeover, phased implementation, pilot implementation or parallel running.
- Documentation is important to the future maintenance of the system and consists of technical and user guides, which have recommended formats. Any changes to the system must be reflected in the documentation.
- The evaluation stage looks at how well the solution meets the requirement specification and then defines how the system needs changing.
- Maintenance goes on throughout the system's operational life and consists of error correction, adding functionality and performance improvements.

Answers to self-assessment questions

Module 1

SAQ 1

Hardware: monitor, mouse, joystick.
Software: web browser, spreadsheet program, flight simulator game.

SAQ 2

Picasa is Google's photo editing program. It can also sort photos, label and tag them. Photos can be shared with other people by uploading to the Picasa website. So it's more of a package than a program. But this package doesn't come in a box.

SAQ 3

a   A school computer has 512 **megabytes** of memory. Of course your school computer may have more memory than this but it won't have 512 gigabytes!

b   A byte is a unit of computer **memory** and it consists of **eight** bits.

SAQ 4

16 bits, 1.5 MB, 2048 kB, 1.2 GB, 1 terabyte.

SAQ 5

a   An operating system is the essential software a computer runs all the time to keep it usable. The OS controls the computer.

b

   i   A graphical user interface uses graphics in the form of icons to stand for more complicated actions that the user wants the computer to carry out.

   ii A command-line interface is a text interface for communicating with a computer.

Module 2

SAQ 1

The human being is what makes data input using a keyboard slow.

SAQ 2

a   Required features might include the type of timber, length, width and height (i.e. the dimensions) of each type of timber required, and the number of that type in the order. Other things might be the method of payment.

b   It is still necessary to have a qwerty keyboard because some details need characters to be typed in like the address for delivery. The alphabet could feature on the concept keyboard but this might make the keyboard confused or cluttered, unless there is plenty of space. Alternatively, if the business has a customer file, then the address will be there and access to the file can be via a simple on/off switch on the concept pad. (There are problems with this that could be discussed, like 'new customer' or 'different address'.)

SAQ 3

A direct input method might include selecting a pre-programmed number from the phone's 'contact list' (or 'phone book'), or 'ring back' function to return a missed call.

SAQ 4

There is no 'right' answer. You could argue that a mechanical mouse or a wired optical mouse would be sensible because it is connected to the computer and hence is not going to go missing. A wireless mouse could get lost easily and would also require frequent battery changing. However, in the dusty conditions of a timber yard the ball of a mechanical mouse is likely to get clogged with dirt very quickly and require frequent cleaning. An optical mouse is easier to clean but does not work on all surfaces and this can cause the cursor to jump across the screen. The mouse could be used for many things, basically for defining the position on the screen that the user wants the cursor to be. The scroll can be used to move through the customer file(s) quickly, the button can be used to select a particular customer, and so on. Examples of input data are the type of timber (what the product it is), the dimensions of the timber (the specifications of the product), how many are ordered, if they need to be delivered, where they need to be delivered, etc.

SAQ 5

a A mechanical mouse is unreliable because in the environment in which it is used it is likely to get dirty and the ball will stick; a wireless optical mouse works better but can be disruptive when its battery runs out and this type of mouse can quite easily get lost.

b The standard advantages and disadvantages are in the text and are significant here. Possible suggestions include that the advantages of using a either a touchpad or a trackerball is that neither require a flat surface to work on, so there is more flexibility in the type of environment in which they can be used. A trackerball can be built into the keyboard or computer so that it will not get lost, and will be easy to use for all workers, even those who might have physical disabilities. However, in the dusty environment you might have the same complication of a mechanical mouse with the ball getting dirty and sticking. A touchpad again can be built into the keyboard or computer but it will not so easily be affected by dust as the trackerball is. However, greasy and sweaty fingers can make it difficult to control the cursor due to the pad's sensitivity, and a touchpad might be too difficult to use for workers with physical disabilities.

SAQ 6

There may be many appropriate responses. One would be to control the positioning of a circular saw when it is cutting the timber. This can then be done from a distance, and is safer, but also allows for fine adjustments to be continually made throughout the cutting process.

SAQ 7

Advantages:
- They are difficult to vandalise compared with something like a mouse.
- They are largely weatherproof so can be in the open air like a station platform.

- They need no computer knowledge to be able to operate them.

Disadvantages:
- Hard to read the screen in bright sunlight.
- Disabled people can find them difficult to use.

SAQ 8

It can be viewed on a screen, emailed, edited, digitally archived, projected, used as wallpaper on a computer, etc.

SAQ 9

Monitoring the buildings remotely at night time.

SAQ 10

Speech-to-data entry using a microphone would be fast and easy, but could be hampered by a noisy environment. Therefore it is more likely to be used by a secretary or receptionist who is working in the office than by someone working in the sawmill or warehouse. Using a microphone and speech-to-data entry might open up a role for someone with physical disabilities, enabling them to do an office computer-based role, which they might be perfectly qualified for but would otherwise struggle to do. As this form of data entry can be unreliable it would probably not be suitable for the person taking orders directly from the customer.

SAQ 11

a OCR – OCR software compares the shape of each character with the shapes that it knows and, when it is matched, the computer stores the fact that it is a letter. Used for converting paper text to computer data.

b OMR – Recognises simple marks in specific positions. On questionnaires for example.

c MICR – Recognises specific types of marks which are also human readable. Account numbers and sort codes on cheques for example.

SAQ 12

Thermometers cannot be used for control; they provide visual output for a human. The system would use a temperature sensor (thermistor). The sensor would not control the heater or make any decisions; this would be done by a computer. The heater would be controlled by the computer, not the sensor (using an actuator). The sensor is electrical but the probes from the sensor can be placed in water.

SAQ 13

Full descriptions and applications are supplied in the main text. Some brief outlines are supplied below:

a   Dot matrix printers use a set of pins to make imprints on the paper by pressing through an inked ribbon. Each different colour needs a different coloured ribbon. An example application is in a mechanic's garage. The printer allows the mechanic to print on two-part stationery to create a customer copy and a shop copy of the work done and the cost. The environment is dirty and greasy and other less robust printers might break.

b   Inkjet printers use a printhead containing different nozzles to squirt different coloured ink at the page as a stepper motor moves across it. An example application is printing photos from a digital camera at home because the printer is cheap and produces high-quality colour output at a reasonable speed.

c   Laser printers use a laser to create electrostatic charge, a drum, toner and heat to bind ink to the paper. Each different coloured toner used needs its own drum. An example application is a school newsletter, because the printer enables high-quality printing at a fast rate, and the ink will not run if the newsletter gets wet.

d   Plotters tend to be line-drawing devices and there are two main kinds, flatbed and drum. They create an output by drawing lines of various lengths and colours. Plotters move their pen around the page in curves or straight lines. In flatbed plotters the paper lies flat whilst the pen is attached to a motor that runs on the paper at any angle, for any distance, curving and returning until the image is complete. In drum plotters the paper is on a spinning drum that drives the paper under the pen at the same time as the pen moves across the drum. This creates the same kind of flexible movement as the flatbed but takes up less space. An example application is architects creating blueprints of new buildings. The printers create clean and sharp images on large pieces of paper.

Module 3

SAQ 1

$1024 \times 1024 = 1\,048\,576$ bytes

SAQ 2

If the user sends an instruction to read a particular file of data, the drive will look in the **index** to find out where it is and then go straight to that part of the disk.

SAQ 3

No, DVD-Rs are not suitable. They can only be written to once, so every time a backup is needed a new disk would have to be used. This would be an expensive method because of all the disks required. The repeated process of labelling the disks and storing them in a managed system is time-consuming and the worker's time could be better spent elsewhere. You could also end up with a considerable storage space issue. DVD-RWs would be more appropriate because the same disk can be written and rewritten to many times. These disks are only suitable for data that you wish to update and replace on a regular basis, e.g. daily.

SAQ 4

On Windows OSs it is the *Recycle Bin*. Deleted files are put here rather than being deleted from the computer. If you accidentally delete a file, you can recover it from the Recycle Bin. Every now and then you should *empty* the Recycle Bin – this is when files are really deleted from your computer and are not recoverable. Other OSs have the equivalent feature.

SAQ 5

a   The *transaction file.*
b   Yes. This would be backed up at least once a day, but more likely several times a day.

Module 4

SAQ 1

a   A router or a modem.
b   A browser to access web pages and an email program to send and receive electronic mail.

SAQ 2

a   LAN = Local Area Network,
WLAN = Wireless Local Area Network,
WAN = Wide Area Network.

b   Geographical coverage. A LAN is smaller than a WAN, which covers large distances. WANs are used to interconnect LANs.

c   The Internet can be considered as a WAN, although it consists of many interconnected WANs and LANs itself.

SAQ 3

The Internet is so fast even when accessing data in other countries because it uses some of the undersea fibre-optic cables as part of its infrastructure. The data travels through the fibre at the speed of light.

SAQ 4

a   A router.

b   A bridge.

SAQ 5

A firewall.

Module 5

SAQ 1

a   Ms Arif

b   Liene Faizan

c   Two

d   Gender; Form tutor

SAQ 2

Date of transfer; school transferred to.

SAQ 3

Just to be on the safe side the 'No. in family' field will have two numeric digits in it. If the database file had been set up with one digit and a child enters school from a very large family of ten or more, then the file structure would have to be changed. This is not trivial – simpler to make it two digits. You should always consider limits when creating database files, sometimes exceptional ones.

SAQ 4

Probably not because in the student file all the numbers are whole numbers and 78.123 is not a whole number.

SAQ 5

$12.34 is currency because the number of digits after the point is 2. The rest are real numbers although 12 could be an integer.

Module 6

SAQ 1

A phone (either a cell phone or a landline).

A computer so that you can:

- access the Internet and see your company's and your client's websites;
- email customers;
- and if necessary video conference with them.

An Internet connection – preferably a broadband connection.

SAQ 2

Encyclopedias give more accurate and reliable information than wikis because their information has been professionally researched and verified. However, their information can be out of date, so they are not necessarily 'better' than wikis.

SAQ 3

You should either look for references to published information in the wiki or try and find another website that confirms the information.

SAQ 4

If you have tried all the usual things like rebooting, going back to a restore point and switching off and on, then the only resort you have is to restore your computer's system from a backup. If you haven't got one, then you will need to reload your entire operating system and applications, then hope your data was on a networked drive and is OK.

SAQ 5

Not blinking is a sign of concentration and leads to sore eyes. Blink more often. Racing drivers wait until they are on a straight before they blink.

Module 7.1

SAQ 1

Too many typefaces and font sizes make a newsletter confusing to the eye and difficult to read.

SAQ 2

You make the image of your school logo transparent. You may have to play around with the amount of transparency (e.g. 10% to 50%) until you achieve a satisfactory result.

SAQ 3

They consist of several smaller posters (but still large) that are joined together.

SAQ 4

You could put a hyperlink on the last page that returned you to the first page. It could be labelled 'Return to start?'

SAQ 5

Email is inflexible. You get all the emails sent to the distribution list whether you want them or not. Social networking websites are more flexible and enjoyable to use and have largely taken over.

SAQ 6

A barometric pressure sensor to be used in a weather station.

SAQ 7

A light sensor to sense when the light fades at dusk and a temperature sensor to sense when the temperature goes below 0 °C.

SAQ 8

Manual timing is better than computerised timing when you want quick and inexpensive timing. Computerised timing is better than manual timing when you want accurate timing.

SAQ 9

The frequency of monitoring (e.g. 3 times per day) and the length of time of the experiment.

SAQ 10

a There needs to be time enough for the last decision to take effect.
b Something might happen that is not spotted quickly enough for something to be done about it.

SAQ 11

In 15 minutes the room might get very hot or very cold. There would be wide variations in the room temperature, especially in very cold or very hot weather.

SAQ 12

A movement sensor has to have a sensitivity control so that only large objects (humans but not dogs and cats) are detected.

SAQ 13

Simulations: do not involve any risks for the participants; enable a scenario to be investigated without the expense of building the real thing; allow variables to be altered to see their effect.

Module 7.2

SAQ 1

a At night or at the weekend.
b You are online to your school's website. The webserver of course may be hosted, but you are still online to it.

SAQ 2

You would search on 'William Shakespeare', '<name of play>' and '<character>' – for example, 'William Shakespeare' 'The Tempest' 'Prospero'.

To search on just 'William Shakespeare' you would put double inverted commas round the search term, for example "William Shakespeare". You could also do this for "The Tempest".

SAQ 3

When a company allows its intranet to be accessed by external companies, it becomes an extranet.

An external company would access another company's extranet via the Internet using a web browser. A username and password would be required. Encryption may be used to make an extranet more secure.

SAQ 4

Using either a word-processing or DTP application you would divide an A4 document into eight or ten credit-card-sized boxes, compose your business card in one of the boxes, copy it to the other boxes, print it onto card, then cut the individual cards out using a guillotine cutter. This is how a printing company would do it. Normally, you wouldn't print onto a single blank business card.

SAQ 5

As soon as you go to an Internet payment website, your web browser encrypts everything. Only the payment website can decrypt your information. It is like having a secure 'tunnel' through the Internet. You can recognise that you are secure by the padlock icon on the browser's status bar and also the address of the secure website will be prefixed by https:// The 's' means 'secure'.

SAQ 6

A medical expert system can hold more information, can be updated regularly and can use computing techniques to aid searches for information. The information can be gleaned from many doctors worldwide. So the doctor using the system is more likely to diagnose patients' conditions correctly than one who doesn't.

SAQ 7

Iron ores are magnetic, so their magnetic field can be detected. The device to measure magnetic field strength is a magnetometer. If this was sunk into the ground in several places across a site, then a map of magnetic field strength, hence probability of iron ore deposits, can be constructed. This map can be input into the expert system knowledge base.

SAQ 8

After Christmas, for example, no one will buy Christmas decorations and crackers and so on. This falls on a set date every year so the stock control system may automatically set the minimum stock level to this without the manager's intervention.

SAQ 9

Cash needs managing – counting, looking after and banking – and there is a delay before it gets banked. EFTPOS transactions go straight to the company's bank account.

Module 8

SAQ 1

The feasibility study and the requirements specification must be agreed during the analysis stage.

If these weren't agreed then the reasons for disagreement would have to be sorted out and the documents revised until the client agrees their content. If they can't be agreed, then the project would be terminated.

SAQ 2

Iteration.

SAQ 3

It is quicker because several modules can be developed in parallel. In testing it is easier for the programmer who coded the module to fix the errors.

SAQ 4

a   Direct changeover.

b   Direct changeover.

SAQ 5

The code that was rewritten would need annotation to explain how it worked. The technical documentation would need amending to explain how data is passed to the module that follows. The user documentation would need amending to show the change to the user interface.

SAQ 6

a   The support staff will have looked at the technical documentation (and possibly the original requirements specification) to check whether the system was designed to do the thing the user tried.

b   The error can be answered in two ways depending on what the user was trying to do: if it is **not** a useful thing then the bug will be closed. A log will be kept (a known error log) so that if any other users try the same thing, it is not re-investigated. If it **is** a useful thing that the user was trying to do, then it will be added to the list of added functionality changes (enhancements) to be made to the system. The change will need to be developed and tested, and then implemented at some point during a maintenance period.

Index

actuators, 34

adaptive maintenance, 164

added functionality, 164

address lists, 99

air conditioning controllers, 118

alphanumeric data type, 70

analogue data, 26, 73–4

analogue-to-digital converter, 26, 74, 106

annotations, 161

architectural simulations, 123

archive, 45

audio software, 3

authentication, 64

automated teller machine (ATM), 140

automatic cooker, control of, 117

backing storage, 11, 37

backing store. *See* storage devices

backup procedure, 43–5

backups, 43

banking applications, 138–40

    automated teller machine, 140

    credit cards, 140

    debit cards, 140

    electronic fund transfer, 138–9

    Internet banking, 139

    telephone banking transactions, 139–40

bar code readers, 24

batch processing, 126–7

bit, 5, 36

blog, 80–81

Bluetooth, 50

Blu-ray disks, 40, 42

booking systems, 136–8

    cinema, 137–8

    theatre, 136–7

    travel, 138

Boolean data, 70

bridge, 56

browser, 48–50

burglar alarms, 120

bus network, 51

business cards, 130

buzzers, 34

bytes, 5, 36

cables, 53–4

car engine fault diagnosis, 145

cathode ray tube (CRT) monitors, 28–9

CD (compact disk), 39, 42

CD-ROMs, 40, 42

CD-Rs, 40, 42

CD-RWs, 40, 42

cell phones, 128–9

central heating controllers, 118

central processing unit (CPU), 4

chess, 80

chess computers, 145

chip-and-PIN readers, 25–6

cinema bookings, 137–8

clubs, 100

Colossus (computer), 1, 7

command-line interface (CLI), 7

communications applications, 89–96

    electronic conferencing, 128

    electronic mail, 128

    fax, 128

    flyers, 92–3

    Internet, 127–8

    Internet telephony, 129

    mobile telephones, 128–9

    multimedia presentations, 94–5

    music, 95–6

    newsletters, 89–92

    posters, 92–3

    websites, 93–4

    work-related, 127–9

communications software, 2

compact disk (CD), 39, 42

computer assisted learning (CAL), 94

computer modelling, 121

computer networks. *See* networks

computer systems, 1–9

    components of, 3

    defined, 3

    development of, 1–2, 7–9

    hardware, 2

    memory, 4–5

    software, 2

    storage device, 5–6

computer-aided design, 2

computers, 8–9

    defined, 3

    laptops, 9

    mainframe, 8

    netbook, 9

    palmtops, 9

    personal, 8

    personal digital assistants, 9

    portable, 9

    smartphone, 9

concept keyboard, 13

confidentiality of data, 62–3

control applications, 33, 34, 110–20

    air conditioning, 118

    automatic cooker, 117

    burglar alarms, 120

    central heating, 118

    control devices, 33–4

    greenhouses, 119–20